Social Class Differences in Britain

a sourcebook

Ivan Reid

Open Books

London

First published in 1977 by Open Books Publishing Limited,
21 Tower Street, LONDON WC2H 9NS

Hardback: ISBN 0 7291 0165 7
Paperback: ISBN 0 7291 0160 6

This book is dedicated to the three Marys in my life

Set in 10/12 pt I.B.M. Journal Medium by Preface Ltd,
Salisbury, Wilts
Printed and bound in Great Britain by Biddles Ltd, Martyr
Road, Guildford, Surrey

Contents

Preface   ix
Acknowledgements   xiii

1   **About this book**   1
Aim and scope   1
How to use this book   5

2   **Social class and its use in empirical research**   13
What is social class?   13
Does everybody use occupation as the criterion of
    social class?   16
Is social class a new idea?   19
Does the public recognise social class?   22
On what basis does the public recognise social class?   26
How social class has been operationalised in empirical
    research   32
Sampling techniques   49
Research methods   56
An overview   60
Suggested further reading on social class theory   61

3   **Distribution, work and income**   63
National distribution of social class   63
Regional distribution of social class   65
Local distribution of social class   71
Distribution of social class by industry   74
Income   75
Number of earners per household and family   77
Expenditure   80
Social class of economically active married couples   82

Sickness and pension schemes 85
Unemployment 87
Working hours 88
Job satisfaction 89
Social mobility 90
Age and social class 96

4 **Birth, health and death** 102
Birth 103
   Gestation 103
   Birth weight 105
   Infant mortality 106
Health 108
   Use of health services 118
Death 123

5 **Family and home** 127
The family 127
Marriage 130
Divorce 132
Class endogamy 134
Children 136
   Number 136
   Age of mother and of marriage at first birth 139
   Family planning 140
   Adoption and fostering 142
Bringing up children 143
The home 155
   Dwellings: type and tenure 156
   Accommodation 158
   Amenities 160
   Domestic amenities 161
   Moving home 162

6 Education 164
Adult social class and education 166
Parental social class and children's education 171
   Pre-school education 171
   Infant school 173
   Primary school 174
   Type of secondary school 178
   Secondary school achievement 185
   Higher and further education 189

7 Politics, religion, leisure and opinion 197
Politics 199
Religion 203
Leisure 210
   Television 210
   Reading 212
   Drinking 216
   Smoking 217
   Cinema and theatre 217
   Clubs and organisations 219
   Holidays 221
   Sport 222
Opinion 225

8 Afterword 234

Appendix
   List and details of research used in this book 237

Bibliography *and* Author index 246

Subject index 259

Preface

This book arose out of my experiences, over the past ten years, in attempting to introduce various kinds of students to sociology. These introductory courses all required a treatment of social class, a fundamental aspect of western society which has had the central attention of sociologists. Existing introductory textbooks in the field had a heavy emphasis on the theoretical aspects of the topic, particularly classical and developmental — the statutory Marx and Weber. Contemporary social class reality, empirically based and about British society, was poorly, if at all, represented. My students and I found this an unedifying situation. I felt a growing need to provide them with some fairly straightforward and systematic data about British social class. Having recognised the need, I initially assumed that, like most of the rest of my ideas, somebody must have had it before. When I was unable to find a book like the one you now read, I wondered why nobody had written one before. Having completed the task, I wonder no longer, but have several cryptic explanations.

Somebody remarked at the outset of this enterprise that the publication would be timely. I've thought about that one. It may be that presenting empirical data has become controversial in the light of the current debate in sociology between those who believe data are the essence of the discipline, and those whose concerns lead them to question, or to reject, existing data. Much of this debate appears to stem from ignorance on both sides, due, in large part, to lack of readily available sources. The display of current knowledge in sociology is too well hidden: it is about time we all had a good look. What I would like to claim — immodestly — is that this book could contribute to the discipline by providing such a view of the empirical treatment of social class.

Like most other authors, I am aware of the support I have received from others. It is clearly appropriate to identify those who have been particularly significant in that role. I am very conscious of the patient support and friendly, encouraging ears of my colleagues and students in the School of Research in Education in Bradford during the preparation of this volume. On reflection, they appear to have survived the experience somewhat better than I, and so it should be. I am grateful to my publishers, especially Helen Fraser, for giving me the opportunity and the encouragement to put my pen where my mouth was, and Henry Hardy. My thanks are due to Brenda Carrington, Gladys Claridge and Pat Reid for conspiring to decode the manuscript into typescript.

I was fortunate in securing the services of several semi-captive groups of students for consumer research. I wish therefore to thank the following: the students of the M.Sc. (Education) and B.Sc. (Applied Educational Studies) courses at the University of Bradford; Peter Squibb of Bingley College of Education; Judith Worsnop of Ilkley College of Education; and particularly their students and my past students at Edge Hill College of Education and elsewhere. My labour was saved, and its fruits certainly enhanced, by Peter Taylor, my sometime student, now Senior Research Officer at the Association of Special Libraries, who kindly and most competently undertook the task of compiling the subject index. Colin Flood Page, Marie Macey, Terry Tordoff and Jim Whittaker also have my gratitude for their labours in reading and commenting on the manuscript.

There are of course numerous 'unsung' heroes connected with this book, for example those who collected the data presented here, but whose names are not given. I am not sure where their reward lies, but they have my gratitude for the hours at windswept doorways. I am aware too that some authors and researchers will seek in vain to find their work reported in this volume. The severe limitation on space and my vagaries in searching and editing should suffice to explain exclusion, but such authors have my commiseration. So too, for that matter, do those who find themselves here but wish they had not. Naturally those who have contributed by their work to the contents of this book are thanked. Hopefully, not too many of them will be deterred from further efforts by current trends in social science towards unquantifiable research.

Finally I wish to thank my family, especially my wife, who combined with a number of more vital roles the very trying one of once more helping me towards a goal.

Ivan Reid
October 1976

Acknowledgements

The author and publisher would like to thank the following for permission to use data presented in this book: George Allen and Unwin Ltd, Hemel Hempstead, and Aldine Publishing Co., Chicago, for data from J. Newson and E. Newson, *Infant Care in an Urban Community* (1963) and *Four Years Old in an Urban Community* (1968); Barrie and Jenkins, London, for data from G. Gorer, *Death, Grief, and Mourning* (1965); the editor of the *British Journal of Psychiatry*, London, and the authors for data from E. M. Goldberg and S. L. Morrison, 'Schizophrenia and Social Class', *British Journal of Psychiatry* 109 (1963); the British Market Research Bureau Ltd, London, and the J. Walter Thompson Co. Ltd for data from *The New Housewife* (1967); the British Tourist Authority, London, for data from *The British on Holiday 1974* (1975), British National Travel Survey 1974; Churchill Livingstone, Edinburgh, for data from N. R. Butler and D. G. Bonham, *Perinatal Mortality* (1963); Peter Davies Ltd, London, for data from J. W. B. Douglas, J. M. Ross and H. R. Simpson, *All Our Future* (1968); Granada Publishing Ltd, St Albans, for data from J. W. B. Douglas, *The Home and the School* (1964); Hamlyn Publishing Group Ltd, Feltham, for data from *Woman and the National Market* (1967); the editor of *Health Bulletin*, Edinburgh, for data from V. Carstairs, 'Distribution of Hospital Patients by Social Class', *Health Bulletin* 24 (1966); the Controller of Her Majesty's Stationery Office, London, for data from *British Labour Statistics Year Book 1973* (1975), *Department of Employment Gazette* (August 1975), *Family Expenditure Survey Report for 1974* (1975), *15–18* (1960), *Higher Education* (1963), *New Earnings Survey 1973* (1974), *Occupational Pensions Schemes 1971*

(1972), *Public Schools Commission: First Report* (1968) and *Report on an Enquiry into the Incidence of Incapacity for Work*, Part 1 (1964) and Part 2 (1965); the editor of *Higher Education Review*, London, for data from L. Donaldson, 'Social Class and the Polytechnics', *Higher Education Review* 4 (1971); the editor of the *Jewish Journal of Sociology*, London, for data from S. J. Prais and M. Schmool, 'The Social-Class Structure of Anglo-Jewry, 1961', *Jewish Journal of Sociology* 17 (1975); Macmillan, London and Basingstoke, for data from D. Butler and D. Stokes, *Political Change in Britain* (1969); Methuen and Co. Ltd, London, for data from R. K. Kelsall, A. Poole and A. Kuhn, *Graduates* (1972); the National Children's Bureau, London, the Longman Group Ltd, Harlow, and the authors for data from R. Davie, M. Butler and H. Goldstein, *From Birth to Seven* (1972); N.F.E.R. Publishing Co. Ltd, Windsor, for data from J. C. Barker Lunn, *Streaming in the Primary School* (1970), E. J. Dearnaley and M. H. Fletcher, 'Cubs and Brownies – Social Class, Intelligence, and Interests', *Educational Research* 10 (1968), and T. G. Monks, *Comprehensive Education in England and Wales* (1968); the Office of Population Censuses and Surveys, Fareham, for data from *Annual Report for Scotland 1973* (1974), *Decennial Supplement, England and Wales, 1961* (1971), *Economic Activity (10% sample)* (1975), *Education Tables (10% sample)* (1966), *Household Composition Tables (10% sample)* (1975), M. Nissel and C. Lewis, *Social Trends No 5* (1974), *Small Area Statistics (Ward Library)* (1975), and *Statistical Review of England and Wales 1972* (1974); the Social Surveys Division of the Office of Population Censuses and Surveys, London, for Crown Copyright data published by H.M.S.O., London, in M. Bradley and D. Fenwick, *Public Attitudes to Liquor Licensing Laws in Great Britain* (1974), M. Bone, *Family Planning Services in England and Wales* (1973), M. Bone and E. Ross, *The Youth Service and Similar Provision for Young People* (1972), *Facts in Focus* (1974), *General Household Survey Introductory Report* (1973), *General Household Survey 1972* (1975), P. G. Gray, J. E.

Todd, G. L. Slack and J. S. Bulman, *Adult Dental Health in England and Wales in 1968* (1970), E. Grey, *A Survey of Adoption in Great Britain* (1971), A. I. Harris and R. Clausen, *Labour Mobility in Great Britain, 1953–63* (1967), K. K. Sillitoe, *Planning for Leisure* (1969), and M. Woolf, *Family Intentions* (1971); Pergamon Press Ltd, Oxford, for data from J. Wakefield and C. D. Sansom, 'Profile of a Population of Women who have Undergone a Cervical Smear Examination', *The Medical Officer* 116 (1966); Routledge and Kegan Paul Ltd, London, for data from K. Dunnell and A. Cartwright, *Medicine Takers, Prescribers and Hoarders* (1972), C. Gibson, 'The Association Between Divorce and Social Class in England and Wales', *British Journal of Sociology* 25 (1974), R. Holman, *Trading in Children* (1975), M. Kahan, D. Butler and D. Stokes, 'On the Analytical Division of Social Class', *British Journal of Sociology* 17 (1966), and P. H. Mann, 'Surveying a Theatre Audience: Findings', *British Journal of Sociology* 18 (1967); Routledge and Kegan Paul Ltd, London, and Humanities Press, New Jersey, for data from D. V. Glass, *Social Mobility in Britain* (1954), and B. Jackson, *Streaming: An Education System in Miniature* (1964); Routledge and Kegan Paul Ltd, London, and Pantheon, New York, for data from M. Young and P. Willmott, *The Symmetrical Family* (1973); the Tablet Publishing Co., London, for data from L. de S. Moulin, 'Social Class and Religious Behaviour', *The Clergy Review* 53 (1968); the 20th Century Fund, New York, for data from W. J. Baumol and W. G. Bowen, *Performing Arts Economic Dilemma* (1969); Georg Westermann Verlag, Braunschweig, for data from M. E. McIntosh and A. Woodley, 'The Open University and Second Chance Education', *Paedogogica Europaea* 9 (1974). Permission to use, and access to, data as well as hospitality, were given by the Joint Industry Committee for National Readership Survey, National Opinion Polls Market Research Ltd, and Social Surveys (Gallup Polls) Ltd.

1

About this book

This booklet is an experiment, to meet a need which has been put something like this: 'You have in your office a great store of facts . . . Some of your publications are costly, and it isn't too easy for the plain man to find his way through them to what he ought to know. Why not produce a short simple statement of the main facts?'

It is not so easy. Much must be left out. Exactness in detail must give place to brevity, but without sacrifice of essential truth in the broad picture presented. The urge to use footnotes, parenthesis, qualifications must be resisted.

George North (1948)

Aim and scope

The aim of this book is to fill a gap in readily available sociological knowledge, a gap which centres around what is certainly one of the most central concepts and concerns of the discipline, that of social class. Indeed it is possible to argue that in terms of the time, energy and space devoted to it, social class is *the* central concept of sociology. This is witnessed by, for example, the number of books on the subject to be found in the sociology section of any library, and the impossibility of finding an introductory text, or a syllabus in the discipline, which does not include the topic. It features prominently too in journal articles and in research, which suggests that it is often recognised as an important variable. Nor is this importance limited to sociology: social class appears to be of considerable interest to market researchers, the Government (particularly with respect to the census and statistical inquiries), the general public, and the mass-media —

where it provides a particularly fertile subject for plays, TV, films, and books.

Given that so much literature exists, it may appear presumptuous not only to add yet another volume, but in so doing to claim that it will fill a gap. This gap, however, lies between the rather grand generalisations concerning social class differences which are to be found in introductory texts, and the very detailed, though often inaccessible, data and findings of empirical studies. Even given the audiences for whom they were written, many textbooks are misleading about social class, their over-simplification amounting to misrepresentation or even to total inaccuracy when compared with contemporary sources. Moreover statements on social class can be, and are, presented simultaneously from vastly different sources. For example, differences in school attainments by social class (based on a number of large national surveys) can be followed by explanations couched say in terms of social class differences in values (based on small-scale studies from another society — typically the U.S.A.). Their juxtaposition implies a similar degree of reliability and importance, which may well be inappropriate. To take an extreme case, the applicability of dated American material to contemporary Britain is obviously of limited value. The overall effect of much of such literature is misleading and confusing, and can lead students to reject the concept of social class because of a lack of really appropriate data. Contact with contemporary statistics and research findings demands not only access to a university library or its equivalent, but also very real efforts of searching and interpretation. Even given the opportunity and motivation, most students and some sociologists would find difficulties in using certain original sources, even, for example, census material. This is because their presentation is normally designed for purposes other than communication with, or use by, students.

This book aims simply to alleviate the situation outlined above by presenting some semi-digested empirical data on social class. More importantly, however, it seeks not only to provide the basis or vehicle for discussions about the operationalisation of the concept of social class in empirical research and the nature and extent of social class differences, but also to reveal something of the actual state of knowledge in the field. In so doing it should lead to a more realistic appraisal by a far larger audience than is at present possible.

In attempting to achieve this aim, it has been necessary to limit the scope of the work in order to contain it within a single volume. The contents are sometimes limited directly by the nature of available sources. It is surprising, for example, that some areas of social class, which one would judge from their treatment in the literature to be more than well catered for, turn out to be otherwise. Similarly, even where information is collected and recorded on a social class basis, it is not always published in that manner. This is particularly true of much census material. Conversely, in some areas it has been possible to choose from a number of similar sources. It is therefore necessary to spell out the criteria upon which data have been selected and used.

1 Only *British* data have been used. Here 'British' has been used to include only England, Wales and Scotland. While the bulk of the data presented, for example from the census, is for the whole of Great Britain, the vagaries of publication and differences in presentation between the two Census Offices has meant that occasionally only Scottish data have been available and therefore used. As a rule of thumb it may be assumed that British or English and Welsh data and studies have been chosen rather than Scottish wherever both have existed.

2 Wherever possible *the most up-to-date and large-scale* research figures attainable have been used. A selection has been made from available sources up to December 1975. The object is to present, as far as possible, a picture of contemporary British social class differences. This is not to deny the importance of the historical/developmental perspective in the study of social class, but merely to assert that the use, or particularly the over-use, of dated material without access to

the contemporary is misleading and confusing. In any case, historical treatments of many of the areas dealt with in this present volume exist elsewhere (see for example Marsh 1965, Halsey 1972).

Large-scale studies have been used since a wider spread of samples and data probably better reflects social class difference in Britain as a whole. At the same time it is true that some of these studies suffer, in comparison with smaller-scale research, from superficiality, and disguise some interesting and illuminating regional variations. Smaller-scale and/or greater-depth studies have been used where large-scale studies do not exist or where smaller studies, in the author's opinion, make a necessary or significant contribution to the aim of the book. Similarly regional variations, where these are central to the concern of the book (for example the geographical distribution of the social classes), have been included (see chapter 3). Other sources already exist (see for example Taylor and Ayres 1970 on North/South variations, and Coates and Rawstron 1971 on regional variations).

3 *Data have been presented in a straightforward way but without oversimplification.* As a general rule figures and percentages have been rounded to the nearest whole number for the sake of clarity. In all cases, however, base figures (normally the sample size) have been provided, usually in the text and always in the appendix. Similarly, wherever possible an average of the percentages for all social classes has been provided to facilitate comparison between them. In no case have the social class categories used in a piece of research or a publication been collapsed. The common combination of social classes into manual/non-manual or middle class/working class categories has thus been avoided. Not only does such a dichotomy oversimplify differences, but it typically disguises variations and trends between social classes.

4 *The text has been designed to be a commentary on the data.* Apart from necessary introductory and linking passages there has been little attempt to provide any exposition of the topics under consideration. This has been done not only with regard for the aims and limitations of this volume but because

it is assumed that readers will have access to other appropriate descriptive and explanatory sources, or that their immediate interest centres, like that of this volume, on the phenomena of social class and social class differences rather than on the contexts within which they have been viewed.

5 *Data have been organised around topics commonly found in textbooks and syllabuses.* This strategy was adopted to make for cogent chapters, and also to facilitate reference to, and from, the type of sources referred to in 4 above. At the same time a system of cross-referencing (see chapter 2, the appendix, the index and text) will enable the reader to make comparisons between different approaches, and to review the areas of research methodology and social institutions, as well as social class itself.

6 *Areas with little available data have not been ignored.* Since part of the aim of the book is to illustrate the state of knowledge regarding social class differences, comprehensive coverage has been aimed for. To some extent this implies not only a review of the available data but also asking what ought to be or might be available. The author has pointed out the lack or paucity of data at places where he felt that the reader might expect evidence to have been presented.

How to use this book

At one level this book is a collection of some of the existing empirical knowledge concerning social class differences in contemporary Britain. At another it is a student text. It is not however a textbook in the traditional sense, more a work- or sourcebook designed to complement and supplement existing books, courses and teaching. This section describes in general terms the layout of the book, and the uses to which it can be put.

An outline
The bulk of the book, chapters 3 to 7, consists of data on British social class differences grouped around typical syllabus topic areas — for example, work, the family, education,

leisure. This is supported by a running commentary on the data. Each of these chapters constitutes a useful source of information on specific topics. Used with introductory texts in sociology and texts on particular topics, they provide a basis for the student to evaluate any statements made.

Chapter 2 and the appendix explain the referencing system used in the book. Together with a discussion of social class as a variable in research, and a review of its importance in sociology and society, chapter 2 contains all the operational definitions of social class used in the studies reported in the book. These are coded with letters referring to the sources of the definition, and to particular modifications or uses. Wherever social class is mentioned in the bulk of the book it is followed by the appropriate code, which allows reference back to chapter 2 and thus to the definition involved. This is to avoid the misunderstandings and confusions which can arise from the simultaneous presentation of sets of social class differences based on different categories of social class. There are two further sections in chapter 2. The first identifies and briefly describes each sampling technique used in the researches reported in the book. The second gives similar treatment to the research methods used. Both research methods and sampling techniques are also coded with combinations of letters in order to facilitate reference to the appendix. It is therefore possible to identify the definition of social class, sample type and research technique used for each research study mentioned in the book.

The appendix lists all the studies used in the text, alphabetically, together with the following information for each:

1 Title
2 Date of publication
3 Date of data collection
4 Sample type
5 Sample size
6 Research technique(s)

7 Definition of social class
8 Table reference (where data from the study are presented in the text)
9 Notes

The appendix enables the reader to classify studies in terms of each of the factors listed. It gives, for example, a picture of the relative use made of different sample types and research methods.

It should be borne in mind that one of the virtues of the format used, and the single axis and emphasis of the book, is that it should encourage the reader to move outwards from an initial interest in a particular topic. It is hoped that the cross-referencing in the index will encourage this. This book should *generate* in the minds of readers some interesting interconnections or correlations between data in different areas. Readers should be aware both of the value of this — in some ways it is the essence of sociology — and also of its dangers, since correlations are not necessarily causations. Indeed in the area of social class they very rarely are. Social class differences on their own generally have no explanatory power. To produce data to show social class differences in children's performance at school is merely to present a statement. To evaluate that statement, we have to ask certain questions, such as 'What does social class mean in this context?', 'What were the criteria of achievement?' and 'How and where was the evidence obtained?' While this book attempts to provide answers to such questions, it does not attempt to explain the reasons why such results should be obtained. It does not approach questions which seek to identify the actual factors, or to describe the processes, involved. For these the reader must turn to other sociological literature.

Looking at the differences
Obviously in a book about social class differences, just these are emphasised, and similarities are overlooked. A valuable

exercise is to review the data, looking for similarities between the social classes. Social class differences are rarely total, since although the majority of one class may differ from that of another, some members of the two classes may be similar. These similarities, or what might be called 'non-data', lead one to speculate why such 'deviance' exists. Does it reflect the crudeness of social class classification by occupation — or are other factors specific to the topic under consideration responsible?

As was stated on p. 4, this book is a commentary on data about social class differences. As such it presents material in a relatively objective way — that is, independently of the observer's attitudes. Though this is how many sociologists try to approach social reality, it is, generally speaking, a somewhat unusual approach. There are some people who are shocked or outraged by the social class differences revealed here; others see them as necessary, if undesirable, realities of our society's way of life; others view them as desirable. Some are fired by a desire to change society in order to bring about greater equality and/or similarity of the social classes. Indeed this can be seen as one of the motives that lead people to investigate social class differences (this is discussed, for example, in relation to education in chapter 6). The author has avoided, at least consciously, presenting data from any particular political or philosophical standpoint, preferring that the reader brings his own to the material, and perhaps develops it while in contact with the book. In no way is he subscribing to the common fallacy that facts speak for themselves. That they do not is witnessed by the endless debates and controversies aroused by almost all, but particularly social, facts. For most people, their beliefs, feelings and ways of understanding are of equal importance to the facts themselves. It is a valuable exercise, therefore, to attempt to appreciate the variety of ways in which the social class differences outlined in this volume can be interpreted. The extremes of these interpretations are marked, on the one hand, by the view that the individual is completely responsible for his situation, and on the other, by complete economic and/or social determinism; and there are countless shades in between.

No mention is made in this book of the statistical significance of the social class differences reported. Briefly, statistical significance is a mathematical concept used to decide whether a difference which has been observed is likely to have happened by chance – or to put it the other way around, the degree of confidence one can have that the difference is a real one and would therefore be found again in further research. Social scientists are usually happy if a test shows that the likelihood of their results having occurred by chance is only one in a hundred, and reasonably content if it is as high as one in twenty. The lack of reference to statistical significance in this text is of course intentional. In the first place, the large size of the samples used in most of the research reported means that quite small differences are in fact significant. For example, Newson and Newson (1968) point out in their appendix 2, with reference to their sample (N = 700), that 'a difference of the order of about 10 per cent between any two percentages will usually prove to be significant statistically' (at the 0.01 level; that is, it is only likely to have occurred by chance 1 in 100 times). As can be seen in the appendix, this study had one of the smaller samples of the studies surveyed. In the second place, statistical significance does not tell one much about the importance of an observed difference in real terms. Very small differences in voting behaviour which are not statistically significant can, and indeed often do, have vitally important outcomes; while much larger differences elsewhere, say in choice of washing powder, may be totally irrelevant except to washing powder manufacturers. It is, then, in 'common sense' terms that the social class differences in this book ought to be viewed and considered.

Exploring social class

Few people will read this book without in some way identifying with its contents. Looking at the data relevant to

oneself, one's family, acquaintances and experiences is likely
to provoke agreement, amazement, disagreement or amuse-
ment. One interesting exercise for the reader is to compare his
own reactions with those of others: do one's friends, colleagues
or fellow students have concepts of social class – and what are
they? Are they willing to identify themselves as being
members of a social class? Do their opinions, habits, and
actions fit their social class ascriptions? A particularly interesting approach is to compare and contrast replies from
structured (pre-coded) questions with those from open-ended
ones (see p. 57).

Several sources exist to assist such exploration: Brown,
Cherrington and Cohen (1975) provide the basis for an
investigation of 'social class stereotypes'; Wakeford (1968) for
'indicators of social class position'; and Straus and Nelson
(1968) for 'social class and power in the family' (the last,
being American, will need modification). All these provide
questions to be used, and procedures for the collection and
treatment of the data. With access to the original source, many
of the studies mentioned in this book can be replicated with
fellow students.

The presentation of data

In order to economise on space nearly all the data in this book
have been presented in the most straightforward way, that is,
in tables of figures. A few tables (see for example tables 3.18,
5.25, 5.26) have been presented as diagrams. Many people find
such graphical presentations very useful in aiding understanding. There are a number of different graphical ways of
presenting data. Apart from the simple bar graphs used in this
text there are straight-line graphs. Both types can be quite
simply produced from the tables in this book using social class
as one axis and the other variable as the other axis. A very
useful scale for such purposes is provided by using 1 millimetre
to represent one per cent. Pie graphs – circles cut into sectors,
the size of each representing a percentage or actual number –
can also be used. More artistic representations, using people or
objects of proportionately varying size, are possible for the

Figure 1.1
Simple bar graph, showing percentage of each social class
reading the *Daily Mirror*

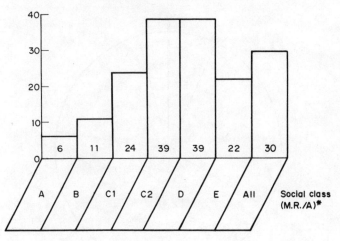

Figure 1.2
Straight-line graph, showing percentage of each social class
reading the *Daily Mirror*

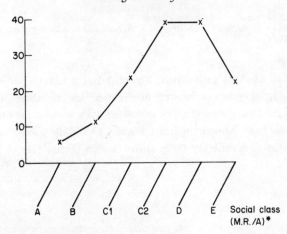

*See footnote to figure 1.3

About this book

Figure 1.3

Pie graph, showing social class composition of readers of the
Daily Mirror

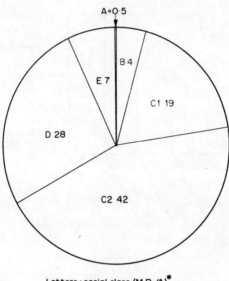

A = 0.5

B 4

E 7

C1 19

D 28

C2 42

Letters : social class (M.R./A)*
Numbers : percentages

*For an explanation of this code see p. 47
(Figures based on table 7.13, derived from *National Readership Survey
1975* 1976)

talented who are so inclined. Figures 1.1, 1.2 and 1.3 are all
based on the data presented in the top line of table 7.13
(p. 213). This shows the percentage of each social class who
read the *Daily Mirror* (figures 1.1 and 1.2) and the social class
composition (profile) of *Daily Mirror* readers (figure 1.3).

2

Social class and its use in empirical research

Social class is a concept readily understood by the average man, but is relatively difficult to define ... In recognising that social class is not a simple factor, but an amalgam of factors that operate in different ways in different circumstances, such a person has arrived at the same view as the professional sociologist.

D. Monk (1970)

Readers of this chapter ought to share with its author the realisation that the topics it deals with are extremely complex. Indeed many whole volumes have been devoted to each of them. No attempt has been made here to review comprehensively the present state of knowledge concerning social class or research methods. It has also been necessary to exclude, almost completely, consideration of the theoretical aspects of social class. The aim of this chapter is, rather, to provide a framework within which the data contained in the following chapters can be viewed. It gives a rather large-scale sketch map of social class and its definitions, and of research methods and sampling techniques as they have been used in post-war empirical research in Britain. Readers who want more detailed treatments will find these quite readily available elsewhere, and the references provided in this chapter will be a starting point for their search.

What is social class?

As almost all introductory books on sociology and social class are at pains to point out, social class is only one form of social stratification. Dictionaries define stratification as an arrangement of layers, or as the relative position of layers. Simply, then, social stratification is an arrangement of society into layers. However, it usually also implies some form of differentiation between, or comparative evaluation of, the layers: reference is being made not only to different groups within society, but to a hierarchy or ranking of these groups. This implied evaluation and ranking can be seen in the definitions of social class outlined below on pp. 32–49. These are ordinarily ranked by number or letter and listed from the 'highest' to the 'lowest'. The very common use of contrasting terms such as 'middle class' and 'working class', 'non-manual class' and 'manual class', reveals the same evaluative connotations. Most sociological treatments of stratification contrast social class with the comparative and historical examples of caste and estate. It is probably much more meaningful, however, to compare it with other forms of stratification in our society, such as the two almost universal forms of stratification – age and sex. To a great extent people of different ages, or different sex, are given, and expect, differential treatment: they have different rights, privileges and duties, and they hold views of the world and of themselves which are related to such differences.

The number of criteria on which social stratification (or categorisation) could be based is theoretically infinite. Any culturally recognisable difference – forms of skill, type and amount of knowledge, religious practice, strength, length of hair, beauty and so on – could be such a basis, depending on the social context. Some kind of social stratification seems almost universal, or even inevitable, in social life. Even among groups of peers certain hierarchies are likely to be perceived. In any group – whether of fellow students, colleagues, or even a family – we are likely to categorise the members by some such differences. To some extent the recognition of such criteria affects people's behaviour towards each other and their behaviour and organisation as a social group. The more visible the criteria of differentiation, the more strict the social stratification, and the more regulated the relationships between the strata. Extreme examples are the armed forces and hospitals, where the wearing of uniform ensures recognition of differences and hence regulates relationships and behaviour.

Clearly, however, social class has a much more elusive character than age or sex. Indeed there appears to be a good deal of discussion, or even confusion, in sociological literature about the nature and meaning of social class. Crisp definitions of social class rarely appear, and the concept is generally seen to be problematic. Even O level sociology textbooks, not unknown for their pat, meaning-defying definitions, treat the concept with caution. Such caution is well advised, since social class is a multidimensional concept, involving not only the identification of what are partly invisible categories in society but also an understanding of the effects of these on the people involved. Fortunately, for the purposes of this book, we can afford to be bolder, and accept as a working definition the following: *social class is a grouping of people into categories on the basis of occupation.*

The main reason why this definition can be accepted here is that our exclusive concern is with empirical research. In British research, as will be seen below (pp. 32–49), almost the sole criterion of social class which has been used is occupation. While British researchers have expressed some reservations about the use of this single factor, it appears to be accepted as a reasonable general-purpose tool for classifying people into social classes. Or, as Monk (1970) has argued, 'occupation has remained the backbone of social grading because no better methods have been found, and because it has still remained a powerful and useful stratification factor, even though the interpretation has become more complex'. It is of interest to note that in Britain there has been little real research concern with the development and use of scales of social class based on other factors, or on multidimensional measures. In some contrast, American sociologists and social anthropologists have developed a number of multidimensional scales. Some of these have been based on combinations of factors such as occupation, income and education, while others have involved more unusual factors such as participation in the community, family prestige, and the contents and condition of living rooms. For a review of these see Gordon 1963. However, it is true that most of these scales have been developed for a particular study, and their general use in other studies has been limited. This is because the use of such scales costs time and money. In terms of research use, occupation, almost certainly because it is easily collected and simple to treat, has remained universally the most popular criterion. Moreover, occupation has been consistently shown to be highly related to most other factors associated with social class, particularly income and education. Occupation, then, is recognised as an element of social class in all sociological treatments of the concept. There are a number of reasons for this which are basically very simple and which can be dealt with briefly. In all societies where they exist occupations are differentially rewarded. Income is obviously an important determinant of possessions, style of life, and place of living in societies based on a cash nexus. Since income is for nearly everyone the main form of wealth, occupation is a good indicator of the economic situation of a person and his family. Furthermore, following an occupation takes up a considerable amount of a person's time and life, and typically places him in a situation where he interacts with particular groups of people in particular ways. It would be surprising if the experience of work did not affect in some way a person's view of the world, his attitudes and opinions. Broadly speaking, too, people are residentially segregated by occupation. People with similar incomes are likely to be able to afford similar housing, and will thus share many other aspects of life with each other. Dockers are likely to have more in common with other dockers than with doctors.

Does everybody use occupation as the criterion of social class?

It is quite reasonable to ask whether the classifying of people into social classes by occupation is an activity peculiar to sociologists. In some ways we all indulge in similar activities in everyday life. One of the earliest and most common enquiries made in a casual meeting is 'What job do you do?' – a question which usually brings a response, and rarely leads to an end of the conversation, or to embarrassment. From this 'knowledge' (of another's occupation) people are likely to make a number of assumptions about that person, his interests, attitudes and so on. These assumptions will be based on one's previous experience of similar people and/or what one has read, seen, or heard about them; they affect the conversation and one's reactions to it. Surprises and mistakes do occur. One could meet a stockbroker who raced pigeons, for example, or a docker who drank only Pernod, but over all our assumptions are borne out. Significantly, when they are not, we do not discard them, but merely dust them off and retain them for the future. We are unlikely to inquire of the next stockbroker we meet how his pigeons are. The experience is accommodated as an oddity. This happens because our categories are resilient, and indeed they probably need to be. Life would become socially and psychologically intolerable if every new encounter had to be built up from scratch. Outside the purely social encounter, many commercial and government organisations require to know our occupations. Since few of us change our jobs dramatically, we may not realise what a crucial role our job plays in the way people and organisations react to us. It is possible to test this by pretending to be something other than what we are, say at a dance or on a rail journey in the company of others. This allows us to compare the responses we get with those we normally receive. Categorisation of people on the basis of small snippets of information is common in social life. One's outward appearance can often affect the treatment one receives in places like banks, garages or large stores. Most of us pay heed to this – for example, when we go for an interview for a job.

What is happening here is clearly not far removed from what the social scientist does when he classifies people in terms of social class. He is assuming that this single piece of information — occupation — is a good predictor of a host of other factors such as income, education, style of life, attitudes, interests and beliefs, which together form his concept of social class. His research is likely to be based on hypotheses (which can be seen as informed guesses, or hunches) rather similar to those used in face to face situations. His categories are just as crude and resilient as our 'real-life' ones, but he is likely to be more systematic in collecting his data, and his judgements can thus be rationally appraised. So common sense, as well as empirical research, would suggest that occupation is a key factor in defining social class. As Berger has written (1963):

Different classes in our society not only live differently quantitatively, they live in different styles qualitatively. A sociologist worth his salt . . . can make a long list of predictions about the individual in question even if no further information has been given. Like all sociological predictions, these will be statistical in character. That is, they will be probability statements and will have a margin of error . . . the sociologist will be able to make intelligent guesses about the part of town in which the individual lives, as well as about the size and style of his house . . . to give a general description of the interior decorating of the house and make a guess about the types of pictures on the wall and books or magazines likely to be found on the shelves of the living room . . . to guess what kind of music the individual in question likes to listen to . . . predict which voluntary associations the individual has joined and where he has his church membership .'. . estimate the individual's vocabulary, lay down some rough rules for his syntax and other uses of language . . . guess the individual's political affiliation and his views on a number of public issues . . . predict the number of children sired by his subject and also whether the latter has sexual relations with his wife with the lights on or off . . . to make some statements about the likelihood that his subject will come down with a number of diseases, physical as well as mental . . . Finally, if the sociologist should decide to verify all these guesses and ask the individual in question for an interview, he can estimate the chance that the interview will be refused.

Most of the present volume is concerned with tracing just such relationships, and illustrating the basis on which such claims can be made.

Is social class a new idea?

A commonly expressed opinion about social class is that if
sociologists, political scientists and the like did not actually
invent the term, then they are certainly active in maintaining
and popularising it. This contention demands some consideration since it is basically untrue. There are some clear historical
indications that divisions in society which exhibit most of the
characteristics associated with social class have long been
recognised. Plato, some three hundred years before the birth
of Christ, wrote about gold, silver, and tin people. The rights
and privileges of these groups he saw as being based on
inheritance, effort and worth to society. Aristotle wrote that
the best administered states had a large middle class — larger if
possible than both the others — which is clearly a reference to
the different degrees of political power enjoyed by the classes.
Romans used the term *classis*, which was a division of people
on the basis of property and taxation. According to the
Roman historian Pliny the classes were judged by wealth
measured in asses of brass. Such historical allusions, and there
are many more, suggest that all the usual concomitants of
class — status, power, wealth and so on — have been recognised
as a basis for dividing people into groups probably for as long
as societies have existed. However, Briggs (1960) has argued
that in Britain the term 'social class', as we understand it,
started to be used only after the Industrial Revolution.
Previously, in the eighteenth century, society was perceived in
terms of broad bands, reflecting the comparatively simple
social structure of what was basically an agrarian society.
Industrialisation not only broke up the existing order of
society, but replaced it with a greater division of labour.
People became much more differentiated in their occupations,
which varied in terms of skills and rewards. These differences,
together with the great migration to the cities (urbanisation),
also brought about separation in residence, style of life and
interests. Certainly the Victorian era was characterised by
what might be termed 'class consciousness' or 'awareness'. It
was not by chance that Marx chose England as the model on

which to base the development of his ideas. However, the flames of class consciousness were probably fuelled not so much by Marx as by the lingering fears created by the French Revolution, and the reaction to those fears on the part of established power. Hence the established Church of England sang

> The rich man at his castle,
> The poor man at his gate,
> God made them, high or lowly,
> And order'd their estate.

and this was echoed in the literature of the day. Dickens wrote

> Oh let us love our occupations
> Bless the squire and his relations
> Live upon our daily rations
> And always know our proper stations.

While certain classical sociologists, namely Marx and Weber, saw social class as a central concept in sociology, other sociologists did not. It was not so much sociologists who were initially involved in the systematic collection of social class data, as medically inspired census workers (see Stevenson 1928 and p. 102 below) and empirically minded social reformers like Booth and Rowntree. Subsequently, government and commercial market researchers have played a major role in empirical research using social class. They have helped in shaping research fashions, but more importantly have sustained the use of the concept and provided much of the data in the field.

In much the same way discussions about the reality and the utility of social class have a history. There are two different ways in which social class can be seen to exist. First, classifications in terms of social class are seen, to some extent, as comparable to those used by a scientist wishing to classify physical phenomena. Such a classification — for example, of moths — needs only to fit the known instances of moths, and to be recognised as useful by other scientists. In this sense it has what can be described as 'objective existence'. It does not rely for its usefulness or legitimacy on whether or not the moths themselves agree with it! Social class too has objective existence, as is clearly witnessed by the data presented in this book in chapters 3 to 7: social class is accepted and used by social scientists and others as a classification of the populations they investigate. The concerns of sociologists, however, are rarely as straightforward as those of other scientists. As has already been suggested, ideas of social class, or social differences, appear to exist, and to have existed, among the general population (see also the following sections of this chapter). Indeed it could be argued that sociologists have only systematised pre-existing knowledge of divisions in human society. Here the second way of looking at the existence of social class comes in. To the extent to which people in society perceive, or accept, social class, it has a 'subjective existence'. Hence we can identify two longstanding concerns of sociologists about the classifications they construct. They are

1 How well do they fit the social reality they are designed to explain?
2 How meaningful are they to the people to whom they apply?

These concerns, which are interrelated, form the basis of much current criticism of sociology, from both inside and outside the discipline. They are far from new. Marx, who is recognised by many as being father to the present interest in, and use of, the idea of social class, clearly recognised them both. His basic idea was that there were two social classes: the bourgeoisie, who owned the means of production, and the proletariat, who did not – as he saw it, the exploiters and the exploited. However, Marx recognised that in the social situation he was describing there was another group who, while not owning the means of production, were saved from exploitation because they had skills and knowledge which the bourgeoisie needed. He used the term 'petit bourgeoisie' to describe such people as doctors and lawyers, who were evidently not being exploited to the same degree as the proletariat. In a similar fashion Marx was concerned that the proletariat did not share his concept of their position in society. They failed to recognise their exploitation because, while they were a class 'in itself' (objective), they were not a class 'for itself' (subjective). To put it more forcibly, as Marx did (but only once), they were suffering from 'false consciousness', that is they did not recognise their 'real' situation, as he had defined it. These sorts of concern continue, and would be seen by some to be of central importance for this book and for the researches from which it uses data. Some sociologists would argue that in the social as opposed to the physical world objective classifications have only limited utility. They argue that a proper under-standing of social reality will only be achieved when social scientists use concepts which have real foundations in the consciousness of the people involved. Whether the efficacy of the concept of social class is dependent on the realisation and acceptance by the general population that social class exists is open to debate. If it is so dependent then the next section of this chapter is vitally related to the rest of the book. If the evidence there is found wanting — which would suggest that the concept does not exist in people's minds — then possibly the utility of the rest of the book would have to be held in doubt. Other sociologists would be more concerned with social class in the objective sense. They would judge its utility by how usefully the concept performed in research: does it for example, reveal consistent and illuminating facts about society?

Does the public recognise social class?

A number of studies have been conducted using representative samples and direct questions about social class. A study by Martin (Glass 1954) asked the following questions: 'How many social classes would you say there are in this country?'; 'Can you name them?'; 'Which of these do you belong to?' Nearly all those questioned (96 per cent of a sample of 1,020) attempted an answer, and four out of five of the replies were accounted for under the headings of 'working class' and 'middle class'. In general, subsequent studies have suggested that over 90 per cent of people questioned are willing to identify themselves as belonging to a social class. In the case of a random sample of adults in England and Wales (Runciman 1964) the percentage was 99, while for Rosser and Harris (1965) with a sample from Swansea it was 93. Similar findings are reported by Kahan, Butler and Stokes (1966), who simply asked their sample (N = 1,775) to volunteer which social class they belonged to. Without prompting, almost all used recognisable and established categories in their replies. The left-hand column of table 2.1 shows that 96 per cent of the respondents' initial replies used either 'middle class' (29 per cent) or 'working class' (67 per cent). When they were invited to say if they belonged to the 'upper' or 'lower' parts of their class, few chose to do so, as can be seen in the right-hand column. In these studies nearly all respondents recognised that there were social classes, had a knowledge of their names, and were willing to identify themselves as belonging to one of them.

A National Opinion Poll study used a somewhat more direct approach, and avoided the self-rating aspect by using the question 'Some people talk about social classes, others say that there is no such thing. Do you think there are different social

Table 2.1
Self-rating on social class (percentages)

	Initial rating	Subsequent rating
Upper class	1	1
Upper middle class	–	3
Middle class	29	25
Lower middle class	1	4
Upper working class	1	10
Working class	67	53
Lower working class	–	4
Other	1	–

(Derived from the text and table 1, Kahan, Butler and Stokes 1966)

Table 2.2
Percentage of respondents thinking that there are different
social classes, and those willing to identify themselves as
belonging to one, by social class

	Social class (M.R.*)				
	A B	C1	C2	DE	All
Yes	93	95	92	87	91
No	6	4	6	10	7
Don't know	1	1	2	3	2
% who identified themselves as members of a social class	95	97	96	94	95
% who did not	5	3	4	6	5

*This code is explained below on p. 47
*(Derived from tables from pp. 14 and 17, National Opinion Polls
1972a)*

classes in Britain today or not?' As can be seen from table 2.2
a somewhat smaller percentage (91) recognised social classes,
and this varied according to the social class of the respondents
(rated on occupation). The higher the social class the larger the
majority who recognised social classes (93 per cent in AB, 87
per cent in DE). It is interesting to note, however, that later in
the study a more forceful question was used: 'Many people do
use the term social class in this country. If you had to say
which social class you belong to, which would it be?' As the
second section of the table shows, the percentage of respondents willing to do this was greater than the percentage who
initially recognised different social classes (over all 95 per cent
compared with 91 per cent). Indeed the table reveals that
about half of those who replied 'No' or 'Don't know' to the
first question subsequently assigned themselves to a class.

A reasonable conclusion would be that the term 'social
class' has a good deal of currency among the population at
large and that people are prepared to use it of themselves.
More interesting is the extent to which the subjective social
class (that which respondents gave themselves) related to the
objective scales based on occupation used by the researchers.

Table 2.3

The relationship between subjective and objective social class

Subjective social class	*Objective social class (M.R.)*†			
	AB	**C1**	**C2**	**DE**
Middle class	82	73	43	35
Working class	13	24	53	59
Don't know	5	3	4	6

(Devised from p. 17, National Opinion Polls 1972a)

Subjective social class	*Objective* social class (M.R./C.)*†					
	I	**II**	**III**	**IV**	**V**	**VI**
Middle class	78	65	60	32	17	9
Working class	22	35	40	68	83	91

*Here relates to social class of head of household in which respondent was living
†In the table the objective social classes AB and C1, and I, II, III and IV, are middle class; C2 and DE, and V and VI, are working class
(Derived from table 4.3, Butler and Stokes 1969)

Table 2.3 shows that in these two studies a sizeable minority of respondents were at variance with the researchers' classifications (full details of these can be found below on pp. 47 and 48). The objective classifications are shown in the headings at the top of the table, and the two subjective classifications in the left-hand column. As can be seen, at the extremes of the scales there is a fair correspondence between the objective and subjective ratings: of social class AB respondents, 82 per cent rated themselves middle class, compared with 35 per cent of those in class DE. Similarly, in the other study 78 per cent of those rated class I compared with 9 per cent of those in class VI viewed themselves as middle class. The situation is much less clear away from the extremes. Indeed in the case of the second study, a majority (68 per cent) of those in class IV (lower non-manual) saw themselves as working class. There is, then, some divergence between people's occupational level and their ideas of which class they belong to. This suggests that factors other than, or as well as, occupation count when people are classing themselves.

On what basis does the public recognise social class?

Both of the studies mentioned went on to make enquiries into how people recognised the social classes. Kahan, Butler and Stokes asked their sample to describe the sort of people they regarded as belonging to the middle and to the working class. From the replies they attempted to identify the implicit frames of reference being used. Clearly, as table 2.4 demonstrates, the major factor was occupation. A majority of respondents (61 per cent) chose this as the criterion for describing the middle class, and a larger one (74 per cent) chose it to describe the working class. These findings are very close to those of Martin a decade before this study, where about three-quarters of the subjects viewed the working class in terms of occupation (Glass 1954, p. 59). However, as the authors remark, occupation cannot be seen as the sole basis of perceived social class. Other factors such as income and education (which are obviously, but not directly, related − see chapters 3 and 6), social graces, parentage etc. were present. These factors were further emphasised by the respondents when they were asked what they saw as being important in relation to social mobility (that is, the movement of people

Table 2.4
Characteristics used to describe the middle class and the working class

Middle class	*% of responses*	*Working class*	*% of responses*
Occupation	61	Occupation	74
Income/level of living	21	Income/level of living	10
Attitudes/hierarchial location	5	Manners and morals	7
Manners and morals	5	Attitudes/hierarchial location	5
Education/intelligence	5	Education/intelligence	3
Family background	1	Other	1
Political	1		
Other	1		

(Derived from table 2, Kahan, Butler and Stokes 1966)

between the social classes: see pp. 90 to 96). It would appear, however, that occupation was seen as the primary basis for social class judgements.

A rather different picture emerges from the somewhat different approach of the National Opinion Poll study. Here the respondents were asked 'Which two of these would you say are most important in being able to tell which class a person is?' They were shown a card with the list of factors reproduced in table 2.5. Note that the order of presentation is shown in parenthesis in the left-hand column, while the table lists them in the overall order in which they were chosen by the respondents (see the right-hand column).

There are, perhaps, two surprising features in this table. First, occupation is ranked over all by the sample in fourth place (24 per cent of the sample chose it), and the top two

Table 2.5

Rank order of bases of social class recognition by social class of respondent*

		Social class (M.R.)				
		AB	C1	C2	DE	All
(4)†	The way they speak	4	1	2	1	1
(1)	Where they live	5	3=	1	2	2
(9)	The friends they have	2	2	3	3	3
(3)	Their job	3	5	4	5	4
(5)	The sort of school they went to	6	3=	5	4	5
(8)	The way they spend their money	7	6	6	6	6
(7)	The amount of money they have	9	8	7	7	7=
(6)	The way they dress	8	7	8	8	7=
(2)	The car they own	10=	10	9	9	9
(10)	None of these	1	9	10=	10=	10
(11)	Don't know	10=	11	10=	10=	11

*Respondents were asked to choose two of the items from the list which appears here; ranking is based on both treated equally
† Figures in parentheses before each item refer to the order in which the items appeared on the card shown to the respondents
(Devised from p. 21, National Opinion Polls 1972a)

rankings are given to 'The way they speak' and 'Where they live' (33 and 28 per cent chose these). Secondly, respondents from class AB most often ranked 'None of these' as being most important. Over all, however, there is a fair degree of agreement across the social classes. Occupation, for example, was ranked 3, 5, 4, 5 across the social classes. The findings here are very different from those of Kahan, Butler and Stokes, and of Martin, reported above, on the prime importance of occupation as a basis of social class. Much of this difference could be accounted for by the nature and structure of the questions used. In the National Opinion Polls study the question refers to what is important 'in being able to tell which class . . . '. This could have directed attention to obvious and outward indications such as speech and residence. Similarly the presentation of the list probably led to consideration of a wider range of factors.

A good deal of debate about the sort of research described above, particularly about its meaning and reliability, is evident in the literature. This amounts almost to a suggestion that 'You asks your question, and you gets your answer' — in other words that the question is the vital factor, different questions producing different responses. Webb (1973), in describing a small-scale study in Liverpool (N = 90), contrasts findings from two distinct types of question. In response to the first, a straightforward request for a self-rating of social class, the middle class respondents appeared to have a stronger class identification than the working class respondents. A further question asked 'What type of people are you thinking of when you talk about people like yourself?' (Webb described this as 'free self-alignment'). In response to this question it was the working class respondents who were most likely to reply in terms of social class. Two quite different pictures had emerged. In his conclusion, Webb restates a point basic to the whole enterprise of social science research: 'If [social] class is a meaningful term in their [the respondents'] normal day to day existence — which the interview best taps — it is perhaps advisable to let the respondents themselves select the term rather than to have it thrust upon them'.

Platt (1971) in reviewing some of the 'affluent worker' study material in this field (Goldthorpe, Lockwood, Bechhofer and Platt 1969) makes a parallel, if somewhat different, set of points. In the affluent worker study the researchers attempted to gain a view of their respondents' 'image of class' with a number of open-ended questions. From the replies the researchers argued that there existed three basic images of social class:

1 A 'power' model, with two classes, based on power and authority
2 A 'prestige' model, with three or more classes, based on life style, social background or acceptance
3 A 'money' model, with one large central class, and one or more small ones, based on wealth, income and consumption

Among the affluent manual workers who were the subjects of this study, the 'money' model was found to predominate. Thus 54 per cent subscribed to model 3 above, 4 per cent to model 1, and 8 per cent to model 2; the remaining 34 per cent were classed as using 'other' models — which is itself perhaps remarkable. A further specific single question asked the respondents to rank six occupations, presented together with their incomes on a card, in order of their 'standing in the community'. A comparison of the respondents' ranking with what was called an orthodox status order (i.e. objective ranking) revealed considerable unorthodoxy. Moreover, in stark comparison with the findings above, in this second context 61 per cent of the affluent manual workers used a 'prestige' model, and only 2 per cent a pure 'money' model. Platt suggests a number of alternative explanations for this incongruence:

1 Respondents distinguished between 'social class' and 'standing in the community'
2 The responses were differently coded (analysed) by the researchers
3 The social range of the occupations presented was very

narrow, and because of this respondents used criteria other than money in discriminating between them

4 Since the class questions were general, and the 'standing in the community' question was specific, the respondents used different frames of reference in answering them

5 The financial information (income) given in the second question directed the respondents' attention away from money

Clearly one has to agree with the author that 'questions which are intended to refer to the same general area of a subject matter may in fact vary and consequently create difficulties of interpretation. In particular caution is necessary in comparing findings from questions of different kinds, and in generalising from them.'

A second type of evidence on the existence of social class in the subjective sense arises from the concern of researchers as to whether their social class definitions, based on occupation, have any agreed or commonly accepted basis. The most famous British study was that connected with the development of the Hall-Jones scale. Hall and Jones said to their respondents 'We should like to know in what order as to their social standing you would grade the occupations in the list given to you' (Hall and Jones 1950). Details of this scale can be found on p. 44 below. The question was basically that which Stevenson claimed to have answered, but presumably without the fieldwork, with reference to the Registrar General's social classification of 1921 (Stevenson 1928; see also p. 102 below). The list contained thirty occupations and the respondents apparently had no difficulty in ranking them according to the criterion supplied. A close correspondence between the standard (objective) classification of the authors and the undirected (subjective) judgement of the sample was found. Hall and Jones concluded that there were no major differences of opinion among those tested, and that the consensus was greater than they had expected.

A somewhat similar, though more sophisticated, approach was adopted by the Oxford study (see Goldthorpe and Hope 1972 and 1974). In the part of this study concerned with the production of a social class classification by occupation, respondents were asked to rank a list of forty occupations on four criteria. These were: standard of living, prestige in the community, power and influence over other people, and value to society. Once again the people involved had little difficulty, in general, in performing the task. Over all, the rankings on the various criteria were related (i.e. similar) and the criterion of prestige was accepted as being the most useful. Hope (1973) also reports that the respondents' ranking remained stable over a period of two or three months. He further states that dividing the sample by age, sex and broad occupational categories confirmed the overall analysis, with some minor differences between the groups.

Such evidence suggests that the public can and will rank occupations with a fair degree of ease and similarity. This facility is not limited to British samples, being evident in other western societies; there is also a similarity in rankings by people in different societies (see for example a review by Lipset and Bendix (1959)). However, nearly all these researches have involved 'non-conforming' respondents whose ranking has been at variance with the majority's. In the past there has been a tendency to dismiss such divergent views as being idiosyncratic, rather than socially or sociologically important. One might expect such differing views of the overall structure to arise from the fact that the respondents were occupying different positions in that structure. However, some studies have revealed these differences within the same occupational level. Young and Willmott (1956) found that some manual workers thought that miners and other manual workers ought to rank alongside doctors and above lawyers and managers. Leaving aside, for the moment, questions of how they understood and responded to the questions involved, a problem remains. Solutions to this may come from current researches that set out to explore how different concepts of

the occupational structure in society differ in socially significant ways. Coxon and Jones (1974), reporting on a preliminary analysis of just such a study (N = 169), suggest that 'it
seems ... that people with similar occupational histories,
rather than current occupational membership, make rather
similar judgements'. Coxon and Jones have also (1973)
questioned the meaning of the ranking of occupations. The
fact that the public agree in evaluating occupations does not,
they suggest, allow one to assume that people share the same
perception (view) of or cognition of (way of thinking about)
the occupations involved. Or, as they illustrate:

In discussing 'images of society' there is a danger of jumping
from the fact that people talk about society in a particular
way (say as a polarised dichotomy) to inferring that they
perceive it that way. But this is by no means inconsistent with
the hypothesis that such people are *just* as aware of social
differentiations and gradations, and can equally make as fine
discriminations around those positions, as a person who tends
to talk in terms of graded hierarchies.

They suggest that the way forward is to examine the cognition
involved in ranking, and to avoid the dangers they see in the
usual forms of ranking exercise. Hence they required their
respondents to indicate 'overall similarity' between pairs of
occupations, and were concerned with the verbalisations they
made while deciding. This sort of research is likely to reveal
some of the thinking and values implicit in the ranking of
occupations.

How social class has been operationalised in empirical research

This section has two purposes. It provides an outline of the
common classifications of occupations into social classes used
in empirical research in Britain. It also provides a referencing
system. This allows the reader to refer from each table in this

book to the definition of social class used in the study in question. The following list is not exhaustive: inclusion signifies only that the particular definition has been used in a study referred to in the text.

The classification of occupations into social classes is an extremely complex business, because there are so many occupations. The Registrar General has a list of more than 20,000 separate occupational titles, which are grouped into 200 occupational units (*Classification of Occupations* 1970), each one of which has a social class classification. Space dictates that only brief outlines of the classifications be presented below. Examples of the actual occupations grouped together to form social classes have been supplied only for the most common classification, that of the Registrar General (see table 2.6 below). Interested readers will find that the full classifications, and instructions for their use, are generally available, and sources for these are included below.

Table 2.6
Typical occupations by social class (R.G. 70)

Social class	Examples of occupations included
I Professional etc.	Accountant, architect, chemist, clergyman, doctor, lawyer, surveyor, university teacher
II Intermediate	Aircraft pilot or engineer, chiropodist, farmer, manager, Member of Parliament, nurse, police or fire-brigade officer, schoolteacher
III Skilled non-manual	Clerical worker, draughtsman, sales representative, secretary, shop assistant, telephone supervisor, waiter
III Skilled manual	Bus driver, butcher, bricklayer, carpenter, cook, electrician, miner (underground), railway guard, upholsterer
IV Partly skilled	Agricultural worker, barman, bus conductor, fisherman, machine sewer, packer, postman, telephone operator
V Unskilled	Kitchen hand, labourer, lorry driver's mate, messenger, office cleaner, railway porter, stevedore, window cleaner

(*Devised from appendixes B1 and B2,* Classification of Occupations *1970*)

Registrar General

The census contains two forms of classification of occupations which are of direct relevance to the present text.

Social class

Since the census of 1911 it has been the practice to group the occupational units of the census into a small number of broad categories known as social classes. The present categories derive from the 1921 census, and the work Stevenson did (see p. 102). Indeed, as has been pointed out above, and as will be obvious from the rest of this section, the Registrar General's social classes form the basis of all the commonly used social class classifications in Britain. The basis and rationale of this categorisation is as follows:

The unit groups included in each of these categories [i.e. social classes] have been selected so as to ensure that, so far as is possible, each category is homogeneous in relation to the basic criterion of the general standing within the community of the occupations concerned. This criterion is naturally correlated with, and its application conditioned by, other factors such as education and economic environment, but it has no direct relationship to the average level of remuneration of particular occupations. Each occupational unit group has been assigned as a whole to a Social Class, and is not a specific assignment of individuals based on the merits of a particular case.

The Social Class appropriate to any combination of occupation and status is derived by the following rules:

(*a*) each occupation is given a basic Social Class
(*b*) persons of foreman status whose basic Social Class is IV or V are allotted to Social Class III
(*c*) persons of manager status are allocated either to Social Class II or III, the latter applying if the basic class is IV or V.

(*Classification of Occupations* 1970)

Until the Census of 1971 the social classes were titled as follows:

    I Professional etc. occupations
   II Intermediate occupations

III Skilled occupations
IV Partly skilled occupations
V Unskilled occupations

The Registrar General recognised that social class I was wholly non-manual and that social class V was wholly manual (*Classification of Occupations* 1960). The other social classes contained both manual and non-manual occupations. Researchers usually ignored the mixed nature of classes II and IV, normally treating II as non-manual and IV as manual. There was some concern about social class III, which clearly contained a large proportion of both types of occupation — some 49 per cent of the occupations of economically active persons in Great Britain in 1971. Researchers quite commonly subdivided this class into III N.M. (non-manual) and III M. (manual). This practice was sometimes indulged in by census and government researchers, who on occasion extended the process to classes II and IV as well. The 1971 census adopted the division of social class III as a standard procedure. Contemporary census material uses the following classification:

I Professional etc.
II Intermediate
III Skilled (N.) non-manual
        (M.) manual
IV Partly skilled
V Unskilled

Examples of the types of occupation which fall into these categories are given in table 2.6. There have been changes from one census to another in the allocation of occupations to the social classes. Details of these changes are to be found in the relevant volumes of *Classification of Occupations* (1950, 1960, 1966, 1970). The most extensive changes occurred between the census of 1951 and that of 1961, and some of the effects of these are displayed in chapter 3 (p. 96). The most important change was the total exclusion of members of the armed forces in 1961. The net result was to increase significantly the 'unclassified' groups. Other changes reflected a re-ordering of occupations. For example, aircraft pilots, navigators and engineers were changed from social class III to II; draughtsmen from II to III; postmen and telephone operators from III to IV; and lorry drivers' mates from IV to V. These changes reflect the fact that the basic social gradient of the classification is being retained within the changing economic and social structure of Britain. An important change in the application of the classification was the use of different age groups (20–64 years in 1951 and 15–64 in 1961).

Code

The letters 'R.G.' following the words 'social class' in the tables and text of this book indicate the direct use of the Registrar General's scale outlined immediately above. The numbers which follow (50, 60, 66, 70) refer to the particular year of the classification used. If any modification to the Registrar General's classification has been made this is indicated by a letter following the two numbers. A key to these letters is provided below and table 2.7 (p. 49) provides a quick reference system for the complete codings.

Modifications

A: social class III (skilled) has been subdivided into III (N.M) and III (M.). This only applies to the Registrar General's classifications prior to 1970, since when this measure has been incorporated.

B: either I and II, or IV and V, or both, have been combined; details are apparent from the table concerned.

C: a collapsed form of classification, consisting of two groups:

Group	*Social classes*
Non-manual	I, II, III (N.M.)
Manual	III (M.), IV, V

D: a collapsed threefold classification:

Group	Social classes
Non-manual	I, II
Skilled	III
Other manual	IV, V

E: a classification used in some of the work of the Registrar General (Scotland), in which the R.G. 70 scale has been modified into a five-point scale by combining III (N.) and III (M.).

F: a simple dichotomy used by Barker Lunn (1970):

Group	Social classes
Upper	I, II, III
Lower	IV, V

Socio-economic groups and class

Since the 1951 census, occupations have also been classified into socio-economic groups. In 1961 the original thirteen groups were replaced by seventeen, and these were used again in 1971. The aim of the grouping is laid out as follows:

Ideally each socio-economic group should contain people whose social, cultural and recreational standards and behaviour are similar. As it is not practicable to ask direct questions about these subjects in a population census, the allocation of occupied persons to socio-economic groups is determined by considering their employment status and occupation.

(*Classification of Occupations* 1960)

The groups are as follows:

1 Employers and managers in central and local government, industry, commerce etc. — large establishments (with 25 or more employees)
2 Employers and managers in central and local government, industry, commerce etc. — small establishments (with 25 or fewer employees)
3 Professional workers — self-employed
4 Professional workers — employed

5   Intermediate non-manual workers
6   Junior non-manual workers
7   Personal service workers
8   Foremen and supervisors — manual
9   Skilled manual workers
10   Semi-skilled manual workers
11   Unskilled manual workers
12   Own-account workers (other than professional)
13   Farmers, employers or managers
14   Farmers, own account
15   Agricultural workers
16   Members of the armed forces
17   Indefinite (inadequately stated occupations)

The last two groups are generally disregarded but the rest of the classification has been extensively used. Government research, particularly the *General Household Survey*, has also made use of a collapsed version referred to here as *socio-economic class*. (Note that the *Classification of Occupations* 1970 also refers to socio-economic class — in that case a 37-category cross-classification between social class (R.G.) and socio-economic groups — but that classification has not been used in research reported in this book.) This collapse is achieved, as shown below, by placing the fifteen groups into six categories. These categories are not identical with social classes, but are clearly parallel, particularly to R.G. 70. In some tables in this text, data collected for all the socio-economic groups shown above has been presented according to the collapsed categories.

Socio-economic class	*Socio-economic groups*	*Descriptive definition*
1	3, 4	Professional
2	1, 2, 13	Employers and managers
3	5, 6	Intermediate and junior non-manual

Socio-economic class	Socio-economic groups	Descriptive definition
4	8, 9, 12, 14	Skilled manual (with own account non-professional)
5	7, 10, 15	Semi-skilled manual and personal service
6	11	Unskilled manual

In the present text the socio-economic classes above are referred to as social classes. They are distinguished both by a separate code, and by the use of ordinary numbers as opposed to the Roman numerals used for social class (R.G.).

Code

'R.G.(S.E.)' identifies a definition as being in terms of socio-economic class. As in the case of social class above a two-figure number follows which indicates the particular classification used (60, 66, 70).

Modifications

A: a five-group classification used by Sillitoe (1969) in a study of an urban population, hence excluding agricultural occupations. A further characteristic that will be noted is that junior non-manual workers are placed between the skilled manual and the semi- and unskilled workers.

Socio-economic class	Socio-economic groups	Equivalent social class	Descriptive definition
1	1, 2, 4	I and II	Professional, employers and managers — large establishments
2	2, 5	II and III	Intermediate non-manual, employers and managers — small establishments

Socio-economic class	Socio-economic groups	Equivalent social class	Descriptive definition
3	8, 9	III	Skilled manual, supervisors, foremen
4	6	III and IV	Junior non-manual
5	10, 11	IV and V	Semi-skilled, unskilled

B: a fourfold collapsed classification used for example by Woolf (1971):

Socio-economic class	Socio-economic groups
Managerial	1, 2, 3, 4, 13
Non-manual	5, 6, 7, 12
Skilled manual	8, 9
Other manual and miscellaneous	10, 11, 14, 15, 16, 17

C: a manual/non-manual dichotomy achieved by combining the Registrar General's socio-economic classes (see above) as follows:

    1, 2, 3: non-manual
    4, 5, 6: manual

D: a five-point classification used by the National Foundation for Educational Research. A notable characteristic of this scale is the inclusion of the armed forces (socio-economic group 16) all of whom were classified as semi-skilled workers.

Socio-economic class	Socio-economic groups	Descriptive definition
1	1, 2, 3, 4	Professional
2	5, 6, 7	Clerical
3	8, 9, 12, 13, 14	Skilled worker
4	10, 15, 16	Semi-skilled
5	11	Unskilled

This book also refers to two pieces of research which used a classification based on the original 1951 census socio-economic groups. These groups were as follows:

1 Farmers
2 Agricultural workers
3 Higher administrative, professional and managerial (including large employers)
4 Intermediate administrative, professional and managerial (including teachers and salaried staff)
5 Shopkeepers and other small employers
6 Clerical workers
7 Shop assistants
8 Personal service
9 Foremen
10 Skilled workers
11 Semi-skilled workers
12 Unskilled workers
13 Other ranks in the armed forces

Code
'R.G.(S.E.)50' denotes this classification.

Modifications
A: a five-group classification used by Butler and Bonham (1963):

Socio-economic class	Socio-economic groups	Descriptive definition
1	3, 4	Professional
2	5, 6, 7	Non-manual
3	9, 10	Skilled manual
4	2, 8, 11, 12	Semi- and unskilled
5	Residual and 1	Remainder

B: a four-group classification used by the Ministry of Education:

Socio-economic class	Socio-economic groups	Descriptive definition
1	3, 4	Professional, managerial
2	5, 6, 7, 8	Clerical and other non-manual
3	9, 10	Skilled manual
4	2, 11, 12	Semi- and unskilled

Department of Employment

This government department uses two quite different and separate occupational classifications for its research and publications. The first of these is extensively used in the *British Labour Statistics Year Book* and the *Department of Employment Gazette.* It consists of a list of some 400 occupations which are arranged into the following main occupational groups:

I	Managerial (general management)	X	Catering, cleaning, hairdressing and other personal service
II	Professional and related supporting management and administration	XI	Farming, fishing and related
III	Professional and related in education, welfare and health	XII	Materials-processing (excluding metal)
		XIV	Processing, making, repairing and related (metal and electrical)
IV	Literary, artistic and sports		
V	Professional and related in science, engineering, technology and similar fields	XV	Painting, repetitive-assembling, product-inspecting, packaging and related
VI	Managerial (excluding general management)	XVI	Construction, mining and related not identified elsewhere
VII	Clerical and related		
VIII	Selling	XVII	Transport-operating, materials-moving and storing and related
IX	Security and protective service	XVIII	Miscellaneous

The above groups are clearly different from social class and socio-economic class as outlined above. They are not capable of translation into social classes as such. They can however be divided into non-manual (the first nine groups, in the left hand column above) and manual (the second nine, in the right hand column). In this way they divide the working population along a commonly accepted basic dichotomy of social class. They are capable, then, of a rough comparison with the collapsed forms of social class (R.G./C) and socio-economic class (R.G.(S.E.)/C) mentioned above.

Code

'D.E.' denotes this classification.

The second classification is used in the *Family Expenditure Survey*. It claims to be derived from the Registrar General's classification (outlined above), but is clearly not identical with it. The seven groupings involved are as follows:

1 Professional and technical workers
2 Administrative and managerial workers
3 Teachers
4 Clerical workers
5 Shop assistants
6 Manual workers
7 Members of Her Majesty's forces

The unusual features of this classification are the lack of differentiation of manual workers and the separate inclusion of Her Majesty's forces.

Code

'F.E.S.' denotes this classification.

Hall-Jones scale

This scale was developed in the late 1940s and was based on a scale used in the pre-war Merseyside survey (Jones 1934). Its development involved a consideration of the subjective social grading of occupations (Hall and Jones 1950), which is discussed above on p. 30. Subsequently it has been used by researchers, notably in a study of social mobility (Glass 1954). The resulting classification of occupations was into seven social classes:

1 Professional and high administrative
2 Managerial and executive
3 Inspectional, supervisory and other non-manual higher grade
4 Inspectional, supervisory and other non-manual lower grade
5 Skilled manual and routine grades of non-manual
6 Semi-skilled manual
7 Unskilled manual

Code
'H.J.' denotes this classification.

Modifications
A: a collapsed classification of four 'social groups' used by Berent (Glass 1954):

Social group	Hall-Jones social classes
I	1, 2
II	3, 4
III	5
IV	6, 7

B: the best known modification — that by Goldthorpe, Lockwood, Bechhofer and Platt (1969) — involved both a more comprehensive classification into eight 'status levels' (shown in the left hand column below), and a simple threefold classification (the right hand column below).

Occupational status level	Summary classification
1 (a) Higher professional, managerial and other white-collar employees	
(b) Large industrial or commercial employers, landed proprietors	
2 (a) Intermediate professional, managerial and other white-collar employees	White-collar
(b) Medium industrial or commercial employers, substantial farmers	
3 (a) Lower professional, managerial and other white-collar employees	
(b) Small industrial or commercial employers, small proprietors, small farmers	
4 (a) Supervisory, inspectional, minor official and service employees	Intermediate
(b) Self-employed men (no employees or expensive capital equipment)	
5 Skilled manual workers (with apprenticeship or equivalent)	
6 Other relatively skilled manual workers	Manual
7 Semi-skilled manual workers	
8 Unskilled manual workers	

(From appendix A, Goldthorpe, Lockwood, Bechhofer and Platt 1969)

National Survey of Health and Development

This survey used a rather interesting classification which, unlike the others quoted in the section, was not based solely on occupation. The families which reared the children who were the subject of this survey were classified by the occupation of the father together with the educational and social class background of the father and the mother. The initials in brackets which follow each social class title below are those used in the tables in this text.

Upper middle class (U.M.)

Father has non-manual occupation

and (*a*) both parents had secondary school education, and middle class upbringing (i.e. had father with non-manual occupation)

or (*b*) both parents had secondary school education, and one parent had middle class upbringing

or (*c*) both parents had middle class upbringing and one parent had secondary school education

Lower middle class (L.M.)

All other fathers with non-manual occupations

Upper manual working class (U.W.)

Father has manual occupation

and (*a*) either or both parents had secondary school education

and/or (*b*) either or both parents had middle class upbringing

Lower manual working class (L.W.)

Father has manual occupation

and (*a*) both parents had elementary school education only

and (*b*) both parents had working class upbringing (i.e. had father with manual occupation)

Code

'N.S.' denotes this classification.

Modifications

A: a collapsed form in which U.M. and L.M. are combined to give 'middle class' (M.C.) and U.W. and L.W. are combined to give 'manual working' (M.W.)

Market research

This book cites the work of a number of commercial social research enterprises, namely National Opinion Polls Market

Research Ltd, British Market Research Bureau Ltd, Joint Industry Committee for National Readership Surveys, and Social Surveys (Gallup Polls) Ltd. These and other such organisations use the same social grading of occupations, fairly full details of which can be found in Monk (1970). The full classification has six 'classes', but the full form is rarely used. The most common form contains only four 'classes' arrived at by combining the first two and the last two:

A   Higher managerial or professional or administrative
B   Lower managerial or professional or administrative
C1 Skilled or supervisory or lower non-manual
C2 Skilled manual
D   Unskilled manual
E   Residual, including state pensioners

An interesting feature of this classification is the inclusion of armed forces personnel, in contrast to their exclusion by the Registrar General. Indeed it provides a good illustration of the grading involved, since social class A contains Lieutenant-Colonels and above; class B, Captains and Majors; and class C1 Sergeants, Sergeant Majors, Warrant Officers, and Lieutenants.

Code

'M.R.' denotes the most common form of this classification, which is as above: AB, C1, C2, DE.

Modifications

A: the full use of the six classes
B: a collapsed form, consisting of two classes: A, B, C1 (non-manual), and C2, D, E (manual)
C: a modification of this scale, used by Butler and Stokes (1969), which involved seven classes, although the seventh was omitted in most of their work:

Butler and Stokes	*Market research*	
I	A	(as above)
II	B	(as above)
III	C1A	Skilled supervisory non-manual
IV	C1B	Lower non-manual
V	C2	(as above)
VI	D	(as above)
VII	E	(as above)

British Broadcasting Corporation

The B.B.C. employs a simple threefold classification of the occupation of the chief wage-earners of families it uses in its consumer research:

Class A: covers about 5 per cent of the population and comprises professionals, directors, executives, senior civil servants etc.

Class B: covers about 25 per cent of the population and comprises bank clerks, teachers, small employers, supervisors, shop managers etc.

Class C: the remaining 70 per cent of the population, comprising all occupations other than those above

Code
'B.B.C.' denotes this classification.

Miscellaneous

One study reported in this book (Baumol and Bowen 1969) used an American classification. This had four categories, as follows:

Professional
Managerial
Clerical and sales
Blue-collar (British equivalent would be working class)

Code
' U.S.A.' denotes this classification.

Table 2.7
Key to codes used to social class definitions

Each code begins with letters (see left hand column). Full details of the classification will be found on the page or pages referred to in the right hand column.

Letters	Source	Page reference
B.B.C.	British Broadcasting Corporation	48
D.E.	Department of Employment	42—3
F.E.S.	*Family Expenditure Survey*	43
H.J.†	Hall-Jones	43—5
M.R.†	Market Research	46—8
N.S.†	National Survey	45—6
R.G.*†	Registrar General's social class	34—7
R.G.(S.E.)*†	Registrar General's socio-economic class	37—42
U.S.A.	Baumol and Bowen	48

*Numbers which follow refer to the year of classification
†Letter which follows oblique stroke (/) denotes which modification has been used

Example of use

In the code 'R.G.60/B' the letters (R.G.) inform one (via columns 1 and 2) that it is the Registrar General's social class classification; the figures (60) that it is the 1960 classification; and the oblique stroke followed by the letter B, that it is a modification of that classification. The right hand column shows the page or pages on which details of this modification are to be found.

Sampling techniques

The census is the only major study dealt with in this book which has attempted to collect information about an entire population — in the everyday meaning of that word. In this case the population was the inhabitants of Great Britain. In social science 'population', or sometimes 'universe', can also be used to refer to all the members of an institution or group, for example a population of university students, of mental hospital patients, of adolescents, of workers etc. A population can therefore vary considerably in size — from, say, all schoolchildren in Yorkshire to the children in the fourth year at Frog Island Secondary School. Most studies in this book have used a sample — that is a proportion of the population which is representative of that population. Social scientists adopt a number of sampling techniques with the aim of reducing the numbers involved while retaining as accurately as possible the characteristics of the whole group. It should be borne in mind that all sampling involves error. Indeed, the whole enterprise of social surveying involves the possibility, if not the probability, of error. As Madge (1953) has pointed out: 'a complete census is not necessarily preferable to a sample survey as it may give openings for inaccuracy, e.g. through the time elapsing in the course of data collection' — to which he could well have added, in relation to the population census, the time that elapses between data collection and publication. (For example, give years after the 1971 census some of the material has yet to be published.) Sampling, then, it usually essential because of time and cost factors, and sampling techniques exist to minimise the errors involved. The following section describes only those techniques used in the studies found in this book.

Direct sampling

This is sampling direct from a population. The purest form, technically speaking, is

Random sampling
The basis of this method is that each person in the population has an equal chance of being selected for the sample. This can

be achieved by numbering each member and drawing out (bingo style) the required number or percentage (say 10 per cent). A less romantic and less time-consuming method would be to use a table of random numbers (see for example Lindley and Miller 1971), which are in effect the results of a previous draw, statistically computed. Much more common in social science research, however, is a technique called

Systematic random sampling

This method is much more straightforward and time-saving. It involves starting at a random number and then selecting every nth person. In the case of a 10 per cent sample, one could begin with the 5th member of the population and then use the 15th, 25th, 35th, 45th etc. This form of sampling is sometimes referred to as quasi-random sampling. Both 'pure' and 'systematic' random sampling are normally referred to in research literature simply as 'random'. This convention has been followed in this text.

Random sampling assumes that the list of the population involved (called a 'sample frame') has no particular order or arrangement which could have any bearing on the investigation. It would be the ideal method for producing a sample to test the quality of beer in bottles leaving a production line. However, most sample frames used in social research are not of this type, but typically have a definite order. Consider, for example, an investigation into schoolchildren: the most readily available sample frame would be their class registers, where the children's names might well be recorded by class (and hence by age and ability), by sex (boys first), and in alphabetical order. In such a case it is usually more appropriate to take a sample from each part (called a 'stratum') of the list – for example, a proportion of the boys and girls from each class – than to treat all the registers together as a single sample frame. As Conway (1967) points out, 'stratified samples have smaller sampling errors than simple random samples of the same size. Also each stratum is adequately represented in the sample . . . '

Indirect sampling

Stratified sampling

The population is divided into a number of strata from each of which a sample is then drawn. A useful bonus of this method is that different percentage samples may be drawn from the different strata. For example the *Monthly Index of Earnings* uses information provided by some 8,000 firms which are stratified according to size: all those employing 500 or more people are included, half of those employing 100 to 499, and a tenth of those employing 25 to 99. This is referred to as a 'variable sampling fraction' — that is, the fraction of each stratum in the sample varies.

Multi-stage sampling

This amounts to taking samples within samples. At its simplest it involves two stages. For example, a sample of British schools might be obtained by first taking a sample of local education authorities in Britain (stage one) and from that a sample of schools (stage two). Further stages could entail a sample of classes within those schools, and a sample of children within those classes. The obvious advantage of such a procedure is that the final sample is concentrated in a few areas, while the dangers of choosing a sample purely by the criterion of convenience are avoided.

A high level of sophistication in sampling can be achieved by combining multi-stage and stratified sampling. In the example above, the first stage, of sampling Local Education Authorities, could involve taking into account such strata as size, rural or urban location, and expenditure. Again, such sampling could be done on a random or systematic basis.

Multi-phase sampling

This involves using a sample (or sub-sample) within a sample for part of an investigation. While a sample may provide certain basic information, a further sub-sample may be chosen to provide more detailed information. This clearly saves fieldwork, and the researcher's general knowledge of the whole sample facilitates comparison between it and the sub-sample or samples. This knowledge also provides an accurate basis on which to construct strata for the selection of the sub-sample. This is a common form of sampling: for example, the 1961 census of all households, each of which was required to complete a questionnaire, asked 10 per cent to complete a different questionnaire providing further information.

All the sampling techniques mentioned above involve random or quasi-random selection which results in a sample of identifiable individuals representing a given population. The value of any investigation depends to a certain extent on what proportion of the population are contacted and actually cooperate in the research. Clearly a low response rate, particularly in a specific part of a sample, is likely to produce distorted findings. While replacements for non-respondents can be sought, this is costly and time-consuming. Two alternatives championed by commercial market researchers exist which are certainly cheaper, though they have been criticised on theoretical grounds and on grounds of utility.

Quota sampling

This is a non-random form of multi-stage or stratified sampling. Perhaps the easiest way to understand this form of sampling is to contrast non-quota with quota sampling. In the first case the interviewer would work from a list of names and probably addresses; with a quota sample he would have a list of characteristics of people he should interview. His list might contain, for example, 'five married, middle class women between the ages of 45 and 65'. He would then set out to find such women and interview them. Obviously his choice would be limited by the availability of people, and would depend upon his diligence and honesty. Clearly, if the interviews were conducted in a city centre during working hours, certain categories within his quota – the housebound woman, or the woman living in the country, for example – would be unlikely to be included. Quota sampling, like random sampling, aims to reproduce a population on a small scale. Quota sampling is dependent on previous knowledge of the population — that is, given the proportions of, say, sex, age and occupation of a population, a quota sample is drawn up by scaling down these proportions to a convenient size. Random sampling works on the assumption that careful sample construction would lead to the same result. In fact both types of samples, when completed, are often justified by being compared to known population characteristics — known, that is, from the census.

Panel sampling

Here a resident, or captive, quota sample is chosen to represent a particular population. Probably the best known example is the B.B.C. audience panel — 3,100 persons from whose responses estimates of audience size for various T.V. and radio programmes are worked out. Similar panels exist to report on branded and consumer goods. They are typically volunteers who are paid for their services.

A certain controversy surrounds the use of quota and panel samples. Social scientists and statisticians criticise them for their theoretical and practical weaknesses while market researchers praise them for their cheapness, speed and convenience. While the problems of accuracy attached to any form of sampling are most noticeable in the case of these two techniques, it is valuable to bear in mind Madge's (1953) strictures on sampling as a whole:

The object of any sampling procedure is to secure a sample which will reproduce the characteristics of the population. This object is never completely attained as two types of error are regularly encountered: those arising from biases in selection . . . those due to chance differences between members of the population included and those who are not included are virtually certain to be present . . . the former can be minimised by good craftsmanship, while the latter can be regulated by appropriate design.

Bias can be introduced either deliberately or by faulty techniques. An example of deliberate bias is the selection of members of a sample on the *a priori* grounds that they are representative. Faulty techniques include: selection by some characteristic which happens to be correlated with properties of the unit which are of interest . . . unauthorised substitution of one person for another by a fieldworker or failure by the investigator to cover all the specified members of the sample.

A key to the types of sampling used in the studies reported in this book can be found in table 2.8. This key is provided for use with the appendix. Together they allow the reader to identify the sampling procedure adopted in each piece of research used in the text. The appendix also contains details of

Table 2.8
Key to types of sampling

Major type	Basis of sampling*	Code†	Notes
Direct	None	P	Signifies a whole population has been used
	Random	DR	
	Other	D	For details see appendix, column 9
Stratified	Random	SR	
	Other or various	S	For details see appendix, column 9
Multi-stage	Random	MSR	
	Other or various	MS	For details see appendix, column 9
Multi-stage/ stratified	Random	MSS	
Multi-phase	Random	MPR	
	Other or various	MP	For details see appendix, column 9
Quota		Q	
Panel		Pan	

*i.e. basis of sampling at the last stage, the actual selection of the sample
†Codes are used in column 4 of the appendix

sample size. Further information in this area can be obtained
from the publications involved, and from books concerned
with social science methodology (see for example Conway
1967, Madge 1953, Mann 1968, Moser 1958, Riley 1963,
Moser and Kalton 1971).

Research methods

The research described in this book used only a limited range
of the methods available to the social scientist. This is mainly
because the studies reported are for the most part large-scale,
and therefore limited, by time and cost, in the choice of
research techniques. Basically, social surveys are concerned
with the answers given to questions by a large number of
people (usually a sample), which are then combined and
separated in various ways. There are a number of different
ways in which the acquisition of such information can be
described. In this section, the term *interview* will be used to
refer to a situation in which the questioner is face to face with
the respondent, and in which the questioner records the
answers. The term *questionnaire* will be used to refer to
situations in which the respondent records his replies on paper
in response to written questions. As will be seen, this
distinction only applies to the way in which the questions are
answered and not to the type of questions asked.

Interviews

A number of types of interview can be identified by the kind
of question asked and the way in which the answers are
recorded.

The unstructured interview (sometimes called a 'depth interview')

In this situation the main aim of the interviewer is to get his
respondent to talk in his own way about the subject or
subjects of the inquiry. The interviewer uses what lawyers

would call leading questions, and subsequently merely guides the interviewee. Answers may be recorded either on tape or by hand. This is a time-consuming method for both parties and is little used in the sort of research which is the basis of this book. Some researchers (for example Barker Lunn (1970)) use it as an initial step from the results of which they subsequently construct questionnaires.

The structured interview

Here the interviewer is provided with a list of questions (a schedule) to ask the respondent. These may be of two types:

1 *Open-ended questions* These are simply questions designed to elicit from the respondent his feelings, attitudes or knowledge in his own words. The interviewer may be expected to write down the answer verbatim, to tape-record the interview for writing up later, or to categorise the answer according to a schedule with which he has been provided.

2 *Pre-coded questions* Here the interviewer provides the respondent with a set of alternative answers to the questions, and invites him to choose. These alternatives vary from simple yes/no to a whole range of responses. In the latter case the interviewer may well show the respondent a card which has the choices printed on it.

Many interview schedules in fact contain both open-ended and pre-coded questions. It is also true that in order to analyse the answers to open-ended questions the researcher has to group and code the answers after the interview stage of his research. Open-ended questions are of course very rich in people's experience and expression, and can be effectively used to add colour to research reports, as any reading of the work of Newson and Newson (1968) will show.

Questionnaires

These are really interviews expressed as forms — or pen and paper alternatives. They can contain open-ended questions but more typically have an emphasis on pre-coded ones. A number of types of questionnaire can be identified by the way they are distributed and completed.

The personal questionnaire

This is delivered to, and/or collected from, one specific individual by another. Usually, however, it is completed by the respondent on his own. The most commonly known example is the census return.

The postal questionnaire

This comes through the post. A notable characteristic of this type is the low rate of returned and completed questionnaires (about 60% is considered acceptable).

The group questionnaire

This is commonly used where the researcher has a captive or semi-captive sample. It is particularly common in educational research areas where classes and groups of students are available.

Questionnaires and interviews are the methods most commonly used in the research reported in this book (see the appendix). A third method is sometimes used:

Documents

These can either be pre-existing documents subsequently used by researchers as sources of data, or documents compiled for the purposes of the research.

Existing documents

These are records and reports compiled and kept for purposes often far removed from research, but subsequently used by researchers.

1 *Existing documentary sources*   These are many and varied. Simple examples would be educational and occupa-

tional applications and records, biographical dictionaries such as *Who's Who*, membership lists etc.

2 *Existing research document sources* Previous research can provide data which are capable of being reworked, or used in conjunction with ongoing research. It can also sometimes assist research into an area for which it was not necessarily designed or intended. A potentially rich field here is the census. As is pointed out elsewhere in this book, many areas of mystery concerning social class could be illuminated if more official statistics were made available (see chapter 5, p. 130, for an example of this).

Created documents

Normally these are the result of a researcher asking respondents to keep a diary or record of particular events or behaviour

Table 2.9
Key to research methods

Major type	Variation	Code*	Notes
Interviews		I	Only used where no further information is available
	Unstructured	IU	
	Structured	IS	Used where both open-ended and pre-coded questions have been used
	Open-ended questions	(OE)	Used to denote where only the type indicated has been used
	Pre-coded questions	(PC)	
Questionnaires		Q	Only used where no further information is available
	Personal	QP	
	Postal	QPO	
	Group	QG	
Documents	Existing	DE	
	Existing research	DER	
	Created	DC	

*Codes are used in column 6 of the appendix; combinations of research methods are referred to with both or all codes involved

over a period of time. The B.B.C. requires its audience panel to report its viewing and listening week by week. The government's *Family Expenditure Survey: Report for 1974* (1975) is based partly on a daily record book of expenditure kept for fourteen consecutive days.

Table 2.9 provides a key to the research methods used in studies reported in this book. The key should be used in conjunction with the appendix. Together they allow the reader to identify the research method or methods used in each piece of research referred to in the text. More comprehensive and extensive treatment of research methods in social science can be found in Madge 1953, Mann 1968, Moser 1958, Riley 1963, Moser and Kalton 1971, and Oppenheim 1966.

An overview

This chapter has covered four main topics. It started with a short discussion, and a working definition, of social class, and went on to look at some of the research concerned with the existence of social class in the minds of the public. These two sections should prevent readers from assuming that sociology's treatment of social class is as naïve as some popular writings and the work of a few sociologists might suggest. Even in looking only at empirical research the discipline was seen to have a continuing, active and deep concern with the notion of social class. While this has as yet borne little fruit in terms of new research methods — only one new scale of social class has recently emerged (Goldthorpe and Hope 1974) — this may be only a matter of time. The continuing abundance in this field of theoretical and descriptive works, which have not been discussed here, reflects an imbalance between theory and research in British sociology.

The third, and central, topic was the description of the operationalisations of social class used in the research mentioned in this book. The chapter allows readers to contrast the simplicity of the operationalisation of social class with the complexity of its theoretical conceptualisation. A further contrast is provided by comparing the contents of this book with those of the theoretical works referenced at the end of this chapter. The discussion has also emphasised the discontent, and perhaps confusion, about social class shared by sociologists and the general public. Both groups, it would appear, subscribe to the existence of social class in broad general terms, while disagreeing about its nature, structure and meaning. Both groups share the basic idea that occupation is a factor in social class, but not the only one. They are therefore equally likely to be unhappy with the use of occupation as the sole criterion of social class, social standing, or status in society. But neither party, apparently, can put forward any simple or complex alternative definition, and both are likely to resort to occupation as the best, the only, or the most convenient 'shorthand' reference-point in terms of which to pin down this extensively used though hazy concept.

Finally, this chapter took a brief look at the methodology used in social class research (also discussed earlier on pp. 28ff). There are problems to do with the whole nature of social investigations using survey methods. These problems centre on the basic unknown – the relationship between what people say in response to questions, and what they do and/or the reality they describe. This is not the place to review such concerns, though the extent to which they detract from the utility or value of the evidence presented in this book is open to debate. Readers should, however, be aware of these issues and view the evidence accordingly. Nevertheless, such issues must remain marginal to this book, whose aim is to present a view of the state of research as it is, not as it might or should be.

Suggested further reading on social class theory

The literature in this field is vast. The following short selection is the author's own and is designed to be useful to students. Readers will find that these works contain abundant further references.

A very good introduction is provided by The Open University (1972) in Block 3 of the *Sociological Perspectives* course (D283), *Stratification and Social Class*: Unit 9 by Salamon, *Major Theories of Stratification*, outlines and contrasts the works of three major sociologists, Marx, Weber and Parsons. The controversy centering on the structural-functional explanation of social class is well summarised in the debate between Davis and Moore, and Tumin, which is to be found in Bendix and Lipset, *Class Status and Power* (1967). A good, clear and brief introduction to the sociological concept of class and its place in Marxist theory is that by Bottomore, *Classes in Modern Society* (1965). Thompson and Tunstall in *Sociological Perspectives* (1971) have most usefully brought together well-edited extracts from the original contributions to the concept of social class of Marx, Engels, Weber, Parsons, Bottomore, Marshall, Runciman, Lipset, Goldthorpe, and Parkin. Together these extracts cover a historical period of some 120 years and provide a basis for comparison. Probably the finest contemporary text in the field is that of Giddens, *The Class Structure of the Advanced Societies* (1973). This is an extremely good critique of theories and theorists, strictly not for beginners. Marx's basic ideas are best read in the original: see Marx and Engels 1848.

3

Distribution, work and income

There can hardly be a town in the South of England where you could throw a brick without hitting the niece of a bishop.

George Orwell (1937)

Each in his place, by right, not grace,
Shall rule his heritage —
The men who simply do the work
For which they draw the wage.

Rudyard Kipling (1902)

National distribution of social class

The only figures relating social class to the entire population of Great Britain are to be found in the census. Theoretically it is possible to allocate each person enumerated in the 1971 census, some 53,979,000, to a social class. As was pointed out in chapter 2 this would be done by classing occupations together. Married women and dependent children would be classified according to their husband's or father's occupation, the retired and unemployed by their last occupation, and so on. However, for the purposes of this section, only the economically active, that is those who are in work or are seeking it, and the retired will be used. The economically active and retired population of England, Wales and Scotland aged 15 years or over in the 1971 census was 30,367,930. Of this number some 26,809,090 persons were classified by social class. The main groups who were not classified were students, members of the armed forces, and those whose

Distribution, work and income

occupations were inadequately described. Of this 26¾ million persons, 17¼ million were men and 9½ million were women. A breakdown of this population by social class is presented in table 3.1. This table presents, then, as accurate a picture as is available of the national distribution of social class. If both sexes are taken together the largest single social class is III(M.), which represents some 28 per cent of the work force and retired, followed by social classes III(N.) and IV with 21 per cent each. Over all, 43 per cent of this population are employed in non-manual occupations and 57 per cent in manual. The differences between the social class distributions of the sexes is very marked, and is clearly related to the fact that men and women have dissimilar job opportunities. Only in social classes II and V is there any similarity in the proportions of male and female. In social class I the males outnumber females by 5 to 1, a situation which is reversed in class III(N.), where the proportion is approximately 1 to 3. Although a much higher percentage of women have non-manual occupations (56 per cent) than do men (35 per cent), the majority of such women work at the routine, lower-skilled end of this job range (III(N.)). This pattern is interestingly reflected in the manual occupations. Here the proportion of men (65 per cent) is larger than that of women (44 per cent) but men are more likely to be in the skilled occupations (III(M.)) – 38 per cent of men compared to 10 per cent of women – than in the semi-skilled occupations (IV) – 18 per cent compared with 26 per cent.

Table 3.1
Percentage of economically active and retired persons, males and females in each social class, Great Britain

Social class (R.G. 70)

	I	II	III(N.)	III(M.)	IV	V	All
Male	5	18	12	38	18	9	100
Female	1	17	38	10	26	8	100
Both	4	18	21	28	21	8	100

(Devised from table 30, Census 1971, Economic Activity (10% Sample) *1975, part 4)*

When looking at the sex differences here, it should be borne in mind that it is almost always male occupation which provides the basis of social class allocation. Lack of collected or published data makes it impossible to examine sex differences in all but a very few of the areas dealt with in this book. (One area where data do exist is that of mothers' occupation and education in relation to children's educational performance – see table 6.18, p. 191.) One example of the lack of such data is to be found in the next section, where the male figures have been analysed to give, separately, the economically active and the retired, while the female figures have not.

Regional distribution of social class

The Registrar General divides Great Britain into ten regions, listed in table 3.2 and displayed on the map on p. 66

Table 3.2

Percentage* of economically active males† in each social class by region of Great Britain

Social class (R.G. 70)

	I	II	III(N.)	III(M.)	IV	V	All
Scotland	4	16	10	40	20	11	
Wales	4	18	9	40	18	10	
North	4	15	10	43	18	11	
Yorkshire and Humberside	4	15	10	43	19	9	
North West	4	16	12	39	19	10	Each
East Midlands	4	16	10	45	18	7	region
West Midlands	4	16	10	43	19	8	= 100
East Anglia	4	20	10	36	22	8	
South East	7	21	15	34	17	7	
South West England and Wales }	5	22	12	36	18	8	
Great Britain }	5	18	12	38	18	9	

*Percentages rounded
†Classified males only
(Devised from table 30, Census 1971, Economic Activity (10% Sample) *1975, part 4)*

Figure 3.1

Percentage of manual workers among (a) economically active males, (b) economically active and retired females, by region of Great Britain

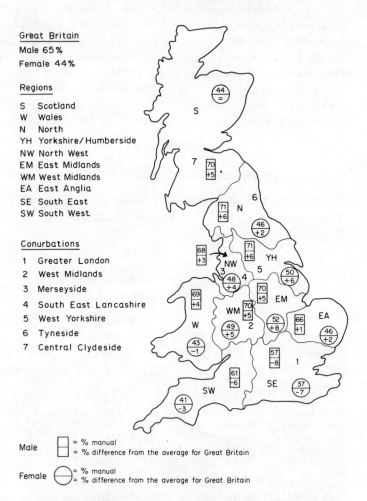

Great Britain
Male 65%
Female 44%

Regions

S   Scotland
W   Wales
N   North
YH Yorkshire/Humberside
NW North West
EM East Midlands
WM West Midlands
EA East Anglia
SE South East
SW South West

Conurbations

1   Greater London
2   West Midlands
3   Merseyside
4   South East Lancashire
5   West Yorkshire
6   Tyneside
7   Central Clydeside

Male ☐ = % manual
= % difference from the average for Great Britain

Female ◯ = % manual
= % difference from the average for Great Britain

(Devised from table 30 and map on page xxv, Census 1971, Economic Activity (10% sample) 1975, part IV)

(figure 3.1). These regions are not equal in size, nor in terms of the proportion of the population of Great Britain living in them. In order to facilitate comparison between the regions, the figures in each row of table 3.2 give the percentages of economically active men from each social class within each region.

As will be seen, the largest region in terms of population, the South East (which includes London), had the most distinctively different distribution of social classes. It had the highest percentage of social classes I, II and III(N.), and the lowest of classes III(M.), IV and V. In consequence, as the map (figure 3.1) shows, it has the lowest working class (manual occupations) percentage of any region, some 8 per cent less than the average for all regions. A similar, though less marked, pattern applied to the South West. Conversely, the North and the Yorkshire and Humberside regions have comparatively high percentages of manually occupied males (71 per cent, or 6 per cent more than the average for all regions), and low percentages of non-manual occupations. There are also interesting differences between the countries involved. England and Wales together have a distribution of 35 per cent non-manual and 65 per cent manual, which is identical to that for Great Britain as a whole. The distributions for Scotland, 30/70, and for Wales, 31/69, are different from those for England and Wales, but similar to each other. With regard to manually occupied males, a line drawn from Bristol to the Wash separates three regions — the South West, the South East, and East Anglia (which in two cases have lower percentages and in the other an average percentage, compared with Great Britain as a whole) — from the other seven regions, all of which have higher percentages.

A somewhat similar picture can be obtained from the figures relating to economically active and retired females (table 3.3). What is interesting here is that in Scotland and Wales the percentage of non-manual females is equal to or above the average for Great Britain. This is in contrast to the male figures. Otherwise, although the figures are different for

Table 3.3

Percentage* of economically active and retired females† in each social class by region of Great Britain

			*Social class (R.G. 70)*				
	I	II	III(N.)	III(M.)	IV	V	All
Scotland	0.9	18	37	10	25	9	
Wales	0.9	22	34	9	26	8	
North	0.7	17	36	10	27	9	
Yorkshire and Humberside	0.7	16	33	13	28	9	
North West	0.7	16	35	12	28	8	Each
East Midlands	0.7	15	32	17	28	7	region
West Midlands	0.7	15	35	12	29	8	= 100
East Anglia	1.0	18	35	10	29	7	
South East	1.4	18	43	8	23	6	
South West	1.0	21	37	9	25	7	
England and Wales } Great Britain	1.0	17	38	10	26	8	

*Percentages other than for social class I rounded
†Classified females only
(Devised from table 30, Census 1971, Economic Activity (10% Sample) *1975, part 4)*

the sexes, the patterning is similar. The map (figure 3.1) shows that regions which have above- or below-average percentages of manual males have similar for females.

The figures in table 3.4, which gives the distribution by social class of retired males, are of particular interest when compared with table 3.2, which is for economically active males. As can be seen, the percentage of retired males in social class I is consistently lower than that of active males, while the percentage in classes IV and V is consistently higher. This is very indicative of a changing occupational structure; i.e. the current structure has a higher proportion of professional occupations and a lower proportion of semi- and unskilled ones. (See section on age and social class, p. 96.) The figures are not directly comparable for two reasons. As will be seen in chapter 4, survival up to and during retirement is related to social class. Secondly, change of residence at retirement is more likely among the higher social classes, though much of this may well occur within the same region.

Another view of the regional distribution of the social classes in Great Britain is given in table 3.5. In this table, instead of the numbers in each social class in a region being expressed as a percentage of the total for each region (as in 3.2, 3.3 and 3.4), they are expressed as a percentage of the total for each social class in Great Britain. For example, 8.4 per cent of all social class I people in Great Britain were in Scotland in 1971. The first column in the table discloses that the regional percentages of economically active social class I males range from 42.6 per cent in the South East to 2.7 per cent in East Anglia. The right-hand column of the table shows the percentage of all social classes in each region, i.e. what percentage each region contains of the economically active male population of Great Britain. Almost a third (32.2 per cent) of such males reside in the South East, and the figures

Table 3.4

Percentages* of retired males† in each social class by region of Great Britain

Social class (R.G. 70)

	I	II	III(N.)	III(M.)	IV	V	All
Scotland	3	18	10	34	22	13	
Wales	3	20	9	38	18	11	
North	2	15	9	44	18	12	
Yorkshire and Humberside	2	15	10	41	21	12	Each
North West	2	17	13	34	21	14	region
East Midlands	2	16	9	43	20	10	= 100
West Midlands	2	16	10	38	22	12	
East Anglia	3	23	10	28	26	10	
South East	4	22	16	29	19	10	
South West	4	26	13	28	20	9	
England and Wales } Great Britain }	3	19	12	34	20	11	

*Percentages rounded
†Classified retired males only
(Devised from table 3.2, Census 1971, Economic Activity (10% Sample) *1975, part 4)*

Table 3.5

Percentage of economically active males* in each social class
by region of Great Britain

Social class (R.G.70)

	I	II	III(N.)	III(M.)	IV	V	All
England and Wales	91.6	91.7	92.0	90.4	89.9	88.2	90.6
Scotland	8.4	8.0	7.8	9.6	10.1	11.8	9.3
Wales	3.8	4.8	3.9	5.1	5.0	6.1	4.9
North	4.6	4.7	5.0	6.7	5.9	7.6	6.0
Yorkshire and Humberside	6.4	7.7	7.9	10.0	9.1	9.8	9.0
North West	11.0	11.2	11.9	12.6	12.8	15.1	12.4
East Midlands	5.4	5.9	5.6	7.4	6.4	5.5	6.5
West Midlands	8.6	8.8	8.5	11.1	10.7	8.9	10.0
East Anglia	2.7	3.3	2.6	2.9	3.6	2.7	3.0
South East	42.6	37.6	40.0	28.3	29.7	26.8	32.2
South West	6.4	7.7	6.5	6.2	6.7	5.8	6.6
Great Britain	Each class = 100						

*Classified males only
(Devised from table 31, Census 1971, Economic Activity (10% Sample)
1975, part 4)

range down to 3 per cent in East Anglia. If each social class
were equally distributed throughout the regions, then the
figures in the separate social class columns would correspond
with the figure in the appropriate right-hand column. For
example, one might expect to find about a third of the
economically active males in each social class in the South
East, since a third of all the economically active males live
there. In fact there is considerable variation. In the South East
region the percentages in social classes I, II and III(N.) are
consistently higher than those for all social classes taken
together, while those for classes III(M.), IV and V are all
lower. Quite the opposite is true of Scotland, where the
percentages for classes I, II and III(N.) are all lower and those
for III(M.), IV and V all higher than the percentage for all
social classes. Other regions display more complex patterns, as
will be seen from the table.

Local distribution of social class

The regions so far dealt with are large geographical areas of mixed social composition. It might be expected that the social class variations within them would be as great as, or greater than, the variations between them which have been outlined above. Such an assumption would be confirmed on a common-sense level by anyone familiar with any town, city or district in Great Britain. Apart from an analysis of social class by region the census includes an analysis of seven conurbations (see figure 3.1). Perhaps surprisingly, comparisons of the social class distribution in conurbations with that in the surrounding region do not reveal great variations. For instance, table 3.6 shows distributions for the Yorkshire and Humberside region, for the West Yorkshire conurbation (Leeds and Bradford and the area around), and for the remainder of the region. The conurbation consists of two large industrial cities and a number of surrounding, mainly mining, towns. The remainder of the region is largely agricultural but includes the cities of Hull, Sheffield and York. As the table reveals, there are differences, but small ones: there are marginally more non-manually and fewer manually occupied males in the conurbation than in the remainder of the region.

Table 3.6

Percentage of economically active males in each social class in the Yorkshire and Humberside region, the West Yorkshire conurbation, and the remainder of the region, by social class

	Social class (R.G.70)						
	I	II	III(N.)	III(M.)	IV	V	All
Yorkshire and Humberside region	3.7	15.3	10.4	43.4	18.1	9.0	100
West Yorkshire conurbation	3.9	15.0	11.3	42.6	18.7	8.3	100
Remainder of region	3.6	15.4	9.9	43.9	17.7	9.4	100

(Devised from table 31, Census 1971, Economic Activity (10% Sample) *1975, part 4)*

Although they are not generally available, it is possible to obtain 'Small Area Statistics' on a ward or grid basis. For example, the City of Bradford was divided into some nineteen wards for the 1971 census. Using this data it is possible to show the ecology of social class in Bradford (see figure 3.2). In Bradford as a whole the distribution of economically active males by social class (R.G.(S.E.)70) was

1	3 per cent	4	41 per cent
2	9 per cent	5	22 per cent
3	16 per cent	6	10 per cent

As the map reveals, these figures hide considerable variation between areas. The range in the case of social class 1, for example, is from 0.6 per cent in the Bradford Moor Ward to 7 per cent in Allerton, and in the case of class 6 from 3 per cent in Wibsey to 22 in Manningham. Similarly, while in Bradford as a whole about 28 per cent of economically active males are placed in non-manual classes and 73 per cent in manual, the ward differences are quite stark. In Heaton the percentages are 44 and 56, and in Manningham and University together 12 and 88. Further variations within the wards would be revealed by reference to census data on a grid basis if this were available. Both ward and grid data are only obtainable on request and payment from the Office of Population Censuses and Surveys. They may, however, be available from local libraries or local authorities.

Such regional, and particularly local, variations in the distribution of social classes are clearly indicative of some sort of residential segregation. Bradford may be accepted as a typical example. Although representatives of all the social classes are to be found in all the wards, some of the wards can be characterised by their predominant social class. Others are more mixed, with a distribution approximating to that of the city as a whole, the conurbation, region or nation. This phenomenon is of course well known to people like head-teachers, social workers, doctors, local authority personnel and the police, who deal with clients drawn from particular areas.

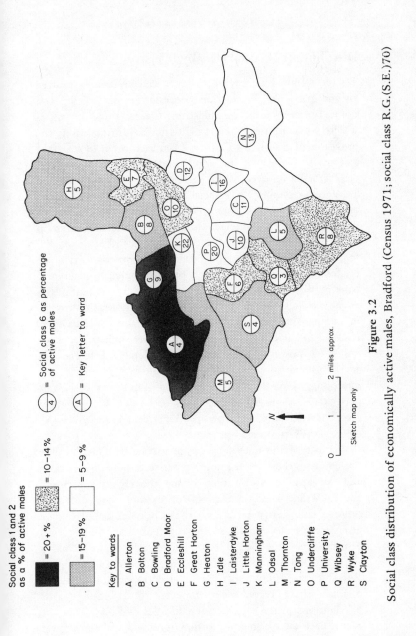

Social class 1 and 2
as a % of active males

■ = 20 + %

▨ = 10 – 14 %

□ = 15 – 19 %

= 5 – 9 %

④ = Social class 6 as percentage of active males

Ⓐ = Key letter to ward

Key to wards

A Allerton
B Bolton
C Bowling
D Bradford Moor
E Eccleshill
F Great Horton
G Heaton
H Idle
I Laisterdyke
J Little Horton
K Manningham
L Odsal
M Thornton
N Tong
O Undercliffe
P University
Q Wibsey
R Wyke
S Clayton

N

0   1   2 miles approx.

Sketch map only

Figure 3.2

Social class distribution of economically active males, Bradford (Census 1971; social class R.G.(S.E.)70)

Distribution of social class by industry

The economic activities of a society can be seen as centred around particular production processes, trades or services, normally referred to as industries. Clearly those industries which are concerned with production as distinct from the provision of a service will differ from each other in structure and in the nature of the occupations involved. Since social class is based on occupation, each industry will be made up of a different combination of social classes. The Registrar General classifies all economic enterprises into twenty-three industrial orders or groups. A selection of ten of these is listed in table 3.7 together with the percentage distribution of the social classes within each. Obviously some industries are predominantly non-manual, and others manual. In insurance, banking, finance, and business services some 87 per cent of the employees fall into social classes I, II and III(N.). Conversely, in mining and quarrying 91 per cent fall into social classes III(M.), IV and V. Even between rather similar types of industries, however, there may be considerable differences in social class distribution. While the industries of mining and quarrying, and that of construction, both have a large percentage of manual employees (91 and 86 per cent respectively), the former has only 1 per cent in social class V, whereas the latter has 14 per cent.

Because of the uneven spread of particular industries over the country, there is a relationship between these distributions and social class distribution among the regions, discussed above. While some industries, for example transport and services, are clearly related to the density of population in given areas, others are based on geographical and/or historical centres. Thus the South East, particularly London, has a concentration of insurance, banking, finance and business. Yorkshire and Humberside has a concentration of textiles and mining. These features are reflected in the social class distributions of the regions (see tables 3.2 and 3.5). Thus the South East has a higher proportion of non-manual and a lower

Table 3.7
Social class composition of industries (percentages*)

	I	II	III(N.)	III(M.)	IV	V	All
Agriculture, forestry, fishing	0.2	48	0.7	5	45	0.6	
Chemicals and allied	9	17	12	25	29	7	
Construction	4	7	3	62	10	14	
Distributive trades	2	37	19	25	13	4	
Insurance, banking, finance, business services	7	29	51	4	5	4	Each industry = 100
Mechanical engineering	5	10	11	51	18	4	
Mining, quarrying	2	3	4	77	13	1	
Public administration, defence	7	20	27	18	15	12	
Textiles	2	10	6	41	29	12	
Transport	2	10	12	48	20	8	

Social class (R.G.70) (column group header)

*Percentages over 1 rounded
(*Devised from table 33, Census 1971,* Economic Activity (10% Sample) *1975, part 4*)

proportion of manual workers than the Yorkshire and Humberside region.

Income

A large proportion of the social class differences dealt with in this book have an economic basis. The ownership of goods and the use of services to some extent depend on ability to pay for them. Of course the relationship is not simple and direct, for the motivation or desire to own or use something is important and can be overriding. Clearly, though, choice and even motivation are affected by wealth. The most common form of wealth in our society is earnings from an occupation. The present treatment of wealth has to be limited to this because of lack of information about other kinds (mainly inherited wealth and unearned income) in a form usable in this book. The Department of Employment publishes very detailed statistics concerning the earnings of people in employment in

Great Britain. At the time of writing the most up to date figures available were for April 1973 (*New Earnings Survey 1973* 1974). This survey was of a random sample of some 172,000 employees 'in all categories, in all occupations, in all types and sizes of businesses, in all industries' in Great Britain. Given the current rates of inflation, the figures involved (but not the relationships) are more dated than their date of origin suggests. Unfortunately too, for the purposes of this book, they are only published by industry group, and for manual and non-manual workers. Thus in this section it is necessary to use this crude dichotomy of social class, which has wherever possible been avoided.

As might be expected, non-manual workers earned more than manual workers and this was true of both sexes (table 3.8). In the case of each sex there is a clear difference in the average earnings of non-manual and manual workers. These differences are interestingly close, being 26 per cent for males and 25 per cent for females. That is, the male non-manual average is 126 per cent of the manual average. Males earn about twice as much as females: the difference between male non-manual and female non-manual is 95 per cent, and between male manual and female manual 93 per cent. It is also clear from the table

Table 3.8

Average gross weekly earnings* for manual and non-manual employees,† male and female

	Social class (D.E.)			
	Full time men aged 21 and 21+		*Full time women aged 18 and 18+*	
	Non-manual	Manual	Non-manual	Manual
Average gross weekly earnings (including overtime)	48.1	38.1	24.7	19.7
Overtime earnings	1.4	6.2	0.2	2.4

*In pounds sterling
†Those whose pay was not affected by absence
(*Derived from table 9*, British Labour Statistics Year Book 1973 *1975*)

that the differences in rates of pay for manual and non-manual workers are in fact greater than this, since a larger proportion of manual workers' pay is for overtime (in the case of males, 16 per cent as compared with 2.9 per cent). The section below on working hours (p. 88) shows considerable social class differences in the number of hours taken to earn the incomes dealt with here.

With regard to sex differences in income two questions can be asked. First, will the legislation on equal pay affect these differences? Secondly, how do the income differences between the sexes relate to those between classes? The differences between classes may be blurred by the fact that many skilled manual workers earn more than many non-manual workers. Do the sex differences increase this blurring, or lessen it?

Both these issues need to be seen in the light not only of table 3.8 above, but also of table 3.1. The latter clearly shows that women and men are employed in very different types of manual and non-manual occupations. The bulk of non-manual female workers are to be found in the more poorly paid section (class III(N.)), whereas the bulk of the manual male workers are in the best paid section (class III(M.)). It seems probable, therefore, that unless the equal pay legislation results in a change in the type of occupation followed by men and women, rather than merely ending discrimination in pay for a given occupation, the bulk of the present differences will remain. If this is so, and if social class continues normally to be measured by male occupation, then the earning differentials between non-manual and manual social classes are likely to be maintained.

Number of earners per household and family

Since the majority of workers in British society live with other people in households (for definition see p. 155 below) individual income is only part of the picture. Households with more than one wage coming in are clearly likely to have a higher per capita income than those with only one. The two

Distribution, work and income

Table 3.9

Percentage of all households with one, two, and three or more
earners in each social class*

Social class (R.G.70)

	I	II	III(N.)	III(M.)	IV	V	All
1 earner	56	51	53	44	48	50	48
2 earners	38	38	38	40	36	33	38
3 or more earners	6	11	10	16	16	17	14

*Of head of household
(*Devised from table 2.2, Census 1971*, Household Composition Tables
(10% Sample) *1975, part 2*)

main situations of this kind are families with working wives, or
with children living at home who are economically active; and
non-family households of working people. Table 3.9 demonstrates that there is social class variation in the distribution of
households with one, two, and three or more earners.
Households without earners have been excluded. The table
shows that the highest percentage of single earner households
is in social class I (56 per cent). The figures waver across the
social classes, with class III(M.) having the lowest percentage
(44 per cent). Two-earner households are slightly more evenly
distributed, while three-earner households vary clearly between a low for social class I of 6 per cent and a high for social
class V of 17 per cent. The non-manual classes all have lower
percentages than the manual classes of households with three
or more earners.

A rather similar picture can be seen in the social class distribution of families (as opposed to households) with differing
numbers of earners (table 3.10). In this case it can be assumed
that most of the third or subsequent earners will be children.
Hence part of the explanation for the social class difference in
the percentages for families with more than two earners is
likely to lie with differences in the educational and occupational experience of children. In social classes I, II and III(N.),

Table 3.10

Percentage of all families with one, two, and three or more
earners in each social class*

Social class (R.G. 70)

	I	II	III(N.)	III(M.)	IV	V	All
1 earner	54	46	46	43	42	44	46
2 earners	40	43	43	42	42	39	41
3 or more earners	5	11	11	15	16	17	13

*Of head of household
(Devised from table 45, Census 1971, Household Composition Tables
(10% Sample) *1975, part 3)*

the proportion of children staying into the sixth form and
entering higher or further education will be greater than in the
other classes (see chapter 6). In contrast to the manual classes,
many of these will not then, or subsequently, earn while still
part of their family of origin. A somewhat different and more
illuminating set of figures can be found in table 3.11, which
gives the average number of earners per person in families in
each social class. Here families without earners have
been included. In this case, although social classes I and II have
a smaller average number of earners per person than all the
other social classes, the usual non-manual/manual split is
absent. The two highest averages were found in classes III(N.)
and IV.

Table 3.11

Number of earners per person in families* by social class†

Social class (R.G. 70)

	I	II	III(N.)	III(M.)	IV	V
Earners per person	0.43	0.47	0.51	0.49	0.51	0.49

*Includes families without earners, and lone parents
†Of head of household
(Derived from table 45, Census 1971, Household Composition Tables
(10% Sample) *1975, part 3)*

Expenditure

As has been shown above there is substantial evidence that the
'higher' the social class the higher the income. This is of course
a generalisation, and for an indication of the range of incomes
involved one should look at table 51 of *Family Expenditure
Survey: Report for 1974* (1975). This shows that while the
average earnings of the social classes were as shown in
table 3.8, each social class (F.E.S.) had within it people whose
earnings ranged from under £12 per week up to more than
£120 per week. One would obviously expect there to be a
relationship between income and expenditure, and would
therefore anticipate similar patterns of social class differences
in expenditure. The most comprehensive figures available are
provided by the Department of Employment in their regular
surveys of the expenditure of some 6,695 households in the
United Kingdom (*Family Expenditure Survey: Report for
1974* 1975). Some caution is necessary in the interpretation
of the figures shown in table 3.12. The expenditure is that of
households, which may well have more than one income. But
most importantly, the classification of occupations, although
based on the Registrar General's, is unique, particularly since
class 6 includes all types of manual workers. Full details of the
classification are given on p. 43 above. Table 3.12 demonstrates that the overall expenditure of social class 6 is lower
than that of classes 1 to 3 and about equal to that of class 4. The
lower level for class 5 reflects differences in income between
'shop assistants' (classified as non-manual by the Registrar
General) and manual workers. A particularly striking feature
of the table is that social class 2 (administrative and
managerial) has higher levels of expenditure than class 1
(professional and technical).

Few clear and consistent patterns can be observed in this
table. Expenditure on housing shows a steady decline from
social class 2 to 6. The other basics – fuel, light, power, food,
and clothing and footwear – show less variation. In the case of
alcoholic drink and tobacco the expenditure in social class 6

Table 3.12
Average weekly expenditure* of households by social class,
United Kingdom 1974

Social class (F.E.S.)

	1	2	3	4	5	6	All
Housing	9.3	10.2	8.4	7.3	6.2	5.7	6.8
Fuel, light and power	2.7	2.8	3.0	2.3	2.1	2.3	2.4
Food	13.0	14.4	11.2	10.9	10.1	12.6	12.6
Alcoholic drink	2.4	2.9	2.0	2.1	2.0	2.8	2.6
Tobacco	1.2	1.7	1.0	1.4	1.8	2.3	2.0
Clothing and footwear	5.2	6.0	4.7	4.4	4.4	4.6	4.8
Durable household goods	4.9	7.3	8.0	4.1	3.9	3.7	4.5
Other goods	4.8	5.5	5.0	3.9	3.1	3.7	4.1
Transport and vehicles	10.8	10.0	10.4	6.4	3.8	6.6	7.5
Services	8.7	7.8	6.7	4.9	2.8	3.9	5.0
Miscellaneous	0.4	0.4	0.3	0.2	(0.1)	0.3	0.3
All expenditure	63.2	68.8	60.5	48.0	40.2	48.3	52.5
Average number of persons per household	3.1	3.3	2.8	2.6	2.7	3.3	3.2

*In pounds sterling, rounded to one decimal place, i.e. to the nearest
10 pence
( ) Based on 10 or fewer readings
(*Derived from table 21,* Family Expenditure Survey: Report for 1974
1975)

households is either the highest of all or nearly so (see also the
section in chapter 7 on leisure, p. 216). Since there is some
variation in the average number of persons in the households
of each class (see the last row of the table) it could be argued
that expenditure per person is a more satisfactory figure to
look at. These figures are presented in table 3.13.

Comparison of the two tables reveals little significant
difference. It is, however, noticeable that expenditure per
person on housing is identical for classes 1, 2 and 3; also that
overall expenditure per person is lowest for class 6, whereas
per household it was lowest for class 5 (table 3.12). Although
the difference here amounts to only 30p, there are other
interesting differences between columns 5 and 6.

Table 3.13

Average weekly expenditure* per person of households by
social class, United Kingdom 1974

Social class (F.E.S.)

	1	2	3	4	5	6	All
Housing	3.0	3.0	3.0	2.8	2.3	1.7	2.1
Fuel, light and power	0.9	0.8	1.1	0.9	0.8	0.7	0.8
Food	4.2	4.4	4.0	4.2	3.7	3.8	3.9
Alcoholic drink	0.8	0.9	0.7	0.8	0.7	0.8	0.8
Tobacco	0.4	0.5	0.4	0.5	0.7	0.7	0.6
Clothing and footwear	1.7	1.8	1.7	1.7	1.6	1.4	1.5
Durable household							
goods	1.6	2.2	2.9	1.6	1.4	1.1	1.4
Other goods	1.5	1.7	1.8	1.5	1.2	1.1	1.3
Transport and vehicles	3.5	3.0	3.7	2.5	1.4	2.0	2.3
Services	2.8	2.4	2.4	1.9	1.0	1.2	1.6
All expenditure	20.4	20.8	21.6	18.5	14.9	14.6	16.4

*See footnote to table 3.12
(Devised from table 21, Family Expenditure Survey: Report for 1974
1975)

Social class of economically active married couples

Since the figures in tables 3.10, 3.11, 3.12 and 3.13 are based
on the social class of the head of the household, they give no
indication of the occupations of other earners in the household. A total picture of the occupations and social classes of
every earner in a household or family together with the head is
not available, but one can look at the social class of married
couples where the wives are economically active. A 10 per cent
sample (N = 499,314) of these was surveyed in the 1971
census.

Table 3.14A shows married couples classified initially by
husbands' social class (the left hand column) and by wives'
social class (the columns headed I, II, III(N.) etc.). From the
top row it can be seen that where husbands in married couples
are in social class I, the following percentages of wives
will belong to this and the other social classes: I, 7 per cent; II,
32 per cent; III(N.), 46 per cent; III(M.), 4 per cent; IV, 9 per

Table 3.14A

Married couples* with economically active wife by social class of husband, and social class of wife (percentages†)

Husband's social class	I	II	III(N.)	III(M.)	IV	V	All
I	7	32	46	4	9	1	
II	2	35	42	5	14	2	
III(N.)	0.7	16	54	17	18	4	Each
III(M.)	0.2	9	34	13	33	11	class
IV	0.1	8	27	11	39	14	= 100
V	(13)	6	19	12	41	23	
All wives	1	16	36	10	28	9	
Economically active and retired females, England and Wales	1	17	38	10	26	8	

*Classified couples only
†Percentages over 1 rounded
( ) Actual number
(Devised from table 52, Census 1971, Household Composition Tables (10% Sample) *1975, part 3)*

cent; V, 1 per cent. The figures in italics show the proportions of cases where the social class of the husband and working wife are the same. These show considerable variation, from only 7 per cent in social class, I to 54 per cent in III(N.). The bottom two rows show that there is considerable similarity between the social class of economically active wives and that of all economically active and retired females in England and Wales.

Some care is necessary in interpreting this table. For example, it may seem surprising that only 7 per cent of the wives of social class I husbands have occupations in that class. However, this is a high percentage if it is borne in mind that only 1 per cent of all married economically active females are in social class I. While some social class I husbands have social class V wives (1 per cent), and some social class V husbands have social class I wives (13 cases), in general the relationships are less mixed. The bulk of married couples where the husband

Table 3.14B

Married couples* with economically active wife by social class
of wife, and social class of husband (percentages†)

Wife's social class	Husband's social class (R.G.70)						
	I	II	III(N.)	III(M.)	IV	V	All
I	*34*	44	9	9	3	(13)	
II	10	*44*	12	22	9	2	
III(N.)	6	22	*18*	37	13	3	Each
III(M.)	2	9	8	*52*	20	8	class
IV	2	10	8	47	*24*	9	= 100
V	0.6	5	6	47	27	*15*	
All husbands	5	20	12	40	17	6	
Economically active males, England and Wales	5	18	12	38	18	9	

*Classified couples only
†Percentages over 1 rounded
( ) Actual number
(Devised from table 52, Census 1971, Household Composition Tables
(10% Sample) *1975, part 3)*

is in social class I or II have wives in the non-manual classes (I,
II and III(N.)), and similarly most husbands in classes IV and
V have wives in the manual classes.

To give the other side of the coin, table 3.14B presents the
same data in a different order. Here married couples are
classified initially by wives' social class (the left hand column),
and then by husbands' social class (columns headed I, II etc.).
Except for this change of axis, this table can be read in the
same manner as table 3.14A. It reveals a similar, but perhaps
more dramatic, view of the correspondence between the social
class of economically active married partners. For example, of
economically active wives in social class I, 34 per cent have
husbands in the same class, and a further 44 per cent in class
II. Some 87 per cent have husbands in the non-manual classes.
At the other extreme 89 per cent of wives in social class V
have husbands in the manual classes.

The relationships revealed here between the social classes of spouses are discussed further in chapter 5 (p. 134). The differences that occur between the social classes of husband and wife have obvious implications for social class research, in view of the fairly consistent use of male social class to characterise families and children. This is particularly pertinent in the field of education, where children's progress and achievement is typically related to the father's social class. As can be seen from tables 3.14A and 3.14B, this could lead to unwarranted assumptions (see chapter 6, p. 190). Two families where the fathers are from the same social class, but where the mothers' social class differs widely, could be providing very different home environments, which may affect the children's educational achievements. In the case at hand — earnings and expenditure — family and household income is obviously related not only to the number of earners but also to their sex and class, and to earners in combination.

Sickness and pension schemes

Apart from the National Insurance Scheme, there exist special occupational schemes for the benefit of employees during periods of sickness and at retirement. Although now somewhat dated, the figures for sick pay schemes shown in table 3.15 display considerable social class variation. For males there is a steady decline from social classes I and II to class V in the

Table 3.15
Percentage of persons covered by sick pay schemes, by social class

| | *Social class (R.G.60/B)* | | | | |
	I and II	III	IV	V	All*
Men	88	57	52	41	57
Married women	88	60	35	53	53
Single women	89	71	36	51	62

*N.B. Includes persons with inadequately described occupations
(*Derived from tables 1, 2 and 3,* Report on an Enquiry into the Incidence of Incapacity for Work, *part 1, 1964*)

percentage covered. In the case of females there is a noticeable dip for social class IV. Single women had the highest percentage of cover over all, and this is particularly noticeable in social class III, where 71 per cent were so covered compared to 60 per cent of married women and 57 per cent of men. Almost certainly the differences are related to the particular types of job involved, and to the different ages of the people.

These figures are interestingly related to those in table 4.6 (p. 111) which shows absence from work because of sickness, by social class. There is an inverse relationship between the rate of reported absence and sickness benefit cover. The classes (I and II) which have the lowest rates of absence also have the highest proportions covered by such schemes. Hence the better paid are likely both to be sick less often, and not to lose income when they are. This is one example of the kind of hidden earnings differential that exists between the social classes. Later figures are available (table 3.16, *General Household Survey 1972* 1975) for socio-economic groups, but these are based on a smaller sample and are for men and women together. Here, the highest level of cover (99.6 per cent) was enjoyed by professional employees, and the lowest (50.2 per cent) by semi-skilled manual workers.

Similar figures for pension schemes are not available. However, a study of thirty-three organisations in the private

Table 3.16
Percentage of non-manual and manual employees covered by pension schemes in 33 organisations, by sex

Social class (D.E.)

	Non-manual	Manual
Men	87	56
Women	56	18

(Derived from p. 7, Occupational Pension Schemes 1971 *1972)*

sector of industry involving half a million employees revealed the differences shown in table 3.16. Both the 'social class' and the sex differences are very clearly marked indeed.

Unemployment

Figures for unemployment on a social class basis are not published. The Department of Employment does, however, produce figures on an occupational group basis, which allow for analysis by non-manual and manual classes. The most up to date published figures at the time of writing were for June 1975: these are shown in table 3.17 together with notified vacancies.

Among unemployed males there was a clear imbalance between non-manual and manual. While the former constituted some 35 per cent of the economically active and retired males in 1971 (table 3.1 above), they amounted to only 17 per cent of the unemployed in 1975. In contrast, the figures for

Table 3.17

Percentage of non-manual and manual unemployed persons and notified vacancies at employment offices, Great Britain, June 1975

	*Social class (D.E.)**		
	Non-manual	Manual	Number of both
Male			
Unemployed	17	83	661,864
Vacancies	36	64	92,381
Female			
Unemployed	49.6	50.4	133,991
Vacancies	43	57	66,615
Both			
Unemployed	23	77	795,855
Vacancies	39	61	158,996

*The Department of Employment does not use the term 'social class' — see p. 42
(*Devised from pp. 776–8*, Department of Employment Gazette *August 1975*)

the manual classes were 65 per cent and 83 per cent. Looking at vacancies, too, one can see that the manual classes are again at a disadvantage: just under two thirds (64 per cent) of the vacancies available were for manual jobs, while some 83 per cent of the unemployed belonged to the manual classes. This suggests that unemployment among manual workers is both more common and less likely to be alleviated.

Female unemployment is split almost equally between non-manual and manual. However, since some 56 per cent of the economically active and retired females in 1971 were from the non-manual classes (table 3.1 above), the situation is similar to, but less marked than, that of males. The percentages for economically active and retired females, and for unemployed females, are 56 per cent and 49.6 per cent for the non-manual and 44 and 50.4 per cent for the manual classes. As for vacancies, female manual workers were relatively better placed than both female non-manual workers and male manual workers, since some 57 per cent of the female vacancies were for manual workers.

Working hours

It was shown above in table 3.8 that there existed a large difference in the average earnings of non-manual and manual workers. The same source reveals that the amount of time spent at work varies in much the same way (table 3.18). About two thirds of the manually occupied males worked over 40 hours a week, while nearly 80 per cent of the non-manual males worked less. The extremes are even more marked: 1 in 5 of the non-manual workers worked 36 hours or less (including 1 in 20 who worked less than 30 hours), compared with the 1 in 100 manual workers. Conversely, while 1 in 3 manual workers had a working week in excess of 48 hours this is true of only about 1 in 20 non-manual workers. The average hourly rates earned were: non-manual, 121.6p; manual 81.7p (including overtime pay and hours). In other words, hour for hour the average non-manual worker earned some 49 per cent

Table 3.18
Percentage of manual and non-manual workers* working
certain average weekly hours

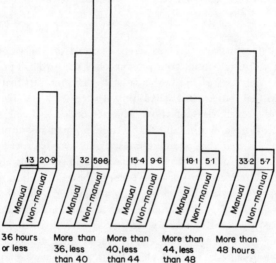

	36 hours or less	More than 36, less than 40	More than 40, less than 44	More than 44, less than 48	More than 48 hours
Manual	1·3	32	15·4	18·1	33·2
Non-manual	20·9	58·8	9·6	5·1	5·7

*Whose pay was not affected by absence
(*Devised from table 120*, New Earnings Survey 1973 *1974*)

more than the average manual worker. This difference is much
greater than the 26 per cent more earnings noted above (table
3.8 and p. 76) without taking into consideration hours
worked.

Job satisfaction

The *General Household Survey Introductory Report* (1973)
gathered information about job satisfaction from some 14,556
working persons aged 15 and over. They were asked 'Which of

Table 3.19
Percentage of persons in each social class reporting themselves
'very satisfied' with present job

	Social class (R.G.(S.E.)70)						
	1	2	3	4	5	6	All
Very satisfied	49	56	72	46	53	58	52

(Devised from table 6.8, General Household Survey Introductory Report *1973)*

the statements on this card comes nearest on the whole to what you think about your present job?' The card had printed on it 'very satisfied, fairly satisfied, neither satisfied nor dissatisfied, rather dissatisfied, very dissatisfied'. The distribution by social class of those who responded as being 'very satisfied' is shown in table 3.19. These are perhaps surprising figures, in that the apparently most highly satisfied social class is 3, while social class 1 is the second lowest. This almost certainly reflects the sex differences in the composition of the social classes and in levels of satisfaction. The *General Household Survey* shows that 61 per cent of females compared with 47 per cent of males were very satisfied with their jobs. Table 3.1 above (p. 64) clearly shows that females were over-represented in social class 3 (III(N.) in that table) and under-represented in class 4 (III(M.) in that table) and in class 1.

Social mobility

People change jobs, and sometimes this change entails a change of social class. Sociologists usually refer to this as intra-generational mobility, that is, upward or downward movement between social classes during a person's working life. Part of a government social survey concerned with this phenomenon looked at the careers of 4,062 men and 1,304 women who were working both in 1953 and 1963 (Harris and Clausen 1967). Not all the people in the sample had worked

Table 3.20

Social class of men in 1963 compared with that in 1953
(percentages)

Social class 1953 (R.G.60/A)	Social class 1963 (R.G.60/A)					
	I	II	III(N.M.)	III(M.)	IV	V
I	94	2	3	—	1	—
II	*	86	7	3	3	*
III(N.M.)	2	10	76	5	6	1
III(M.)	1	4	4	78	10	3
IV	—	4	3	14	73	6
V	—	1	1	10	20	68

*Less than 0.5 per cent
(Derived from table 52, Harris and Clausen 1967)

continuously through the decade, but most of those who had
not were women. The results for men and women are shown
separately in tables 3.20 and 3.21. In these tables the figures in
italics show the percentage of people in each social class
who remained in that class throughout the survey. The top
row of table 3.20 shows that, of the men who were in social
class I in 1953, 94 per cent were still in that class in 1963,
2 per cent had moved to class II, 3 per cent to class III(N.M.),
and 1 per cent to class IV. Social classes III(N.M.) and III(M.),

Table 3.21

Social class of women in 1963 compared with that in 1953
(percentages)

Social class 1953 (R.G.60/A)	Social class 1963 (R.G.60/A)					
	I	II	III(N.M.)	III(M.)	IV	V
I	(4)	(1)	—	—	—	—
II	—	86	7	2	5	*
III(N.M.)	—	6	84	2	5	1
III(M.)	—	2	7	65	19	7
IV	—	2	6	8	74	9
V	—	—	5	5	20	70

*Less than 0.5 per cent
( ) Actual number
(Derived from table 52, Harris and Clausen 1967)

for obvious reasons, displayed most movement in both directions. It is noticeable, however, that males in class III(N.M.) were equally likely to move up or down (12 per cent in both directions), whereas males in class III(M.) were slightly more likely to move down (upward 9 per cent, downward 13 per cent).

Table 3.21 reveals once again the very small numbers of economically active women in social class I. Over all, a slightly larger proportion of women than of men changed social class. This may well be due both to breaks in working, mainly for child rearing, and to mobility associated with husband's occupation. In the case of women the greatest amount of movement took place in social class III(M.), and this was mainly downward (26 per cent compared with 9 per cent). Indeed over all, in comparison with the men, there was less upward mobility.

It is interesting to note, from the same source, that social mobility typically involves a change of employer (only 2.4 per cent of the male mobility took place within the same employment). Of the men in the sample who had remained in the same employment, some 97.6 per cent experienced no mobility, 1.9 per cent upward mobility, and 0.5 per cent downward mobility (Harris and Clausen 1967, table 54). Job mobility, which does not necessarily mean social mobility, is a comparatively frequent phenomenon that also shows social class differences. In 1973 some 17.4 per cent of all male employees had been with their present employer for less than twelve months, but the non-manual figure was 19.3 per cent while the manual was 13.9 per cent. It must be remembered, however, that these figures include males commencing employment during that year. The figures for females were higher, at 26.2 per cent for all employees, and the social class difference is marginal and reversed, at non-manual 25.6 per cent and manual 26.7 (table 25, *New Earnings Survey 1973* 1974).

The other form of social mobility referred to by sociologists is *inter*-generational — that is, the change in social class between two generations, the data being normally but not always limited to males (that is, father and son). The largest

Table 3.22

Social class of sons in relation to that of fathers (percentages*)

Sons' social class (H.J.)	Fathers' social class (H.J.)							
	1	2	3	4	5	6	7	All
1	49	16	12	11	14	–	–	
2	12	25	22	13	23	4	2	
3	8	10	20	18	35	6	4	Each
4	2	4	14	24	40	9	7	class
5	1	2	9	16	50	13	10	= 100
6	1	1	4	11	44	24	15	
7		0.5	0.7	5	8	45	17	25	

*Percentages over 1 rounded
(Derived from table 2, p. 183, Glass 1954)

British study on this was carried out in 1949 (Glass 1954), and is at present being replicated, though data are not available at the time of writing. Table 3.22 shows the relationship between the social class of sons and that of their fathers. Thus the top row shows that, of men in social class I, 49 per cent had fathers who were in that class, 16 per cent had fathers in social class 2, 12 per cent in class 3, and so on. The figures in italics display for each social class the percentage of sons and fathers with the same social class. About half the men in social classes 1 and 5 had fathers from the same class, as did about a quarter of those in classes 2, 4, 6 and 7, whereas in social class 3 only a fifth did. Recruitment from within a class is highest, then, in professional and high administrative occupations (class 1) and skilled manual and routine non-manual occupations (class 5). It is lowest among inspectional, supervisory and other higher grade non-manual occupations (class 3). Although the figures in table 3.22 are clearly indicative of a high level of social mobility in five of the seven classes, attention needs to be paid to the extent of movement involved. Extreme movement is very rare. For example, only 3.2 per cent of sons of fathers in social classes 1 and 2 had jobs in classes 6 and 7. Conversely, none of the sons in class 1 had fathers in classes 6 and 7.

Clearly, social mobility is related to the job opportunities available to sons, and to the differences between these and the job opportunities which were available to their fathers. The people involved in this study lived through a period in which there was a depression and a world war (for some, two world wars). Since this study there have been considerable economic changes, together with some developments in education, and one could speculate as to how these will affect the current social class relationship between sons and fathers.

A further and later view of this type of social mobility is provided by the work of Butler and Stokes (1969). In their study they investigated social class both by classification of occupation and by self image (see chapter 2). They were mainly concerned with movement between the middle (non-manual) and the working (manual) classes. The top half of table 3.23 shows the sons and their fathers classified into social classes by occupation — i.e. objective classes. The lower half shows the sons' perceived (i.e. subjective) social class, both present and childhood. As can be seen, there was a reasonably close correspondence between the figures yielded by objective and subjective criteria of class. The figures in italics are the percentages of those who were socially mobile

Table 3.23
The relationship between fathers' and sons' social class, by
(1) classification of occupation and (2) sons' perception
(percentages)

1 Occupational classification	Sons' social class (M.R./C)		
Fathers' social class (M.R./C)	I–III	IV–VI	All
I–III	13	*10*	23
IV–VI	*16*	61	77
All	29	71	100

	Present class self image		
2 Perceived childhood class	Middle	Working	All
Middle	18	*5*	23
Working	*11*	66	77
All	29	71	100

(Devised from table 5.1 and footnote to p. 127, Butler and Stokes 1969)

(top half of the table), or who perceived themselves as socially mobile (bottom half of the table). Of the sample (N = 1,603) some 26 per cent had moved across the middle/working class divide, on the occupational criterion, and there was a net upward movement of 6 per cent. A smaller percentage, 16, perceived themselves to have been socially mobile. About three quarters of the sample were placed in, and identified themselves as belonging to, the same broad social class category as that of their parents.

A cautionary note has already been struck (see chapter 2, p. 35) about comparisons between the 1951 and 1961 censuses. The re-classification in 1961 contained fewer unit groups, and the derivation of social class used industrial status as well as occupation. Also, the armed forces were excluded from the new classification. An interesting exercise by the Registrar General in his *Decennial Supplement, England and Wales, 1961* (1971), 'Occupational Mortality Tables', reveals that the re-classification by itself meant a movement, on average, of about 30 per cent from each social class. A sample of 1 in 200 of the economically active men in 1961 was classified by social class on both the 1950 and the 1960 classifications. Table 3.24 compares these classifications, showing the 1950 one on the top axis, and the 1960 one on the left-hand axis. The figures in italics are the percentages of each social class which received the same classification in 1960 as they would have done in 1950. The top row reveals that, of men classifiable as social class I in 1950, 70 per cent were so classified in 1960, 20 per cent were classified as class II, 5 per cent as class III, and 5 per cent were not classified. The overall net result was a considerable apparent change in the social structure of Britain. This may be seen by comparing the right hand column in the table, the social class distribution according to the 1960 system, with the bottom row, the distribution by the 1950 system. All classes show a decline in their percentage of the total between the 1950 and 1960 classification, except for class IV which grew by 6.5 per cent. The re-classification also resulted in the non-classification of

Table 3.24

Economically active men in 1961 allocated to social classes
derived from 1950 and 1960 classifications of occupations
(percentages)

Social class (R.G.60)	*Social class (R.G.50)*					Percentage of sample
	I	II	III	IV	V	
I	70	4	(21)	(2)	–	3.9
II	20	71	3	(7)	(3)	14.4
III	5	23	78	21	7	49.8
IV	–	2	14	69	21	19.9
V	–	–	(17)	6	63	8.6
Not classified	5	(2)	3	3	9	3.5
Percentage of sample	4.5	16.4	53.5	13.4	12.1	100

( ) Actual numbers
(Devised from table D.1, Decennial Supplement, England and Wales,
1961 *1971)*

some 3.5 per cent of the economically active. Thus the
appearance of social mobility is created simply by altering
one's classificatory scheme. The bulk of the apparent movement took place within adjacent social classes and rarely
crossed the non-manual/manual line (though this line is not
always clear, since social class III is not divided in that way).
For example, as was pointed out above, of the 25 per cent of
social class I who were re-classified, 20 per cent went to class
II and 5 per cent to class III. Such changes make straightforward social class comparisons between the census of 1951 and
that of 1961 of doubtful utility. Fortunately the changes that
occurred in the 1971 census were of a comparatively minor
nature (*Classification of Occupations* 1970).

Age and social class

Several references have been made in this chapter to the fact
that the occupational structure of our society changes over
time. With respect to social mobility, for example, it was
suggested that the available stock of jobs on offer to would-be

employees was different for fathers and sons. A view of the actual situation is gained by looking at the age structures of the social classes, or alternatively at the social class compositions of the age groups of the economically active and retired. The figures for men are in tables 3.25A and 3.25B. The first table should be read vertically: hence, the left-hand column shows the percentage of social class I males in each age group. The second table should be read horizontally: hence, the top row shows the percentage of economically active males aged between 15 and 24 in each social class. The two tables show a clear pattern. At the extremes, for example, table 3.25A shows that social class I has a higher percentage of the younger age groups (27 per cent are aged 25 to 34) and a lower percentage of the older groups (only 13 per cent are between 55 and 64). Social class V is quite different: 13 per cent of its members are aged 25 to 34, and 19 per cent between 55 and 64. Table 3.25B shows that while 7 per cent of those aged 25 to 34 are in social class I, the proportion in this class declines to 4 per cent of those aged 55 to 64 and 3 per cent of those over 65; and while 6 per cent of those between the ages of 25 and 34 are in social class V, this proportion increases to 10 per cent of those aged 55 to 64, and 13 per cent of those over 65. Clearly, then, an immediate conclusion must be that the social classes have different age structures. As will be seen in the next chapter, this difference is crucial when comparing the social classes in terms of factors which are themselves obviously related to age – in this case sickness and death (see p. 112).

Considerable care is called for in interpreting these tables, mainly because our knowledge of the factors involved is limited. In the case of social class I the figures, which have been discussed, reflect *both* the increased share of such jobs in the occupational structure, and the increasing number of persons gaining higher education and professional qualifications. On the other hand, the slight rise through the age groups in the percentage of social class II (mainly managerial) jobs may well reflect the movement of men into such jobs as they become

Table 3.25A

The percentage* of economically active and retired males† in each social class by age group

	Social class (R.G. 70)						
Age group	I	II	III(N.)	III(M.)	IV	V	All
15—24	12	9	21	19	15	18	16
25—34	27	18	19	20	15	13	18
35—44	22	20	15	18	16	14	18
45—54	17	21	16	18	18	16	18
55—64	13	18	15	15	19	19	16
65 and over	9	14	14	11	17	20	13
All ages				Each class = 100			

Table 3.25B

The percentage* of economically active and retired males† in each age group by social class

	Social class (R.G.70)						
Age group	I	II	III(N.)	III(M.)	IV	V	All
15—24	4	10	15	44	17	9	
25—34	7	18	12	41	15	6	
35—44	6	20	10	40	16	7	Each
45—54	5	21	10	38	18	8	group
55—64	4	19	11	34	21	10	= 100
65 and over	3	18	12	31	22	13	
All ages	5	18	12	38	18	9	

*Percentages rounded
†Only those classified by social class included
(*Devised from table 29, Census 1971,* Economic Activity (10% Sample) *1975, part 4*)

older and more experienced. In the same way the larger percentage difference in the 15—24 age group between those with skilled jobs (classes III(N.) and III(M.)) — 59 per cent — and those with semi-skilled jobs (class IV) — 17 per cent — compared with the 55—64 age group (where the percentages are: skilled, 45 per cent; semi-skilled 21 per cent) are partly due to inter-generational changes in job and training opportunities. However, they are also likely to reflect intra-generational social mobility (see p. 90) — that is, the movement of individuals from one social class to another during their working life. Whether this is so would be revealed only by longitudinal studies of people's careers, while here only a cross-sectional picture is presented. Likewise it is probable, but not demonstrated, that the rise in the percentage of social class V through the age groups (the older having the higher percentage) is in fact partly due to the movement of some men to such jobs late in their working careers as a result of deteriorating health and/or ability to cope with other jobs. This is shown to be true in a study of schizophrenics reported in chapter 4 (p. 117).

The figures for women, presented in identical form, are in tables 3.26A and 3.26B. In the case of women, however, not only do the cautions outlined above apply, but so do others. Obviously, women typically break their employment for family reasons, and the timing and extent of such breaks almost certainly varies according to social class. See, for example, chapter 5, which illustrates social class variation in age of marriage, age of motherhood, and size of family. The tables show again what was seen above in tables 3.1 and 3.3. Very few economically active women are to be found in social class I, and a very large proportion in class III(N.) — which includes jobs like typist and shop assistant. This class III(N.) percentage is particularly high in the 15—24 age group, where 55 per cent of women are so employed: almost a third (32 per cent) of women in social class III(N.) are of that age. This proportion declines rapidly with age — at ages 25 to 34 only 39 per cent are so employed (15 per cent of class III(N.)) — presumably as women leave employment to raise families. In contrast, the percentage of women in classes IV and V (semi-skilled and unskilled) rises very steeply with the age groups — the older groups having the highest percentage. Of women aged 15 to 24 some 21 per cent are so employed, compared with 43 per cent of those between 55 and 64. This is due not only to differences in educational standards and job

Table 3.26A

The percentage* of economically active and retired females†
in each social class by age group

Social class (R.G.70)

Age group	I	II	III(N.)	III(M.)	IV	V	All
15—24	15	17	32	24	16	5	22
25—34	24	17	15	12	14	11	14
35—44	20	19	17	16	20	20	18
45—54	18	20	19	21	24	26	21
55—64	13	16	11	16	18	25	15
65 and over	11	12	6	11	9	13	9
All ages			Each class = 100				

Table 3.26B

The percentage* of economically active and retired females†
in each age group by social class

Social class (R.G.70)

Age group	I	II	III(N.)	III(M.)	IV	V	All
15—24	0.7	13	55	11	19	2	
25—34	2	21	39	9	24	6	
35—44	1	18	35	9	28	8	Each
45—54	0.9	16	34	10	29	10	group
55—64	0.8	18	28	10	30	13	= 100
65 and over	1	23	25	13	27	11	
All ages	1	17	38	10	26	8	

*Percentages over 1 rounded
†Only those classified by social class included
(Devised from table 29, Census 1971, Economic Activity (10% Sample)
1975, part 4)

opportunities of older women compared to younger, but also
probably to the fact that fewer women originally employed in
skilled occupations return to their former jobs.

In this chapter there has been an almost complete reliance on
government and census material. This is justifiable not only on
the grounds that such material is the most comprehensive and
extensive available, but because it also typically forms the

basis for much social research. Readers who are unfamiliar with the methodology, scope and limitations of the census will find these admirably and succinctly covered by Benjamin (1970). A further useful reference is Cox 1970, which also sets the census in a historical and comparative context within the discipline of demography.

4

Birth, health and death

Birth, and copulation, and death,
That's all the facts when you come to brass tacks:
Birth, and copulation, and death.

T. S. Eliot (1932)

This chapter is about a topic which has a long history of social class analysis. The relationship between wealth and health was well established and recognised by the turn of the century, partly as a result of the work of those pioneers of the social survey, Booth and Rowntree (for a short account of their work see Abrams 1951). Stevenson, the 'inventor' of the Registrar General's social class classification of 1921, which is the basis of the present one, was particularly interested in the influence of wealth and culture on mortality (death rates), natality (birth rates) and disease (Stevenson 1928). He argued that previous work in the field had applied only the criterion of wealth (surveys had been made of whole districts chosen to represent wealth and poverty). This criterion placed publicans, well known for living less long than others, above clergymen, who lived longer than average. Stevenson argued that this conflict showed that culture — in this case habits of diet and hygiene — was also important in relation to health. Similarly he recognised that wealthy districts contained relatively poor people — servants and the like — while poor districts contained relatively wealthy ones, such as pawnbrokers and publicans. For these reasons he saw the need for a 'scale of social position (largely but by no means exclusively a matter of wealth or poverty, culture also having been taken into account) based on occupation'. This would allow for the classification of whole populations in terms of individuals. Indeed he went on to argue that his social classes were meaningful because the mortality statistics fitted them. That is, the highest social class had the lowest mortality, and there was a fairly regular increase class by class so that the lowest class had the highest mortality. This type of distribution is commonly referred to as a gradient.

This chapter shows how social class pervades almost every vital aspect of man's experience in Britain. It outlines social class differences in experience from before birth, through birth and life, to death. Its concern is particularly with what might be described as the medical aspects of life.

Birth

Gestation

This, otherwise referred to as pregnancy, is a measure of the period of time between the conception of a child and its birth. While birth is an obvious and easily recorded event, conception is not necessarily so, and gestation is therefore a somewhat imprecise measure. A study by Butler and Bonham (1963) of all the children born in Britain during a week in 1958 (n = 17,205) was based on medical reports, and seems to provide reliable and reasonable evidence. It showed, perhaps surprisingly, that even this natural and physiological event demonstrated variation along social class lines. (In fact an earlier study had provided evidence for this (Douglas 1948).) Normal (here called 'mature') gestation is recognised as lasting for 38—41 weeks, and some 71 per cent of the pregnancies of women with husbands in the sample came into this category. As can be seen in table 4.1, the distribution of mature gestation varies from 80 per cent in social class I to 66 per cent in class V. Similarly, the higher the social class, the lower the

Table 4.1

Duration of gestation by social class of mother's husband
(percentages)*

Social class (R.G.(S.E.)50/A)

Gestation period	1	2	3	4	5	All	No husband
28—37 weeks							
(curtailed)	7	8	9	9	10	9	13
Mortality ratio	400	469	439	470	521	456	372
38—41 weeks							
('mature')	80	77	72	70	66	71	55
Mortality ratio	40	36	45	55	65	48	60
42+ weeks							
('prolonged')	11	11	12	12	13	12	11
Mortality ratio	50	66	74	79	66	75	107

*Percentages rounded. Note that the columns do not total 100 per cent,
because of the lack of information concerning the length of gestation
for some births. Over all this was true of 8 per cent of the births.
*(Derived from table 40.1, Butler and Bonham 1963 [*Perinatal
Mortality]*)

rates for shorter ('curtailed') and longer ('prolonged') gesta-
tions. The length of gestation is importantly related to survival
at birth. This is indicated in table 4.1 by the *mortality ratio*.
This is a figure which relates the death rate in a particular
group of a population to the death rate in a population as a
whole, using a base of 100. In this table, then, the base figure
100 corresponds to the infant death rate in the whole
population that was surveyed. In fact, of the 17,205 births
covered, 666 involved or were followed by the death of the
baby. Since the figures are ratios, a figure of 200 would mean
twice the overall death rate, and 50 half of it. Reference to the
table shows that the range involved is from 36 for 'mature'
gestation by class II, to 521 for 'curtailed' gestation by class V.
The table clearly shows the much higher incidence of death in
curtailed gestation, and a higher though less extreme incidence
in 'prolonged' as opposed to 'mature' gestation. The relevant
figures for 'all social classes' are: curtailed, 456; prolonged, 75;
mature, 48. The social class relationships are somewhat less
simple and linear than the distribution of the length of
gestation.

Follow-up studies on this population have suggested that length of gestation is an important factor in the subsequent development of the child. Davie, Butler and Goldstein (1972) show that it is related to various factors such as school performance (reading and social adjustment), clumsiness, handicaps, and ability to copy designs. These relationships are complicated by the fact that there are social class variations both in length of gestation and in the other measured variables. However, to take as an example reading ability at the age of seven, the authors write:

... the effect of length of pregnancy ... was small but clear. After allowing for all other factors except birth weight the best readers were those born at the 'expected' time (normal gestation), and the worst were those born more than two weeks early, the difference being equivalent to about three months of reading age. (p. 177 and see Davie 1969)

Birth weight

This is another measure associated with length of gestation, and was recorded in the same study. Table 4.2 again displays a fairly regular social class variation. It reveals markedly lower mortality ratios for birth weights over 2,500 grams (5lb 8½oz) than for weights under this. The order of this difference varies very little along social class lines, the mortality ratio for the lower birth weight being some 16—18 times greater than that for the higher except in class I where it is 21 times greater. The

Table 4.2

Birth weight by social class of mother's husband (percentages)*

	Social class (R.G.(S.E.)50/A)						
Weight	1	2	3	4	5	All	No husband
2,500 grams and under	4	5	7	7	8	7	11
Mortality ratio	854	740	763	807	931	795	739
Over 2,500 grams	96	94	93	92	91	93	89
Mortality ratio	40	42	48	53	56	49	66

*Percentages rounded
(*Derived from table 45, Butler and Bonham 1963* [Perinatal Mortality])

mortality ratios for each birth weight rose from social class I to V (from 854 to 931 and from 40 to 56 respectively). The incidence of lower birth weight varies in the same way, accounting for some 4 per cent of births in social class I, and 8 per cent in class V. Again follow-up studies have shown that relationships exist between birth weight and subsequent development similar to those outlined for gestation. It should be remembered that length of gestation and birth weight are related; premature babies (of short gestation) will typically be of under 2,500 grams.

Infant mortality

This refers to deaths of children between birth and the age of one year. The Registrar General for Scotland in his Annual Report publishes figures for infant mortality by social class. Hence the *Annual Report for Scotland 1973* (1974) provides the most up to date large-scale figures available. The *Statistical Review of England and Wales 1973* (1975) contains infant mortality data but not by social class. Infant mortality is normally recorded under three headings. *Stillbirths* are babies who display no life at birth. *Neonatal* deaths are those that occur between a live birth and the end of the week following it. *Post-neonatal* deaths are those that occur between the first week and a year following a live birth. The figures in table 4.3 relate to the 74,392 recorded live births and the 873 stillbirths in Scotland in 1973. It should be noted that they are expressed as a rate per 1,000, which may be conveniently converted into a percentage by moving the decimal point one place to the left. Hence the stillbirth rate for 'all social classes', which is 12, can be viewed as 1.2 per cent of all births. Table 4.3 shows that the stillbirth rate more than doubles between social class I and V (7 compared to 16). The differences between each social class are progressive and uniform, the increase being at the rate of about two per class.

Neonatal and post-neonatal deaths are expressed separately in rates per 1,000 live births (that is total births minus stillbirths). Table 4.4 shows these by social class. The distri-

Table 4.3
Stillbirth rates* per 1,000 total births by social class,
Scotland

Social class (R.G. 70/E)

	I	II	III	IV	V	All
Stillbirth rates per 1,000	7	9	11	14	16	12

*Rounded
(Derived from table D1.4, Annual Report for Scotland 1973 1974)

bution is somewhat different from that of stillbirths. In both neonatal and post-neonatal deaths it is only social class V that is markedly different from the other social classes. For example, the rate of post-neonatal death per 1,000 for social class I is half that for classes III and IV; while the rate for class V is more than twice that of classes III and IV, and almost five times that of class I. The rates for social classes III and IV are identical, and the difference between these and that for class II is small.

This section has demonstrated that social class, in this case that of the father, is related to the length of gestation, birth weight, and chances of survival at and just following birth. It has not attempted to explain why this should be. One can see, however, that even before life, and certainly at birth, social

Table 4.4
Neonatal and post-neonatal death rates* per 1,000 live births
by social class, Scotland

Social class (R.G. 70/E)

	I	II	III	IV	V	All
Neonatal death rate per 1,000	9	10	12	12	18	13
Post-neonatal death rate per 1,000	3	4	6	6	14	6

*Rounded
(Derived from tables F1.3 and F1.4, Annual Report for Scotland 1973 1974)

class affects individuals. In general terms, the figures suggest that the higher the social class of a father, the easier and safer life is for his child.

Health

In this section two aspects of health are considered. Both are concerned with epidemiology — 'the study of the distribution and determinates of diseases and injuries in human popula- tions' (Mausner and Bahn 1974). Our approach will be limited to viewing only social class distributions and a single 'deter- minate' factor — the use of medical facilities. A much fuller treatment of epidemiology and its uses, together with examples related to Britain, is available in Morris 1964. A general idea of the level of health enjoyed by the social classes can be gained from the *General Household Survey*. This is, now, an annual attempt by the government to survey some 15,000 households (for definition see p. 155) in Great Britain (England, Wales and Scotland). By contrast with the census, there is no legal obligation to take part. The number of persons involved, and the response rates, vary both over all and in relation to particular aspects of the interview schedule. In the *General Household Survey 1972* (1975) the following question about health was asked:

Do you suffer from any long-standing illness, disability or infirmity?

IF YES: Does [it] limit your activities compared with most people of your own age?

This question was designed to obtain some measure of the incidence of chronic sickness. Clearly the answers are to some degree dependent on the subjective feelings and the knowledge of the respondent. It could be argued that this, far from detracting from the validity of the data, actually enhances it, since attitudes towards sickness are at least as important as clinical symptoms. The responses in table 4.5A demonstrate that there is a marked difference between the incidence of non-limiting and that of limiting long-standing illness. This varies along social class lines: in social class 1 exactly half of those reporting a long-standing illness see it as limiting, whereas in class 6 the figure is about two-thirds. The incidence of both types of illness increases regularly across the social classes, class 1 having the lowest rate and class 6 the highest. Obviously age is a crucial factor in chronic sickness. Table 4.5B contrasts two age groups by social class in respect

Table 4.5A

Rates per 1,000 reporting (1) long-standing illness,
(2) limiting long-standing illness, by social class

	Social class (R.G.(S.E.)70)						
	1	2	3	4	5	6	All
Long-standing illness	130	168	192	192	265	317	206
Limiting long-standing illness	65	90	104	113	162	208	121

Table 4.5B

Rates per 1,000 reporting limiting long-standing illness by
social class and age

	Social class (R.G.(S.E.)70)						
Age group	1	2	3	4	5	6	All
15–44	40	62	49	66	68	113	62
45–64	113	118	173	196	256	272	190

(Derived from table 5.10, General Household Survey 1972 *1975)*

Table 4.5C

Observed rates of those reporting limiting long-standing illness
by social class and sex, as a percentage of expected rates

	Social class (R.G.(S.E.)70)						
	1	2	3	4	5	6	All
Males	74	78	86	103	120	156	100
Females	69	75	85	105	119	118	100
Males and females	72	76	85	104	119	134	100

(Derived from table 5.11, General Household Survey 1972 *1975)*

of limiting illness only. Generally, progressive incidence from social class 1 to 6 is confirmed, except for classes 2 and 3 in the age range 15—44, which are reversed. By comparing the upper and lower lines it is possible to get an idea of the increase due to age. Over all (see the last column) this is in the order of 1:3, and this is also true for classes 1 and 4; classes 2 and 6 have somewhat lower differences (1:2—2½) and classes 4 and 5 somewhat higher (1:3—4).

The data from the second line of table 4.5A have been recast and are shown as a percentage of the expected rate in table 4.5C. This is a similar process to that which produces standardised mortality ratios (see p. 112). Simply, the 'expected rate' is the rate which would be expected in each group (defined by class, sex etc.) if it had the same rate as that recorded for the whole population. The observed rates for the groups, however, vary, some being higher and others lower: here the observed rate is expressed as a percentage of the expected rate (100).

Table 4.5C reveals a very clear distinction between the non-manual classes (1, 2 and 3) and the manual (4, 5 and 6). The former have lower rates than expected, the latter higher, for each sex and for both sexes together. The figures also show a clear linear progression across the social classes, from the lowest rate for class 1, to the highest for class 6. It is also noticeable that the gradient involved is steeper for men (from 74 to 156) than for women (from 69 to 118). Over all, however, women had much higher rates of long-standing illness per 1,000, at 215, than men whose rate was 115 (table 5.10, *General Household Survey 1972* 1975).

The same source provides a further measure of ill-health — this time of its effect on the working population only. Respondents were asked about absence from work due to ill-health in a particular two-week period, and about the number of days lost from sickness in the year (table 4.6).

The social class differences here are very marked, particularly at the extremes. The rate of reported absence in social class 6 is almost five times greater than that in class 1, and the

Table 4.6

Working persons aged 15+ by social class: (*a*) rates per 1,000
reporting absence from work due to illness/injury in two
reference weeks; (*b*) average number of working days lost per
person per year

	Social class (R.G.(S.E.)70)						
	1	2	3	4	5	6	All
(*a*) **Reporting absence per 1,000**	21	39	48	56	68	99	55
(*b*) **Average days lost per person**	3	6	6	9	11	18	8

(Derived from table 5.19, General Household Survey 1972 *1975)*

average number of days lost is six times higher. Another
noticeable feature is the large increase in rates between social
classes 1 and 2, and similarly between 5 and 6. Caution is
necessary in interpreting these figures since they are not pure
measures of sickness. Clearly, they have to do with attitudes
towards sickness and work, with work habits, conditions and
demands, and so on. The *General Household Survey Introductory Report* (1973) showed that people who were dissatisfied
with their jobs were more likely to have been absent from
work than those who were satisfied. Objectively, too, occupations vary in terms of health and injury risk, and also in terms
of the possibility of continuing to do them if one is ill or
injured. Generally speaking, these differences follow social
class lines. Simply, some manual occupations are more
hazardous than most non-manual ones, and also more de-
manding in terms of physical fitness. In a similar way
occupations vary in their levels of absenteeism, some having
what amount to sets of informal norms for this. The
conditions of employment, financial considerations and the
welfare state make the relationship between 'sickness' and
absence from work more complex than might at first appear.
    Rather morbidly, though not surprisingly, much of our
knowledge concerning the incidence of particular diseases
among the population of Britain stems from our knowledge of

the causes of death (though there have been many small-scale clinical studies of particular conditions). The registration of deaths, as required by law, includes the cause of death and the deceased's last occupation. The Registrar General puts these facts together with the information gathered from the census for England and Wales to produce 'Occupational Mortality Tables'. These are published in a *Decennial Supplement*, the most recent of which covers deaths between 1959 and 1963 and the population as in the census of 1961. This was published in 1971. Many problems arise in analysing these findings. The simple recording of the incidence of death by cause and by social class would be rather meaningless, mainly because age is an obvious factor in death, and, as was demonstrated in chapter 3 (pp. 96 to 100), the age structures of the social classes are not the same. Therefore, in order to make comparisons between the social classes more meaningful *standardised mortality ratios* are produced. These are computed using the following formula:

$$\frac{\text{observed deaths}}{\text{expected deaths}} \times 100$$

'Expected deaths' is the number of deaths one might expect to find in a particular social class if the age-specific death rate for the whole population (everyone aged 15—64 years in England and Wales) was replicated in the group in question. For full details of the calculations involved see *Decennial Supplement, England and Wales, 1961* (1971). The S.M.R. for any given population is taken to be 100. The figures for groups within that population are then expressed as a ratio of this (see p. 104).

It should be recognised, as Nissel (1971) points out, that although death rates of various types have been traditionally used as indicators of levels of health, they clearly may not tell us much about the living members of a population. Thus the Registrar General in his introduction (*Decennial Supplement, England and Wales, 1961* (1971) points out that many of the

Table 4.7

Standardised mortality ratios for cancer in men and married women between ages 15 and 64, by social class

	Social class (R.G.60)					
	I	II	III	IV	V	All
Men	73	80	104	102	139	100
Married women	89	92	103	100	124	100

(Derived from tables 5A and 5B, Decennial Supplement, England and Wales, 1961 *1971)*

currently registered deaths 'reflect damage caused by infections in the pre-antibiotic era, and mirror the social class differences known to exist in those decades'. They remain however, the only major source of data in this field.

The most outstanding feature of the *Decennial Supplement* is the general positive gradient of S.M.R.s along social class lines — they rise from class I to class V. An example of this is given in table 4.7 for cancer deaths. As can be seen, not only does the S.M.R. increase between social classes I and V but the S.M.R.s for classes I and II are both lower than those for classes IV and V.

Another table (E.1) in the *Decennial Supplement* lists 84 selected causes of death for men, and shows that in 49 cases the S.M.R.s for classes I and II are both lower than those for classes IV and V. The interpretation of this sort of figure is difficult. There are clearly two aspects of social class which are involved:

1 Wealth, personal habits, diet, home environment, physical exercise and mental stress (the latter two are general occupational factors)
2 Specific occupational hazards

These are not entirely separable, though wives, it has been suggested, could be seen to reflect mostly the first aspect. Thus occupational hazards may be isolated, to some extent, by comparing the rates of cause of death of men and married women in the social classes, though the usefulness of such a comparison is limited by our lack of knowledge concerning how many of the married women worked, and at what type of occupation. However, mortality differences may also indicate differences in the availability and/or use of medical care. Further, there is the question of selection in and out of occupations on the basis of health. Finally, it may be that diagnosis varies according to social class and doctors' ability and inclinations. Doctors may, for example, be restrained from putting 'syphilis' or 'suicide' on the death certificate of a well known member of the community. Bearing these factors in mind, look at table 4.8, which presents S.M.R.s for some selected causes of death (the figures relating to cancer are in table 4.7, those for maternal deaths in table 4.19, and those for suicide in table 4.20).

Perhaps surprisingly, given the introduction of the National Health Service, the Welfare State and advances in medicine, these social class differences in mortality have been shown to have increased (Townsend 1974). Although the exact extent of the increase remains debatable — because of changes in the classification, collection and processing of data — the trend of growing inequality between the social classes in mortality has been established.

A rather similar picture of the relationship between social class and illness was displayed in the *Report on an Enquiry into the Incidence of Incapacity for Work* (1964, 1965). The second part of this study was an analysis of the medical certificates presented for absences from work of four or more days. Some 5 per cent of all insured and employed men (N = 620,000) and 2½ per cent of similarly placed women (N = 90,000) were surveyed for the year ending June 1962. The study was rigorous and included a check by Regional Medical Officers on a sample of the doctors' diagnoses. The figures in table 4.9 are the age-standardised rates per 1,000 persons in each class. The figures for men can be treated with considerable confidence. A number of reservations about the figures for women are made in the report. These mainly concern the fact that only a certain proportion of all women

Health

Table 4.8

Comparison of social class standardised mortality ratios for selected causes, in men and married women aged 15—64

Social class (R.G.60)

Cause	Men's social class					Women's social class				
	I	II	III	IV	V	I	II	III	IV	V
Tuberculosis	40	54	96	108	185	41	61	102	112	178
Diabetes	81	103	100	98	122	43	67	95	121	183
Coronary disease	98	95	106	96	112	69	81	103	107	143
Influenza	58	67	89	114	162	46	74	97	121	171
Pneumonia	48	54	88	102	196	64	69	95	114	172
Bronchitis	28	50	97	116	194	33	51	102	118	196
Pneumochoniosis (occupational)	5	9	109	181	95	–	–	–	–	–
Appendicitis	104	79	104	105	108	80	98	104	100	108
Cirrhosis of liver	106	136	86	85	137	94	132	92	92	115
Accidents in home	95	78	81	104	226	107	91	87	99	171

N.B. S.M.R.s refer to males and females separately; in each case the S.M.R. for all social classes is 100; social class of married women is based on husband's occupation

(Derived from table E1, Decennial Supplement, England and Wales, 1961 1971)

Table 4.9

Number of employed persons commencing one or more new
spells of incapacity for work, expressed as a rate (standardised
for age) per 1,000 in each social class, Great Britain

Social class (R.G.60/B)

Men	I and II	III	IV	V	All
Diseases of respiratory system	91	145	157	177	144
Influenza	39	62	64	70	60
Pneumonia	1	2	2	2	2
Bronchitis	15	35	44	57	37
Chronic sinusitus	3	4	4	4	4
Asthma*	1	1.7	2.1	2.4	1.8
Arteriosclerotic/heart disease*	3.3	3.4	3.2	3.3	3.3
Psychoses/psychoneuroses	4	7	8	13	7
Arthritis and rheumatism	7	25	30	40	25
All causes	181	282	307	349	281
Married women					
Diseases of respiratory system	157	166	199	174	174
Influenza	52	62	72	87	61
Bronchitis	19	35	47	35	38
Psychoses and psychoneuroses	19	18	25	17	19
Arthritis and rheumatism	13	20	31	23	23
All causes	364	371	439	432	393
Other women					
Diseases of respiratory system	173	173	195	215	178†
Influenza	61	64	75	72	66†
Bronchitis	23	26	36	38	28†
Psychoses and psychoneuroses	10	14	21	28	15†
Arthritis and rheumatism	10	13	23	26	15†
All causes	331	319	369	405	331†

*Actual rates (all others rounded)
†Including unclassified
(Derived from tables A9 and B9, Report on an Enquiry into the
Incidence of Incapacity for Work, *part 2, 1965)*

were insured — no more than three out of ten employed
married women, who themselves represented only about one
tenth of married women of working age. Once again the
general linear relationship between social class and disease and
illness can be seen. There is, in most cases, a steady increase in
the rate of incapacity per 1,000 from classes I and II to V, the

only major exception being heart disease among men, where the social class rates vary hardly at all, and psychoses and psychoneuroses among married women, where a peak occurs for social class IV rather than V. The latter figure is marginally lower than that for other classes. Comparison of the sexes reveals generally higher rates for women than for men. This is particularly noticeable in the case of psychoses and psychoneuroses, where the male rate for all social classes is 7, for married women 19, and for other women 15.

A good illustration of how problematic it is to relate social class directly to illness was provided by a study of schizophrenia (Goldberg and Morrison 1963). This is a reminder that social surveys often present what amounts to only a single frame of a moving film. A number of previous studies of hospital admissions of schizophrenics had shown the lowest social classes over-represented. The top half of table 4.10 shows this for a sample of first admissions in 1956, by comparing 'observed' with 'expected' numbers. For social class V these are 90 and 39. However, the lower half of the table shows that the social class distribution of the patients' fathers was very similar to that of the general population. It

Table 4.10
Social class distribution of schizophrenic patients and their fathers

Social class (R.G.50)

	I	II	III	IV	V	Not known
Patients						
Observed	12	21	178	52	90	18
*Expected**	12	44	203	55	39	
Fathers						
Observed	14	42	192	66	55	2
Expected†	8	42	192	68	59	

*From 1951 census distribution
†From 1931 census distribution
(Derived from table I, Goldberg and Morrison 1963)

Table 4.11

Total tooth loss among adults* by household social class

Social class† (R.G.66/A)

	I	II	III(N.M.)	III(M.)	IV	V	All
Percentage without teeth	15	31	25	34	46	47	37

*Aged 16 years and over
†Individuals were classified by social class of head of household in which they lived
(Derived from table 4.5, Gray, Todd, Slack and Bulman 1970)

was suggested that this was the result of social 'drift' (downward social mobility) on the part of schizophrenics — that is, that their complaint was not a result of their social class but rather its cause. Goldberg and Morrison, in a very detailed clinical study, have traced this decline in occupational status both between father and patient and in the patient's own history. It seems extremely likely that 'social drift' is a feature of many forms of chronic and progressive illness.

Less serious aspects of health have also been surveyed, with rather similar results. A study of adult dental health (Gray, Todd, Slack and Bulman 1970) displayed a very clear relationship between social class and total tooth loss (table 4.11). Not only is total tooth loss shown to be progressive across the social classes from I to V, but there is a clear distinction between manual and non-manual. In social class III, the manual percentage is 34 and the non-manual 25. Once again, however, the measure not only reflects the condition of dental health in the social classes, but is related to the use of the health services, and the treatment that they provide. It is this area — the use, provision and quality of health services — which must be considered next.

Use of health services

At a simple level, the use of health services might be expected to vary according to the health of an individual or group. Thus the rates by social class for consulting a doctor would be expected to follow the distribution of reported incidence of

Table 4.12

Observed rates of (*a*) consulting a general practitioner (N.H.S.), (*b*) attending 'outpatients' at a hospital, as a percentage of the expected rates, by social class

| | *Social class (R.G.(S.E.)70)* | | | | | | |
	1	2	3	4	5	6	All
(*a*) Consulting G.P.	95	93	98	103	107	116	100
(*b*) Attending 'outpatients'	95	94	107	102	99	113	100

(Derived from tables 5.29 and 5.35, General Household Survey 1972 *1975)*

illness and injury (table 4.5C above). The figures from the *General Household Survey 1972* in table 4.12 do in fact show a progressive rise in the use of a doctor and in the attendance of outpatients' departments from social class 1 through to 6. Hence a broad conclusion would be that the non-manual social classes (1, 2, 3) used doctors less often, and the manual (4, 5, 6) more often, in comparison with the rate for the population as a whole. This conclusion is supported by the work of Dunnell and Cartwright (1972). Their sample kept a two-week diary of their symptoms and noted their health on the scale 'excellent, good, fair, poor, O.K.'. These two measures together with general practitioner consultations varied directly along social class lines as can be seen in table 4.13. The authors confirm the suggestion here that the working classes (III M., IV and V) have a greater need for medical care, and make more use of general practitioners, by showing that this is true even for individuals from different classes who report the same number of symptoms. They further report that the class differences shown here were not related to age differences. This social class gradient is an interesting finding, since a study of 106 general practices (Logan and Cushions 1962) and one of a sample of 1,397 patients from twelve areas (Cartwright 1967) revealed no such gradient. In both these studies, the age and sex variations between the social classes were found to account for most of the apparent differences in social class rates of consulting a doctor. One contributory factor which

Table 4.13

Number of reported symptoms, self-rated health, and general practitioner consultations by social class

| | \multicolumn{6}{c}{*Social class (R.G.66/A)*} |
	I	II	III(N.M.)	III(M.)	IV	V
Mean number of symptoms reported in two weeks	3.4	3.7	3.6	4.0	4.0	4.6
Percentage who rated health fair or poor	17	28	28	36	37	43
Estimated mean number of general practitioner visits in year	2.9	3.1	3.3	3.6	4.0	4.2

(Derived from table 30, Dunnell and Cartwright 1972)

should be borne in mind, however, is that manual workers may be more likely to need medical certificates for short absences from work. This would lead to higher consulting rates for manual workers, and hence go some way towards explaining the social class differences which can be seen in table 4.14. In the case of men there is a general rise in consulting across the classes, particularly high rates for classes 5 and 6, and a fairly clear distinction between the rates for the non-manual and manual classes. The rates for women are much more similar to one another, with a small peak occurring in class 4. Since it can be assumed that a larger proportion of the men than of the

Table 4.14

Observed rates of consulting a general practitioner (N.H.S.) as a percentage of expected rates by sex and social class

| | \multicolumn{7}{c}{*Social class (R.G.(S.E.)70)*} |
	1	2	3	4	5	6	All
Male	93	98	93	99	118	140	100
Female	98	89	101	107	101	100	100
Both	95	93	98	103	107	116	100

(Derived from table 5.29, General Household Survey 1972 1975)

women were in employment, the separate patterns for the
sexes could be seen as supporting the view that the need to use
doctors is partly related to occupation. Over all, the rate for
females was higher than for males. In Great Britain in 1972 the
rates per 1,000 who consulted a general practitioner were 97
for male and 129 for females, the overall rate being 113
(table 5.28, *General Household Survey 1972* 1975). The
average number of consultations per person also varied along
social class and sex lines. The overall rate for males was 3.2;
for social class 1 it was 2.7 and for class 6, 4.4. The overall rate
for females was 4.3; for social class 1 it was 3.8 and for class 6,
4.6. Notice the much smaller differences between the rates for
the sexes in social class 6 compared to those in social class 1.

Social class differences in the use of hospital services for
in-patients have also been reviewed (Carstairs 1966). This
survey involved analysing the records of all patients (other
than maternity and mental cases) in all Scottish National
Health Service hospitals in 1963. Table 4.15 looks at the social

Table 4.15

Standardised discharge ratios* and mean stay ratios† of
hospital patients by social class, Scotland

	Social class (R.G.60)					
Male	I	II	III	IV	V	All
Standardised discharge ratio	93	84	92	105	149	100
Standardised mean stay ratio	78	88	99	103	112	100
Female§						
Standardised discharge ratio	99	95	92	100	156	100
Standardised mean stay ratio	88	93	99	103	107	100

*The standardised discharge ratio is the result of a comparison of the
actual rates of hospital discharge for each social class with the rate that
would be expected if the age structure of each social class was the same
as that for the whole population. The actual rate is then expressed as a
rounded percentage of the expected rate. Thus if the actual and the
expected rates were identical, the standardised discharge ratio would be
100 (which is the score for social class IV females)
†The standardised mean stay ratio is calculated and rounded in the
same way as the standardised discharge ratio
§In the case of married women, the social class is their husband's
(Derived from table 2, Carstairs 1966)

class and sex differences on two measures: the first is the actual use of hospital facilities, and the second the length of such use. As can be seen, for both measures and both sexes there is a fairly steady rise across the social classes from I to V, particularly for length of stay. What is particularly noticeable is the difference in the discharge ratios between social classes I, II and III on the one hand, and social classes IV and V on the other. The figures for the latter classes are markedly higher. It is necessary to bear in mind that these differences in admission to, and length of stay in, hospital do not reflect only differences in rates of illness and disease, though these do exist, as was seen in tables 4.8 and 4.9. Differences in physical and social environment are also likely to be relevant. Poor housing and lack of amenities and privacy are likely to limit the possibility of home treatment. This could well lead to more frequent admission and a longer stay in hospital in social class V where these provisions are most limited (see chapter 5). At the other end of the scale people in the upper income brackets make greater use of private hospital services.

The use of other — perhaps less obvious — health services also appears to be related to social class. For example, an analysis of women undergoing cervical smear tests (N = 4,048) revealed an over-representation of social classes I, II and III and an under-representation of classes IV and V by comparison with the general female population (Wakefield and Sansom 1966: see table 4.16).

Table 4.16
Social class of women undergoing cervical smear examination
(percentages)

	I	II	III(N.M.)	III(M.)	IV	V
	Social class (R.G.60/A)					
Examination 1965*	7	19	16	42	11	6
Census population 1961*	2	14	49		27	9

*Both sets of figures refer to an area of Lancashire
(Derived from table 3, Wakefield and Sansom 1966)

This study suggests that there were social class differences in terms of where such tests took place. In classes I and V the highest proportion were done by family doctors, in class II by family planning clinics, and in classes III and IV by local authority clinics. Rather similar findings are reported later (table 5.17) for mothers' use of infant welfare clinics, immunisation and dentists.

A further question which arises is whether the social classes receive different types and qualities of treatment from the health services. Clearly this is a difficult research area. Cartwright (1964) found some differences between working class and middle class areas in terms of doctors' qualifications, the size of their list of patients, and whether they also held hospital appointments. In a later study of a sample of patients (Cartwright 1967) she failed to find consistent results. The area is perhaps best surveyed by Rein (1969), who concluded:

These scattered findings are inconclusive, but they are suggestive and support the general conclusion of this review that in Britain the lowest social classes make the greatest use of physician and hospital medical care services and that the care they receive appears to be of as good quality as that received by other social classes.

However, Hart (1971) has argued that there exists 'massive but mostly non-statistical evidence in favour of Titmuss's generalisations'. These were:

We have learnt ... that the higher income groups know how to make better use of the service [i.e. the N.H.S.] : they tend to receive more specialist attention; occupy more of the beds in better equipped hospitals; receive more elective surgery; have better maternal care, and are more likely to get psychiatric help and psychotherapy than low-income groups – particularly the unskilled. (Titmuss 1968)

Death

Unfortunately for our purposes the life tables published by the Registrar General (see table 92, Nissel and Lewis 1974) are not

Table 4.17

Mean annual death-rate per 100,000 men by age group and
social class

Age group	I	II	III	IV	V	All men
15—19	67	99	90	110	132	93
20—24	67	97	103	114	170	114
25—34	82	81	100	119	202	112
35—44	166	177	234	251	436	241
45—54	535	545	708	734	1119	707
55—64	1699	1820	2218	2202	2912	2171
65—74	4666	5100	6347	5702	6715	5452

Social class (R.G.60)

(Derived from table 3A(i), Decennial Supplement, England and Wales,
1961, *1971)*

produced on a social class basis. It is not possible, therefore, to
make definitive statements about life expectancy or age of
death for the social classes. As has been shown above,
however, the majority of standardised mortality ratios for
particular causes of death are markedly higher for social classes
IV and V. Table 4.17 further illustrates this trend by presenting annual mean death rates per 100,000 men. Based on the
recorded deaths from all causes in England and Wales between
1959 and 1963, the figures represent the average number of
persons dying per year in each age group of each social class.

In all age groups the mean annual death rate increases
across the social classes from class I to V. Indeed in all age
groups other than 55—64 and 65—74 the death rate of social
class I is about half that of class V. This clearly indicates that
life expectancy and age of death is related to social class. The
social class chances of surviving through adulthood into old
age are similar to those of surviving birth (see tables 4.3 and
4.4 above).

A further perspective is added by table 4.18 which gives
S.M.R.s for all causes of death for ages 15—64 years. The
S.M.R.s for men and married women show a remarkable
similarity in pattern — a progressive gradient from social class I
to V. The married women's rates are of particular interest.

Table 4.18

Standardised mortality ratios of men, married women (by husband's occupation), and single women, aged 15—64, by social class

Social class (R.G.60)

Group	I	II	III	IV	V	All
Men, 15—64 years	76	81	100	103	143	100
Women, married, 15—64 years	77	83	103	105	141	100
Women, single, 15—64 years	83	88	90	108	121	100

(Derived from table 1, Decennial Supplement, England and Wales, 1961 1971)

Since they are based on husband's social class by occupation, they could be seen as reflecting all the aspects of social class identified as associated with health (see p. 113), other than specific occupational hazards. However, caution is necessary. We have no knowledge from these tables of the proportion of these women who worked, or of the occupations in which they were employed. However, it should be noted that the single women's rates show a shorter, more level distribution (from 83 in social class I to 121 in class V, compared with 77 to 141 for married women). It is also noticeable that the interval between social classes IV and V is smaller in the case of single women (108 to 121 compared with 105 to 141 for married women).

Apart from the general figures for death and mortality rates, there are those for specific causes of death. Some of these can be seen in tables 4.7 and 4.8 above. There are, however, two further causes of death which are of special interest for this book. These are maternity and suicide. The first links up with infant mortality (tables 4.3 and 4.4 above). While maternity deaths are few in number — 847 were recorded between 1962 and 1965 — they appear to be related to social class (see table 4.19) in the same way as most other causes of death, including infant mortality.

Suicide has been of considerable interest to sociology since the now classic work of Durkheim (1952; originally published

Table 4.19

Standardised maternal mortality ratios* and mean annual
maternity deaths per 1,000 total legitimate births, of married
women by social class

	Social class (R.G.60)					
	I	II	III	IV	V	All
Standardised maternal						
mortality ratio*	55	73	90	120	178	100
Mean annual death rate	0.16	0.22	0.23	0.32	0.44	0.26

*S.M.M.R.s are similar to S.M.R.s but based on the number of
maternities
(Derived from tables 6A and 6B, Decennial Supplement, England and
Wales, 1961 *1971)*

in Britain in 1915). The most recent figures available, shown in
table 4.20, are at considerable variance with those previously
reported. Giddens (1971), commenting on the male S.M.R. for
suicide for ages 20 to 64 up to 1950, writes 'Suicide is the
most frequent in the two highest classes' (that is classes I and
II), and 'tends to go up again in the lowest social class'. Clearly
the present figures reveal quite a different picture, with a
steady increase in the ratios across the social classes. What is
interesting, however, is that the S.M.R.s for both married and
single women do display the pattern described by Giddens.

Table 4.20

Standardised mortality ratios for suicide of men, married
women, and single women, aged 15—64, by social class

	Social class (R.G.60)					
	I	II	III	IV	V	All
Men	91	94	87	103	184	100
	(134)*	(110)	(89)	(99)	(119)	
Married women	110	98	101	84	109	100
Single women	132	104	86	82	160	100

*Figures in brackets are S.M.R.s for ages 20—64 for 1950, from table
5.6, Giddens 1971
(Derived from table 4, Decennial Supplement, England and Wales, 1961
1971)

Table 4.21

Mean annual suicide death rates per million persons living,
by sex

	Age group				
	15—24	25—34	35—44	45—54	55—64
Male	58	113	147	199	297
Female married	26	52	76	119	150
Female single	24	113	164	204	239

(*Derived from table 2,* Decennial Supplement, England and Wales, 1961
1971)

The same source reveals that there are large sex differences in
the incidence of suicide. A comparison of male with married
female figures in table 4.21 shows that the male mean annual
death rate from suicide is twice as large.

The single women's figures are more similar to those of the
men, exceeding them at ages 35—44 and 45—54. Hence there
is an extremely marked difference between single and married
women, of the same order as that between men and married
women. It is interesting to note that the difference between
married and single women continues to support one of
Durkheim's original findings: 'Whereas without the effect of
family life married persons should kill themselves half again as
often as the unmarried by virtue of their age, they do so
perceptibly less' (1952, p. 173).

In contrast to the number of anthropological studies of
death in pre-literate societies, very few studies on any scale
have been made of death in western societies. There are only
two of direct relevance to us here. The first suggests that there
are few social class differences in the experience of death
(Cartwright, Hockey and Anderson 1973). Their conclusion
was that 'death in many respects appeared to be the equaliser
it is so often reported to be'. In their review of the
circumstances of some 800 deaths, the main differences they
pointed out concerned housing standards. Apart from this, the
dying working class individual, in comparison with the middle

Table 4.22
Social class variations in mourning (percentages)

	Social class (M.R.)			
	AB	C1	C2	DE
Wore full mourning to funeral	18	31	29	40
Wore only tie or armband	39	29	38	26
Wore no mourning	43	40	34	34
Percentage of those who wore mourning who wore it for more than 3 months	14	31	22	42
Paid respects to body of deceased	48	68	67	77

(Devised from tables VII and XXV, Gorer 1965)

class one, needed financial aid more often (26 compared with 14 per cent), died in a private nursing home less often, and was less likely to receive domiciliary visits (i.e. visits at home) by consultants (professional classes, 29 per cent; unskilled, 6 per cent).

The other study (Gorer 1965) was more concerned with the significance of death for those who remained. As table 4.22 shows, the manual classes (C2 and DE) appeared to be more involved than the non-manual with the formal aspects of mourning. It should be noted, however, that this survey was relatively small (N = 359), is now somewhat dated, and refers to a changing area of social custom.

5

Family and home

> The rich man at his castle,
> The poor man at his gate,
> God made them, high or lowly,
> And order'd their estate.
>
> Mrs C. F. Alexander, *All Things Bright*
> *and Beautiful* (Hymn 573, *Hymns*
> *Ancient and Modern* 1950)

The family

The family is almost certainly the oldest, the most basic and the most common of human institutions. Nearly all societies, throughout history and across the world, contain families. In our society the family has a legal status for all and a religious (or symbolic) significance for most. The latter is witnessed by the relative stability and popularity of church or religious weddings, despite the marked decline in church attendance. Of the 42,018 marriages in Scotland in 1973, 27,620 had a religious form and 14,395 were civil (*Annual Report for Scotland 1973* 1974). The legal and formal importance of the family and marriage is brought out by the fact that one's marital status is, along with one's sex, age and occupation, one of the most commonly demanded pieces of personal information required for official purposes by a whole host of agencies. The census regards it as a vital statistic, and classifies a whole series of other factors by it. The 1971 census contains a volume – *Age, Marital Condition and General Tables* (1974) – which deals with marital condition by sex and age, relates this to geographical area and gives it extensive historical coverage from 1851 to 1971. Many other forms of large-scale social research report their findings on a similar basis, particularly in the case of women. Unfortunately for the purposes of this book, not all such research cross-tabulates marital status or family data directly with social class. This is curious, since the evidence is collected but not made available. The census, for example, collects both but only rarely puts them together. At marriage, the occupation of bride and groom and of their parents must be recorded, and at birth that of the father. Similarly, court proceedings, including divorce, usually contain a reference to the defendant's occupation. This information is not, however, presented in the statistical returns. Geographical and historical variations exist: for example, the Registrar General for Scotland produces more tables by social class than the Registrar General for England and Wales, while divorces were recorded by occupation in the Civil Judicial Statistics until 1921.

Marriage

Although there is a popular tendency to think of the family in terms of parents and children, legally a family is constituted by marriage.

Incidence of marriage

The 1971 census of Great Britain contains figures which show that 56 per cent of the entire male and 62 per cent of the entire female population are or have been married; that is, they are either married, widowed or divorced (*Age, Marital Condition and General Tables* 1974). A better view of the incidence of marriage can be gained by excluding children and young people. The relevant figures for the population aged over 19 in 1971 show that 83 per cent of males and 88 per cent of women were married, widowed or divorced. The census does not analyse marital status by social class and it is therefore not possible to make much comment about the incidence of marriage within the classes. Some researchers who have used a representative sample of the population have shown the percentage of married persons by social class (see for example Gorer 1971, table 1A). These reveal very marginal differences, but are usually confused by factors associated with sampling. For example, in the case cited, people aged 45 and over were excluded from a random sample. Perhaps all that can be said is that there is no evidence to suggest that the incidence of marriage within the social classes varies much.

Age at marriage

A number of sample surveys, involving either married women or the general public as a whole, have substantiated the hypothesis that members of the working class, and particularly working class women, marry at an earlier age than do the members of the middle class. (See for example Pierce 1963, Gavron 1966, Gorer 1971.) A more extensive and up to date though somewhat different set of figures can be found in the 1971 census (*Household Composition Tables (10% Sample)* 1975, table 47). This table is an analysis of married couples by the spouses' ages and the social class of the husband, which has been recast as table 5.1. The top line of the table shows that

Table 5.1
(*a*) Married couples under 20 as a percentage of all married persons; (*b*) married males under 20 as a percentage of all men, by social class*

		Social class (R.G.70)						
		I	II	III(N.)	III(M.)	IV	V	All
(*a*) Married couples	under 20	0.3	0.4	0.5	0.8	0.8	1.2	0.7
(*b*) Married men		0.03	0.07	0.2	0.3	0.3	0.6	0.3

*Of husband

(Devised from table 47, Census 1971, Household Composition Tables (10% Sample) *1975, part 3)*

the percentage of married couples, both of whom are under 20 years of age, increases across the social classes from 0.3 in class I to 1.2 in class V. While there is a difference between the manual and the non-manual classes, the largest observable difference is for class V, where the percentage is some four times higher than in class I, half as high again as in class IV, and nearly twice the overall percentage. The second line of the table reveals a very similar pattern among married men. Since male occupation has been used to define social class the data do not allow one to draw conclusions about the married women, who may or may not have similar occupations to those of their husbands (see below, p. 134). Clearly, then, early marriage is related to social class: the manual classes, particularly the unskilled (class V), more often marry early than do the non-manual classes.

Divorce

Divorce is the most obvious and dramatic indication of marriage breakdown, but by no means the only or necessarily the most common one. National figures on divorce by occupation of the husband were published yearly until 1921 and research in the early part of this century suggested that only some 29 per cent of all divorces were working class (as defined by husband's occupation at the date of marriage — McGregor 1957). The most recent available data — *Statistical Review of England and Wales 1967* 1971 — is an analysis of a sample of divorces in 1966 of spinster and bachelor (i.e. first) marriages by social class of husband at time of divorce (N = 4,152). This reveals a markedly different situation.

Table 5.2 allows one to compare the incidence of divorce with that of marriage. If there was no social class variation then the figures in the two rows of the table would be the same. Actually the figures show that for social classes I, II, III and IV the proportion divorcing is lower than the proportion in the married population, whereas in the case of class V it is higher. Divorce is then more common in class V. The pattern

Table 5.2

The distribution across the social classes of (*a*) each 1,000
divorces (1966), (*b*) each 1,000 married men (1961)

Social class (R.G.60)*

	I	II	III	IV	V	Other	All
(*a*) Divorces†	23	72	455	171	98	181	1,000
(*b*) Married males	36	162	485	194	75	47	1,000

*Of husband at time of divorce
†Of first marriages only
(Derived from table C.14, Statistical Review of England and Wales
1967 *1971, part 3)*

of actual rates (that is the top line in relation to the bottom) is
uneven across the classes. Caution is necessary in generalising
from these figures, however, since it is not possible to make
allowance for any variation in the marriage rates for the social
classes, and in any case the social class used here is the
husband's at the time of divorce, not at the time of marriage.
A more detailed view can be gained from a sample study
(N = 598) of divorces in 1961 (Gibson 1974). By comparing
the number of divorces within each social class with the still
married population in that social class a divorce rate was
calculated. In table 5.3 social class I has the lowest rate (22)
followed by classes II and IV (25). The high rate for social
class V (51) echoes the findings in table 5.2, being twice that
for classes I, II and IV. Table 5.3 also reveals that within social

Table 5.3

Divorces per 10,000 married women aged under 55 in each
social class*

Social class (R.G.60/A)

	I	II	III(N.M.)	III(M.)	IV	V	All
Divorce rate	22	25	43†	29†	25	51	30

*Of husband
†32 for class III as a whole
(Derived from table III, Gibson 1974)

class III (overall rate 32) there is a marked difference between the non-manual (43) and manual (29) rates.

Class endogamy

Considering the evidence given elsewhere in this book concerning the relative segregation of people in different social classes in, for example, housing, employment, education, interests, leisure activites and so on, it is perhaps quite reasonable to suppose that there would be some relationship between the social class origins of marriage partners. An intriguing though now dated study on this topic was reported by Berent for the Population Investigation Committee (Glass 1954). Tables 5.4A and 5.4B show the percentage of husbands and wives by social class origin who married people from the same social class (figures in italics) or different social classes. Of the 5,100 marriages surveyed some 44.9 per cent had husbands and wives from the same social class background.

Each of these tables should be read horizontally, from left to right. Thus, for example, in table 5.4A the top row displays the social class origins of the wives of husbands in social class I. Of these wives 37 per cent were themselves of class I origins, 36 per cent were from class II, 21 per cent from III, and 6 per cent from IV. Table 5.4B, which should be read in the same way, shows the social class origins of the husbands

Table 5.4A
Relationship between husbands' social class
origin and that of their wives (percentages)

Social class (H.J./A)

		Wives		
Husbands	I	II	III	IV
I	*37*	36	21	6
II	6	*34*	41	18
III	3	20	*54*	24
IV	<1	15	43	*42*

(Derived from table I, p. 325, Glass 1954)

Table 5.4B

Relationship between wives' social class
origin and that of their husbands (percentages)

Social class (H.J./A)

Husbands

Wives	I	II	III	IV
I	47	28	21	4
II	11	36	38	15
III	3	23	53	22
IV	2	18	42	38

(Derived from table I, p. 325, Glass 1954)

of wives who came from each social class. Hence the top row
shows that of wives of social class I origin 47 per cent had
husbands from the same class.

This relationship is much closer than would be expected by
chance — that is, if choice of marriage partner was completely
unrelated to social class. In other words one is more likely to
marry someone from the same or an adjacent social class than
from a distant one. It should be noted that social class III here
includes both routine non-manual and skilled manual workers,
which may well blur differences. Berent, by combining this
analysis with another — of the spouse's education — finds that
83 per cent of marriages showed correspondence between
spouses either in social origin or in educational level, 71 per
cent at least in educational level, and 45 per cent at least in
social origin, only 7 per cent showing no correspondence. The
higher accord on education than on social origin is of interest
given the relationship between the two (see chapter 6).

A similar relationship was demonstrated by the Registrar
General's study of couples divorcing in 1966 (*Statistical
Review of England and Wales 1967* 1971). Of the 3,596
divorcing couples whose parents were classified, in this case
using five social classes (R.G.), an average of 30 per cent came
from the same social class background. This overall percentage
is lower than that in Berent's study, but given that the social
class classifications in the two studies, and the couples

involved in them, were different, it is perhaps surprisingly close. Indeed the Registrar General's figure for husbands and wives both coming from social class III origins is 55 per cent, which is almost identical to the 54 per cent in table 5.4A above. We can conclude with the Registrar General that 'It is of interest to note that despite trends to increased social mobility and more open social structure, there is a marked persistence of homogamy by couples in the sample.'

Children

Number

There are no figures that are both contemporary and national to illustrate social class differences in the typical number of children per family. The most up to date national figures (table 5.5) of the distribution by social class of children shows that the majority of households in all social classes have no dependent children. Of course most of these households will either have had children who are not now dependent, or will have them in the future. A more useful set of data for the

Table 5.5

Percentage* of households by number of dependent children in each social class†

Number of children	Social class (R.G.70)						
	I	II	III(N.)	III(M.)	IV	V	All
0	48	58	66	52	63	67	62
1	17	16	15	19	15	13	15
2	22	17	13	18	13	10	14
3	8	7	5	8	6	6	6
4	3	2	1	3	2	3	2
5 or more	0.8	0.7	0.5	2	2	2	1

*Percentages over 1 rounded
†By chief economic supporter: households whose supporter is retired are included, classified by previous occupation of retired person; households supported by students and other economically inactive people are omitted
(*Derived from table 17,* Social Trends No 5 1974: *source — Census 1971, 1% tables*)

Table 5.6

A comparison of the number of children* in 'professional' and
'unskilled manual' households (percentages)

Social class						Children					11 and
(R.G.60)	1	2	3	4	5	6	7	8	9	10	more
I Professional	8	43	29	15	4	0.8	†	†	0	0	†
V Unskilled	6	19	24	19	14	7	4	2	1	0.8	

*Under the age of 21
†Less than 0.5 per cent
(Derived from table A10, Davie, Butler and Goldstein 1972)

purpose at hand is a survey of all children born in a week of
1958 (Davie, Butler and Goldstein 1972), which shows the
number of children under the age of 21 in the families of the
15,000+ children (when aged 7) in the sample (table 5.6).
From this source it is possible to show the dramatic difference
between the average size of the 'professional' as compared to
the 'unskilled' family, a feature which can also be discerned
from table 5.5. In comparing these sorts of figures, however,
an assumption is being made, either that the families are
complete, or that a similar number in each social class is
complete (or incomplete). The last national figures available
on completed family size, for marriages which took place in
1925–9, showed that the average number of children born
into non-manual workers' families was 1.73, and into manual
workers' families 2.49 (*Royal Commission on Population*
1949). A more recent perspective can be gained from a study
of family intentions (Woolf 1971) which contains information
on the number of live births to women married not more than
once, who were married before 1950 and who were not over
the age of 44 at the time of the survey (1967) (N = 1,155).
These women were, by then, most likely to have completed
their families.

In table 5.7 a clear relationship is shown: the higher the
social class the smaller the family. It is particularly dramatic at
the extremes: while the managerial class has 8 per cent of
childless wives, and 11 per cent with four or more children,

Table 5.7

Percentage of women by number of live births and husband's social class

Number of live births	Social class (R.G.(S.E.)66/B)			
	Managerial	Non-manual	Skilled manual	Other manual
0	8	11	8	3
1	20	19	18	16
2	45	34	31	31
3	16	18	20	18
4 or more	11	18	23	32

(Devised from table 3.13, Woolf 1971)

the figures for the semi- and unskilled ('other') manual classes are 3 and 32 per cent respectively. This study also provides some evidence that the traditional relationship between family size and social class may be changing. If the trends illustrated in table 5.8 were to be realised and continued, the highest mean family size would be associated with managerial occupations, since their expectations of family size have remained comparatively stable while those of the manual group have declined. The table reveals that for both manual groups the decline in expected family size occurs between those married in 1955—9 and those married in 1960—4, the 'skilled manual'

Table 5.8

Mean most likely number of children expected, by date of marriage and husband's social class

Date of marriage	Social class (R.G.(S.E.)66/B)				
	Managerial	Non-manual	Skilled manual	Other manual	All
All dates	2.5	2.4	2.6	2.8	2.6
1945—9	2.3	2.3	2.5	3.1	2.5
1950—4	2.5	2.4	2.8	2.8	2.7
1955—9	2.5	2.5	2.7	2.8	2.7
1960—4	2.6	2.4	2.5	2.6	2.5
1965 and later	2.6	2.4	2.4	2.5	2.5

(From table 2.15, Woolf 1971)

change occurring from 1950—4 onwards, and the 'other manual' after 1959.

Age of mother and of marriage at first birth

In table 5.1 it was shown that marriage took place in the lower social classes at an earlier age than in the higher. A similar and expected relationship exists with regard to the age at which wives become mothers. The Newsons (1963) in a study of 700 families in Nottingham produced clear evidence (table 5.9) that mothers are younger in the manual classes. This can be seen not only in terms of earlier marriage, but also in relation to the fact that the interval between marriage and the first birth (and to some extent between subsequent births) is shorter for manual mothers than for non-manual (table 5.10 and Woolf 1971).

Table 5.9

Percentage of mothers under age of 21 at birth of first child by social class

	Social class (R.G.60/AB)				
	I and II	III(N.M.)	III(M.)	IV	V
Mothers under 21	24	25	40	46	53

(Derived from table XII, Newson and Newson 1963)

Table 5.10

Length of interval between marriage and first live birth by social class

	Social class (R.G.(S.E.66/B)			
	Managerial	Non-manual	Skilled manual	Other manual
Mean years: married 1950—9	2.7	2.9	2.5	2.1
Mean years: married 1960 or later	1.7	1.7	1.6	1.4

(Derived from table 3.13, Woolf 1971)

Family planning

One factor which is commonly assumed to be related to family size and spacing is the use of contraception. This is not a straightforward factor, since some families were limited before contraception was available, and some methods of contraception in common use today are far from being a reliable means of avoiding pregnancy. At a simple level it can be said that the use of contraceptives lessens the likelihood of unwanted pregnancies and is more likely to result in families of a planned size (assuming of course that 'planned' means 'limited'). Table 5.11 shows that the manual classes are the least likely to use contraceptive methods, and that when they do they are more likely to use the less reliable methods. It is the families of these social classes that have the largest families.

Over all nearly all (92 per cent) of the non-manual classes were using mechanical or chemical contraceptives compared

Table 5.11

Percentage of women at risk* currently using various methods of contraception, by social class

Chemical and mechanical methods	*Social class (R.G.66/D)*			
	I, II and III(N.M.)	III(M.)	IV and V	All
Pill	28	24	21	25
Condom	38	35	36	36
Diaphragm	10	3	4	6
Coil (I.U.D.)	6	5	4	5
Spermicides	10	4	2	5
Total	92	71	67	77
Other methods				
Coitus interruptus	12	23	22	19
Safe period	8	6	3	6
Abstinence	3	3	7	4
Total	23	32	32	29
No methods	2	7	10	7

*Married women neither sterile, pregnant, nor planning to be pregnant
Note   Percentages do not add up to 100 because some informants used more than one method
(Derived from table 3.5, Bone 1973)

with 67 per cent of the semi- and unskilled manual, of whom 10 per cent used no methods. It should be remembered that none of the women in this sample were planning to get pregnant. Taking this last point into account, and noticing that the number of expected children for the non-manual and manual classes are very similar (if not lower for the latter) (table 5.8), one can conjecture that the dissimilarity in the two classes' use of effective contraception methods is a factor in the dissimilarity of their respective completed family sizes (tables 5.6 and 5.7).

A similar pattern emerges in the use of contraception by unmarried women who do not reject pre-marital intercourse (Bone 1973). The percentage using contraceptive methods of all types was 48 in classes I, II and III(N.M.), 40 in class III(M.), and 33 in classes IV and V.

A further aspect of family planning which has grown in importance since the Act of 1967 is abortion. Since there are no available figures for pregnancy by social class it is not possible to show what proportion of pregnancies in each social class are terminated. However, of the 108,505 legal and notified abortions in 1972, 74,779 were classified by social class and reveal the variations shown in table 5.12.

If it is assumed that Bone's (1973) figures on the social class of women likely to be 'at risk' (see table 5.11 for definition) are crudely applicable, it appears that abortion is

Table 5.12
Legal abortions by social class of mothers (percentages)

	I	I and II	II	III	IV	IV and V	V
			Social class (R.G.66)				
All abortions	3	—	21	54	17	—	5
Approximate female population	—	26	—	52	—	19	—

*Based on a sample of married women aged 16 to 40, by husband's social class, and single women aged 16 to 35, by father's social class (*Devised from table 9,* Statistical Review of England and Wales 1972 *1974, and tables 1.1 and 1.2, Bone 1973*)

probably more equally spread across the social classes than
contraceptive methods are. Caution is necessary, however,
since the woman's social class was known for only 69 per cent
of the abortions.

Adoption and fostering

At the opposite end of the spectrum there are families who are
unable to produce children of their own, and some of these
seek to adopt children. (Of course, it is also true that some
parents with children of their own adopt other children.)
Interesting social class differences can be seen in the figures in
table 5.13. Social classes I and II provide a third of prospective
adopters from 20 per cent of the adult population, but less
than 10 per cent of the children for adoption. In contrast the
semi-skilled and unskilled classes provide only 14 per cent of
prospective adopters, but represent nearly 30 per cent of the
population. Although caution is necessary in the interpretation
of the figures relating to natural mothers (because of the high
percentage not recorded by social class), it is noticeable that
in relation to the proportion of the country's population they
comprise, and particularly to the number of prospective
adoptive parents they provide, classes I and II are under-

Table 5.13
Social class of natural mothers and prospective adopters
(percentages)

	Social class (R.G.60/AB)					N/A and
	I and II	III(N.M.)	III(M.)	IV	V	other
Natural mothers						
offering child	9	32	7	19	2	30*
Prospective non-family						
adopters	33	17	32	12	2	5
Population of Great						
Britain	20	48		20	9	3

*Includes 17 per cent with no information, 9 per cent housewives, 4 per
cent students
(Derived from tables 3(18) and 2(15), Grey 1971)

Table 5.14

Foster parents, natural parents of foster children, and parents
of primary school children by social class (percentages)

	Social class (R.G.66)				
	I	II	III	IV	V
Foster parents*	3	15	44	24	14
Natural parents*†	2	7	30	20	40
Primary school parents	4	14	59	16	6

*Average of private and local authority foster parents
†Where known, excluding students
(Devised from tables 2.2 and 8.1, Holman 1975, and pp. 99–100,
Children and their Primary Schools *1967)*

represented. Further, whereas nearly a third (32 percent) of
natural mothers offering their child are from social class
III(N.M.), and only 7 per cent from III(M.), the percentages
are markedly different for prospective adoptive parents (17 in
III(N.M.); 32 in III(M.)).

A further way in which children become part of a family
(albeit sometimes only temporarily) is by fostering, which
shows a different pattern from that of adoption (table 5.14).
Both the natural and the foster parents are clearly more
numerous in the lower two classes, in relation to the general
population of parents. These figures, together with those on
adoption, suggest that whereas adoption apparently attracts
the professional, fostering is more attractive to the semi- and
unskilled social classes.

Bringing up children

Social class differences in the care of babies and young
children have received quite detailed attention in social
research in Britain since the Second World War. Two large
national cohorts of children – all those born in Great Britain
in one week in 1946, and all those born in one week of
1958 – have been and are being followed through life, the first
under the auspices of the Population Investigation Committee

and the second mainly under the sponsorship of the National Children's Bureau, both of which have produced a number of publications used in this text. A smaller-scale but more detailed study has been conducted by a husband and wife team on two overlapping samples of 700 mothers in Nottingham (Newson and Newson 1963, 1968).

It is worth bearing in mind that much of the evidence contained in these studies is based on mothers' answers to questions in interviews. Some doubts have been raised about the accuracy of such reports (see for example Yarrow, Campbell and Burton 1964; Davie, Butler and Goldstein 1972). Respondents from different social classes may differ in their awareness of what is a socially acceptable answer, may vary in their familiarity with current professional opinion and literature about child-rearing and in their anxiety about giving what they consider to be socially acceptable answers. A further point is that, given the purpose of this book, and the nature and extent of the material to hand, the data that have been selected tend to emphasise social class differences. It should be remembered that in many areas of child care social class differences are very small or non-existent.

Infant feeding

In the 1930s the majority of babies were breast-fed. Interest in feeding methods arose when it was discovered, in 1946, following the introduction and popularisation of modified cows' milk, that only 45 per cent of babies were breast-fed at the age of two months (Douglas 1948). The social class variations recorded then were also found by Davie, Butler and Goldstein (1972) for children born in 1958 (see table 5.15). While over two-thirds of the babies were breast-fed initially, only 43 per cent were breast-fed at the end of the first month. Generally speaking, the higher the social class of the mother the greater the likelihood of initial breast-feeding (social class I, 78 per cent; social class V, 64 per cent). Even more marked is the variation in the length of time that breast-feeding was continued. Table 5.15 shows a more marked drop in the

Table 5.15

Percentage of mothers breast-feeding their child at age 0—1 by social class

Social class (R.G.60/A)

	I	II	III (N.M.)	III(M.)	IV	V	All
Not breast-fed	21	26	24	33	35	36	31
Breast-fed under 1 month	78	73	75	67	65	64	68
Breast-fed over 1 month	59	50	51	41	39	36	43

(Derived from table A 110, Davie, Butler and Goldstein 1972)

percentage of social class V mothers who breast-fed (44 per cent of all those who initially breast-fed stopped within a month) than in that of breast-feeding mothers in social class I (25 per cent). This tendency can be followed through to three and six months, by reference to the Newsons' work (table 5.16). At six months the percentage of social class I and II mothers still breast-feeding is almost three times as great (20 per cent) as that in social class V (7 per cent). The same study also shows, however, that the length of time a feeding bottle continues to be used varies in the opposite direction along social class lines — that is, the higher the social class the less likely the baby is to receive bottle feeding at the age of one year. Clearly, then, the higher the social class, the more frequently early weaning from milk or liquids occurs.

Table 5.16

Percentage of mothers breast-feeding their child at age 3 and 6 months and giving bottle at one year by social class

Social class (R.G.60/AB)

	I and II	III(N.M.)	III(M.)	IV	V
At 3 months	39	34	24	22	12
At 6 months	20	12	11	11	7
Bottle, one year	50	53	71	79	85

(Derived from tables XVI and XVII, Newson and Newson 1963)

The use of medical and other services

Local authorities provide under statute a number of clinics and services for babies and children. The use of these is general and widespread: for example, some 77 per cent of all mothers reported having been to an infant welfare clinic, and some 93 per cent of all children were immunised against diphtheria (see table 5.17). There are small but real social class differences in the use of clinics, particularly in terms of regularity. In table 5.17, for example, it is noticeable that while there is little variation from the average for all social classes in 'some attendance' (77 per cent), it is social classes III(N.M.) and III(M.) who are most likely to report having been regular attenders. In relation to infant welfare clinics, 66 and 60 per cent respectively reported regular attendance compared with 54 per cent of each of the other social classes, except for social class V for which the figure was 48 per cent. For both types of clinic social class V had the smallest percentage of mothers who were regular attenders, though these mothers

Table 5.17

Percentage of mothers reporting use of (*a*) infant welfare clinics, (*b*) toddlers' clinics, (*c*) immunisation and dental services, by attendance and social class

			Social class (R.G.60/A)				
Attendance	I	II	III(N.M.)	III(M.)	IV	V	All
(*a*) No	26	25	17	21	25	25	23
Yes, regularly	54	54	66	60	54	48	57
Yes, occasionally	19	20	17	18	20	26	20
(*b*) No	46	44	36	43	46	52	44
Yes, regularly	17	19	23	20	18	14	19
Yes, occasionally	35	35	40	36	35	31	35
(*c*) Immunised against smallpox	93	85	83	73	68	64	75
Immunised against diphtheria	99	97	96	94	91	87	93
Attended dentist	83	80	81	76	72	68	76

(*Derived from tables A71, A74, A76, A80 and A82, Davie, Butler and Goldstein 1972*)

used infant welfare clinics marginally more 'occasionally' than social classes I, II and III.

A much more straightforward picture emerges in relation to immunisation and dental care. In each case there is a linear decline in percentage from social class I to V. The figures for the middle classes (I, II, III(N.M.)) are above the average for all social classes, and those for working classes below.

Talking and social adjustment

There is little systematic evidence on any scale about social class differences in the way in which children are taught, or learn, to talk. The medical examination of children in the National Child Development Study included a speech test and an intelligibility of speech report, which gives an indication of how successfully children learnt to talk. The speech test required children to repeat a series of short sentences designed to cover English letter sounds and most of the combinations of sounds used in normal speech. The stricture on the nature and conduct of the test mentioned in the footnote to table 5.18 should be noted. As can be seen in table 5.18, almost two-thirds of the children from social class I (65 per cent) made no mistake in the speech test, compared with rather more than one third in social class V (36 per cent) – figures

Table 5.18
Speech test scores and intelligibility of speech rating of children by social class (percentages)

	Social class (R.G.60/A)						
Speech test errors	I	II	III(N.M.)	III(M.)	IV	V	All
0	65	58	56	46	44	36	49
1–9	34	40	42	51	52	58	48
More than 10	1	2	2	3	4	6	3
*% fully intelligible**	94	92	90	85	82	78	86

*The authors argue that these differences may, in part, be due to the preference on the part of the doctors involved for 'middle class speech' (p.93)
(Derived from tables A147 and A149, Davie, Butler and Goldstein 1972)

which vary quite markedly from the average for all social classes (49 per cent). There is an increase in the percentage of children making errors from social class I to social class V, particularly noticeable in the group making 10 or more errors. Here the percentage for social class I is only a sixth of that for social class V.

One assumed objective of the socialisation of the child in the |family| is to prepare him for life in other groups. In our society the first other group universally entered into is the school class. The source which provided the data on speech above also gives Bristol Social Adjustment Guide (B.S.A.G.) scores (Stott 1963) for the children in the study. In this test teachers choose from a series of behaviour descriptions those which best fit the child in question. A score is given such that the higher the score the more deviant the behaviour, producing three groups: 'stable', 'unsettled' and 'maladjusted'. It should be noted that these are not clinical terms, but merely an indication of behaviour, and that while many of the behaviour deviations noted in the B.S.A.G. are abnormal by any standard, a proportion of them reflect school and teacher norms which are likely to be 'middle class'. As table 5.19 shows, there is an increasing percentage of 'unsettled' and 'maladjusted' children from social class I through to social class V. What is very noticeable, however, is that while there is little real difference in the percentages for the 'middle classes' (I, II, III(N.M.)), a marked difference occurs in each case

Table 5.19

Percentage of stable, unsettled, and maladjusted children according to B.S.A.G. by social class

			Social class (R.G.60/A)				
	I	II	III(N.M.)	III(M.)	IV	V	All
Stable (0—9)	77	73	73	63	59	51	64
Unsettled (10—19)	17	19	19	23	24	27	22
Maladjusted (20+)	6	9	8	14	16	22	14

(Derived from table A232, Davie, Butler and Goldstein 1972)

between III(N.M.) and III(M.), the latter being similar to social class IV. However, there is again a markedly higher percentage in social class V.

Sex and modesty

Children early become aware of their own bodies, and conscious of their bodily functions; later they are curious about other bodies in the family. The parents, and more especially the mother, have the power to some extent to control, ignore, or encourage such interest. Some of the evidence from the Newsons' studies (1963, 1968) shows that mothers from different social classes behave differently in this respect. Most children display an early and often continuing interest in their own genitals. Table 5.20 shows that middle class mothers are markedly more tolerant of this than are working class mothers, especially at an early age. While 75 per cent of social class I and II compared with only 7 per cent of social class V did not discourage genital play at age one, by age four it was discouraged or punished by a clear majority of all mothers of all social classes. There is a difference, however, in the manner in which it was discouraged, with the working class, particularly social class V, much more likely to punish or to threaten the child (social class I, 5 per cent; social class V,

Table 5.20
Mothers' attitudes towards children's genital play at one and four years of age, by social class (percentages)

	I and II	III(N.M.)	III(M.)	IV	V	All
			Social class (R.G.60/AB)			
Discouraged at age 1*	25	50	57	69	93	—
Ignored/permitted at age 4	17	11	10	5	10	10
Discouraged at age 4	78	71	54	54	42	59
Punished or punishment threatened at age 4	5	18	36	41	48	31

*Actual cases only (i.e. excluding cases which are not applicable because child has not been observed in genital play)
(*Derived from table 36, Newson and Newson 1968*)

48 per cent). To some extent this difference reflects a social-class-linked preference for punishment (see table 5.23 below).

The Newsons suggest (1968, p. 391) that if a child is allowed to see his parents unclothed, this 'may be considered a stage further on in permissiveness' from viewing other children naked. Certainly the social class differences here are more marked, as is shown in table 5.21, so much so that the majority attitude of social classes I and II with regard to seeing both parents naked was the minority attitude for the population as a whole. Interestingly enough the second row in

Table 5.21

Mothers' attitude towards child aged four years (*a*) seeing parents unclothed, (*b*) being given the facts of life, by social class (percentages)

	Social class (R.G.60/AB)					
	I and II	III(N.M.)	III(M.)	IV	V	All
(*a*) *Seeing parents unclothed*						
May see both parents	59	45	27	24	15	32
May see same sex parent only	22	23	22	22	17	22
May see neither parent	19	32	51	54	68	46
(*b*) *Knowledge of facts of life*						
Child knows at four	44	26	15	14	15	20
Mother would tell if asked	44	47	30	39	10	34
Mother would not tell yet	12	27	55	47	75	46
Of those who would not tell yet						
Avoid without falsehood	4	8	14	7	9	11
Give falsehood	8	19	41	40	66	35

(*Derived from tables 39, 40 and 41, Newson and Newson 1968*)

the table displays a very similar set of figures — around 22 per cent for all social classes. The top row shows the clear 'permissiveness' of the middle classes, while the 'modesty' of the working classes is displayed in the third row. A further and similar aspect of this area concerns the basic knowledge of reproduction which at age four amounts to 'a baby comes from mummy's tummy'. As table 5.21 shows, there exist social class differences both in the extent of children's present knowledge, in the likelihood of their being given the facts, and in the likelihood of being given a false explanation. In each case the higher the social class the more likely the child is to be favoured with accurate knowledge.

As the Newsons write, in lighthearted vein, 'it has been suggested to us that attitudes towards sexual modesty might be a better index of social class affiliation than the more conventional occupation of father' (p. 408).

Discipline and obedience

According to mothers' reports, children from different social classes vary in their degree of obedience and disobedience at the age of seven (Davie, Butler and Goldstein 1972: see table 5.22). Perhaps surprisingly, over all some 40 per cent of children were seen as never being disobedient, with a range from 45 per cent in social class I to 36 per cent in social class V. The class V children were more likely to be seen as

Table 5.22

Frequency of disobedience of child* by social class
(percentages)

Social class (R.G.60/A)

	I	II	III(N.M.)	III(M.)	IV	V	All
Frequently	2	3	3	4	4	5	4
Sometimes	52	54	55	55	57	58	55
Never	45	43	42	41	38	36	41

*As reported by their mothers
(Derived from table A227, Davie, Butler and Goldstein 1972)

frequently disobedient (5 per cent as compared with 2 per cent in social class I). Given that these figures are based on mothers' reports, and that the study lacked a definition of 'disobedience' (whose meaning can vary widely), too much weight should perhaps not be put on them. The same report does, however, contain references to specific kinds of behaviour — 'fighting' and 'destroying belongings' — which show similar social class distributions (tables A 225 and A 217, Davie, Butler and Goldstein 1972).

The Newsons' study (1968) reviewed mothers' attitudes towards methods of discipline and punishment, and these are summarised in table 5.23. A first observation from the top

Table 5.23

Mothers' attitudes towards, and use of, punishments for child aged 4 years, by social class (percentages)

		Social class (R.G.60/AB)				
	I and II	III(N.M.)	III(M.)	IV	V	All
Smacking						
Disapproves of smacking	20	14	16	16	22	17
Smacks less than once a week*	33	23	20	24	11	22
Smacks once a week to once a day*	61	68	70	66	79	68
Reasons for smacking						
To enforce obedience	56	63	70	63	79	67
For lies	27	37	38	44	42	38
For smacking mummy	43	50	63	60	64	58
Other punishments						
Threat of authority figure	10	23	29	29	46	27
Threat to send away or leave	10	34	29	27	30	27

*Mothers reporting smacking never, or once a day, are small in number (3 and 7 per cent) and show no social class variation
(Derived from tables 44, 45, 46, 48 and 49, Newson and Newson 1968)

section of the table is that smacking is a very common practice among mothers of four-year-olds, and that a sizeable proportion of those who disapprove of it actually indulge (compare the first line in the table with the second and third added together). The main social class difference in this part of the table is that mothers in social classes I and II are over-represented in the 'smack less than once a week' category — 33 per cent as compared with the average for all classes of 22 per cent — and in social class V under-represented at 11 per cent. The latter are over-represented in the more frequent smacking category — 79 per cent compared with the average for all social classes of 68 per cent. The second part of the table refers to specific reasons for smacking. In each case here, according to the Newsons, social classes I and II are more likely to use methods other than smacking, usually verbal methods. Over all then, with respect to both general and specific use of smacking, social classes I and II are less likely, and social class V is more likely, to smack than would be expected from the average for all social classes. Finally, in the third section of table 5.23 there is a clear social class difference in the use of threats. In the case of threats involving authority figures there is a steady increase in their use across the classes from 10 per cent in classes I and II to 46 per cent in class V. There is an interesting variation in the otherwise similar pattern for threats to send away or to leave the child: their most common use occurs in social class III(N.M.), and they are less often used in social class V.

Fathers' role

A major difference between the social classes in child rearing appears in the degree of involvement of the father. As might be expected, this also varies with the age of the child. The Newsons' studies (1963, 1968) show that while the father's participation does increase with the age of the child, the social class differences remain. Generally speaking, the figures in table 5.24 show a larger percentage of high participating fathers as one moves up the social classes, together with an increase in such fathers between the child's first and fourth birthday. This increase is most marked in social class V (from 36 to 49 per cent), and is reversed in the case of social class IV, where the percentage drops from 55 to 44. In the case of fathers with 'little' or 'no' participation it is interesting to note that when the child is one year old the percentage in social classes I and II (19 per cent) is much larger than in the other middle class group (III N.M.), and similar to that in social class IV. The Newsons went on in their second study (1968) to ask the mothers how their husbands compared with themselves in strictness with the child (see table 5.24). The Newsons argue that mothers in the higher social classes are less likely to think their husbands are stricter than they are, and that this is

Table 5.24

Extent of father's participation in child care,* and the comparative strictness of parents, by social class (percentages)

Father's participation	Social class (R.G.60/AB)				
	I and II	III(N.M.)	III(M.)	IV	V
At age one year					
High	57	61	51	55	36
Little or none	19	6	16	18	36
At age four years†					
High	64	59	48	44	49
Little or none	4	5	10	14	10
Parental strictness					
Husband stricter	22	31	46	35	52
Wife stricter	23	22	22	27	28
Agree on strictness	55	47	32	38	20

	Father's participation	
	High	Moderate or low
Husband stricter	32	47
Wife stricter	25	22
Agree on strictness	43	31

*As reported by mother in interview
†Includes 275 of the sample at one year
(Derived from table XXXI, Newson and Newson 1963, and tables 53 and 54, Newson and Newson 1968)

because they agree on strictness (in social classes I and II disagreement was 45 per cent; in social class V, 80 per cent). The bottom section of the table shows that the level of participation by the father is related to the wife's agreement on strictness. Where the father is high on participation, 43 per cent of all mothers said that they agreed with their husbands on strictness, compared with 31 per cent where fathers participated at a moderate or low level.

The home

So far the family has been treated as if it had a clear definition — that, for example, it begins with marriage, develops with children, and so on. It is fairly obvious on reflection, however, that for a number of reasons it is not true that nearly all people in Britain live in families — by any standard definition of that word. Some people live alone, or with others who do not constitute a family; some live in institutions, temporarily or permanently; while many families are broken through death and divorce. For these sorts of reasons, and because of the demands of large-scale social research, most work in this field is done in relation to households rather than families. The Office of Population Censuses and Surveys uses the following definition of 'household': 'a group of people, who all live regularly at the address ... and who are all catered for by the same person for at least one meal a day' (Atkinson 1971). The *General Household Survey Introductory Report* (1973) was concerned with 'private households', therefore excluding institutional dwellings such as hotels, hospitals, boarding schools, barracks, prisons etc. It found that the average households in Britain contained 3.67 persons, and that the most common number of people in a household was two (31 per cent of all households). It is not possible to say how many of these households are actually families, though it can be noted that 58 per cent of the private households included young people under the age of 15. The following section, then, is mainly concerned with the relationship between social class and private households, which of course include but are not exclusively families.

Dwellings: type and tenure

The *General Household Survey Introductory Report* (1973) found that in 1971 79 per cent of households lived in houses, 19 per cent in flats, maisonettes or rooms, and 2 per cent in business and 'other' premises (e.g. caravans and houseboats). Almost half (49 per cent) of the dwellings were owned by their occupants, the rest being rented, mainly from local authorities (councils) (31 per cent of all household dwellings).

In chapter 3 a strong relationship was displayed between

Table 5.25

Type of house by social class of head of household (percentages)

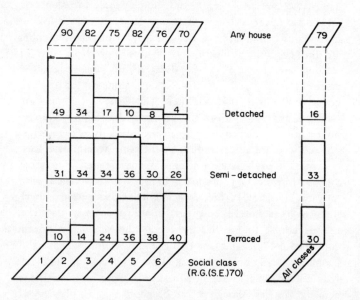

	1	2	3	4	5	6		All classes
Any house	90	82	75	82	76	70		79
Detached	49	34	17	10	8	4		16
Semi-detached	31	34	34	36	30	26		33
Terraced	10	14	24	36	38	40		30

Social class (R.G.(S.E.)70)

(*Devised from table 5.38,* General Household Survey Introductory Report *1973*)

social class and income, via occupation. It is to be anticipated, then, that social class will be related to the sort of dwellings that households live in, and whether these are rented or (being) bought. Tables 5.25 and 5.26 show that in fact all social classes live in all types of houses, and use all types of tenure. Perhaps surprisingly, about one in five of the unskilled households are owner occupiers, some 4 per cent of them living in detached houses, while 3 per cent of professional households rent their homes from a local authority. These facts do not, however, reflect the general picture, which is clearly displayed in the tables. The higher the social class the more likely the household is to live in a house, as opposed

Table 5.26
Home tenure by social class of head of household
(percentages)

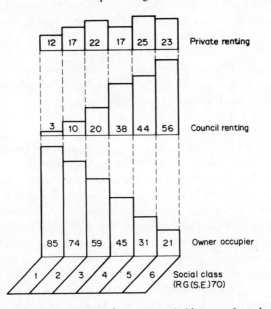

(*Devised from table 5.18(b)*, General Household Survey Introductory Report *1973*)

to a flat, and the more likely the house is to be detached rather than terraced, and the household to own or be purchasing it. It is worth noting that the semi-detached house appears to be occupied to a similar extent by all the social classes, the figures varying little from the average of 33 per cent, and that a similar proportion of each social class rents its home from a private landlord. It can be expected, however, that there will exist big variations in the types of semi-detached house, and in the rents paid, and consequently in the accommodation provided. That this is so, and that the variations are class-based, is supported by the figures which follow concerning the accommodation and amenities provided for the households in their homes.

It should be remembered that the six social classes shown here are far from equal in size (see p. 64) and that no conclusions concerning the numbers of each type of dwelling in Britain can be drawn. The *General Household Survey* makes no social class breakdown of dwellings other than houses, flats and rooms. A Consumer Council study (1967) showed that caravan households were predominantly composed of members of the skilled and other manual classes — the non-manual, especially the professional, being under-represented in relation to the general population.

Accommodation

A basic measure of accommodation is provided by relating the number of rooms available to the number of people living in them. The census of 1961 suggested that more than 1.5 persons per room represented overcrowding, and that in Great Britain 3.8 per cent of households were so overcrowded. Of course this figure related to all types of household, and a better picture of family accommodation can be gained from surveys of families with children. The National Child Development Study (Davie, Butler and Goldstein 1972), which surveyed the homes of over 15,000 children illustrates a strong relationship between social class and overcrowding. As can be seen in table 5.27, virtually no families with professionally

Table 5.27
Percentage of families by people per room and social class

	Social class (R.G.60/A)						
	I	II	III(N.M.)	III(M.)	IV	V	All
Number of							
persons per room							
Less than 1	86	79	72	52	46	28	58
Between 1 and 1½	13	17	22	31	34	35	28
More than 1½ (i.e. overcrowded)	1	4	7	16	20	37	15

(Derived from table A48, Davie, Butler and Goldstein 1972)

employed heads lived in overcrowded accommodation, while over a third (37 per cent) of families with unskilled heads lived in such accommodation. A more sophisticated measure of accommodation is the bedroom standard (Gray and Russell 1962), which relates the number and type of people in a household to the available bedrooms, according to the following rules:

A bedroom is allocated to

(a) Each married couple
(b) Each other person over age of 21
(c) Each pair of same sex persons aged 10–20
(d) Each other person aged 10–20 with children under 10 of same sex (otherwise given bedroom on own)
(e) Each pair of children under 10 (remainder given own bedroom)

This measure was used in the *General Household Survey*, which produced the figures in table 5.28. Here, although the social class relationship is clear (i.e. the lower the class the less likely the household is to meet or surpass the bedroom standard), the differences are not so well marked. As has been suggested, this is partly because table 5.28 refers to all types of households. It is worth noting that, over all, almost 60 per cent of all households had bedroom accommodation above the

Table 5.28

Percentage of households by bedroom standard and social class

	Social class (R.G.(S.E.)70)						
	1	2	3	4	5	6	All
Above bedroom standard	76	71	62	56	53	53	59
Equals standard	23	26	33	36	38	36	34
Below standard	1	3	5	8	9	11	7

(Derived from table 5.31, General Household Survey Introductory Report *1973)*

standard, and accordingly could be said to under-occupy their accommodation. Large family households, with three or more children, fared poorest, 25 per cent being one bedroom short and a further 6 per cent at least two short, while of small adult households 44 per cent had two or more bedrooms to spare.

Amenities

Although there is a whole range of amenities which can be regarded as necessary for households in Britain , including, for example, electricity, gas, drainage, central heating and so on, the most commonly chosen amenities for social research are baths, W.C.s (toilets) and hot water systems. In table 5.29 'bath/shower' has been defined to include a hot water supply and 'W.C.s' refers to both inside and outside flush toilets. It shows that of households with professional heads 96 per cent had sole use of bath and W.C., and that this percentage declines along social class lines so that of unskilled manual households only 79 per cent were so served. These figures reflect again the type of housing lived in and are related to the amount of income available for the purchase of accommodation.

There is pretty clear evidence to show an improvement in standards of provision of both accommodation and amenities throughout this century, and particularly since 1960. Although this information is not available on a social class basis, the following figures suggest overall improvement in all types of accomodation. In England and Wales in 1960 6 per

Table 5.29

Percentage* of households with provision of amenities by social class

	Social class (R.G.(S.E.)70)						
	1	**2**	**3**	**4**	**5**	**6**	**All**
Sole use of bath/shower and W.C.	96	95	88	88	82	79	88
No bath/shower, sole use W.C.	0.2	2	5	7	12	14	7
No bath/shower, shared W.C.	†	†	†	1	2	2	0.9
No bath/shower, no W.C.	Nil	0.5	0.5	1	2	1	0.9

*Percentages over 1 rounded
†Less than 0.5%
Note Columns do not add up to 100 because of other arrangements
(Derived from table 5.44, General Household Survey Introductory Report *1973)*

cent of owner-occupiers, 14 per cent of council tenants and 15 per cent of other renters were living below the bedroom standard; by 1971 these percentages had improved to 4, 8, and 9 respectively (*General Household Survey 1972* 1975).

Domestic amenities

There is some evidence from market research sources which reveals social class differences in the ownership of domestic amenities or consumer durables. As is to be expected these show that the higher the class the higher the frequency of ownership (table 5.30). Over all this tendency is such as to suggest that ownership is merely the result of being able to afford to purchase or rent the amenity. The similarity in television ownership, and the differences between the social class percentages of ownership for different items, suggest that the factors of perceived needs and values are also involved. The centrality of money is emphasised by table 5.31, which refers to newly married women under the age of 35. Here, as we would expect, the comparable percentages are lower for each social class than those in table 5.30.

Table 5.30

Percentage of households owning consumer durables by social class

| | Social class (M.R./D) | | | |
	AB	C1	C2DE	All
Washing machine	75	68	56	61
Electric refrigerator	73	57	37	46
Steam iron	40	37	31	33
Electric kettle	65	55	42	48
Food mixer	35	17	7	13
Vacuum cleaner	96	91	76	81
Television	91	92	89	90

(Derived from table 2, Young and Willmott 1973; source – Woman and the National Market 1967)

Table 5.31

Percentage of married women aged 16–34 who owned consumer durables by social class

| | Social class (M.R./B) | | |
	A, B, C1	C2, D, E	All
Dining room suite	79	71	73
Refrigerator	63	29	38
Washing machine	72	63	65*
Vacuum cleaner	85	67	71
Sewing machine	51	37	41

*The overall percentage for washing machines is higher than in table 5.30
(Derived from table 7.2a, The New Housewife 1967)

Moving home

Evidence that we live in a mobile society is provided by the *From Birth to Seven* study (Davie, Butler and Goldstein 1972), which showed that some 64 per cent of all the families involved had made at least one move in the previous seven years (table 5.32). These families had a child or children under seven at the time of the study. With regard to actual moving, there is little social class variation, only social class I varying appreciably from the average (63 per cent had between

those provided by local authorities. Empirical research into social class and education — the concern of this chapter — was initially systematised in the inter-war period, mainly through the interest of psychologists, notably Burt (1937, 1943), in relating intelligence and educational performance to social background and class. Since the Second World War the field has blossomed, and between the mid 1950s and 60s became a veritable industry, with a wealth of government and academic social science research into a host of topics, and using a variety of approaches.

Two factors coincided to promote this flourishing interest in social class and education. The first was a continuing concern about social equality in education among some educationalists, the public and politicians. In the 1950s and 60s this focused particularly on how the 1944 Education Act (which in abolishing the payment of fees in secondary schools was seen as removing an obvious source of social inequality) actually worked out in practice. The ensuing empirical research revealed, briefly, that many working class children were still being kept out of grammar schools, but by 'academic' rather than financial criteria, and that those who did get in progressed less well than expected. This led to suspicions that academic selection involved social selection, and that equal educational opportunity did not necessarily result in equality of achievement. The debate caused by this research culminated in calls for the abolition of selection, the introduction of comprehensive schools, and more subtle educational reforms of the curriculum and of teaching methods. The second important influence was the emergence and development of sociology and in particular of the sociology of education. Whether the discipline merely heightened existing interest or actually created the new research developments is open to debate. It seems probable, however, that sociology did more than just provide a body of empirically minded researchers who thought social class an important concept for explaining how society worked. It also needs to be recognised that the theoretical emphasis in the application of sociology to education was, at least to the end of the 1960s, very clearly that of structural functionalism. (Simply, structural functionalism is a particular sociological perspective according to which society is viewed as a set of interrelated social systems or parts.) As Banks (1968) has written: 'One of the major strengths of the structural functionalist approach to education is the placing of educational institutions firmly in their relationship with the wider social structure . . . Consequently . . . the sociology of education has developed as a largely macrocosmic study . . .' Certainly during the late 1950s and the 60s researchers tried to explain classroom performance, and the functioning of schools and of the educational system, in terms of their relationships with other parts of society. Most important among these were family and social background, and a commonly considered aspect of this was social class. This interest resulted in a fairly substantial body of data which described reasonably well the relationship between parental social class and children's educational achievement. Explaining the results was harder, however, particularly when it came to demonstrating how social class actually affected children's educational performance – and this situation remains true today. The task of this chapter will be initially to demonstrate how and to what extent the social classes differ in their educational experience and achievement, and subsequently to look at the relationship between parents' social class and the educational achievements of their children.

Adult social class and education

The most extensive data on this derive from a 10 per cent sample of those enumerated in the 1961 census, of whom only the males are considered here (N = 1,545,456) (*Education Tables (10% Sample)* 1966). Perhaps surprisingly this was the first census to include questions about education. Unfortunately for our purposes, although more extensive treatment was given to the topic in the 1966 and 1971 censuses, the only source

Table 6.1

The terminal educational age† of economically active males in each social class, England and Wales 1961 (percentages*)

	Social class (R.G.(S.E.)60)						
	1	2	3	4	5	6	All
Under 15 years	13	47	42	68	72	86	60
15 years	9	14	18	24	21	11	21
16 years	20	17	20	6	4	2	10
17—19 years	21	15	13	2	2	0.5	6
20 years and over	37	7	7	0.6	0.5	0.2	4

*Percentages over 1 rounded
†Percentages are based on persons who stated their terminal educational age, and exclude those whose education was not completed at time of the census
(Devised from table 3, Census 1961, Education Tables (10% Sample) 1966)

at the time of writing remains the 1961 census. This is because the 1966 data were not produced in a suitable form for social class analysis, while the 1971 figures have yet to be published. The data presented in table 6.1 give the age at which economically active males in each social class completed their full-time education. It gives no indication of the type of course followed or its outcome. It has to be borne in mind that this table refers to males aged between 15 and 65 (i.e. the products of some fifty years of educational change, including the raising of the statutory minimum school leaving age to 14 in 1921 and 15 in 1947). Some distortion is also likely since the age structures of the social classes are different (see chapter 3, pp. 96—100). How long someone has spent in full-time education will depend greatly on his age, for while the table reveals that 60 per cent left full-time education when they were under 15, the percentage of 15- to 24-year-olds was 7, of 25- to 44-year-olds 58, and of those over 45, 80. Over all, however, the trend is clear: the higher the social class the longer the period of full-time education. The most marked social class differences are to be seen between those who finished their education at the age of 16 or over (i.e. having completed at least secondary or selective education) and those who left at a lower age than this (i.e. at the minimum age). Of those surveyed some 20 per cent over all finished their education at 16 or more years, but the figure varied from social class I, where it was 78 per cent, through classes 2 and 3 (about 40 per cent), and classes 4 and 5 (about 7 per cent), to class 6, where it was just less than 3 per cent. These figures do not, however, give a complete picture, since they do not include part-time or mature educational courses.

The actual educational qualifications held by members of the social classes have been surveyed, albeit on a smaller scale (*General Household Survey 1972* 1975). Table 6.2 presents a somewhat similar picture to that in table 6.1. The higher the social class the smaller the percentage without any formal educational qualifications, and the larger the percentage of those with higher qualifications. What is of particular interest in both this table and in table 6.1 is that while there are clear

Table 6.2

Highest educational qualification by social class, males, Great Britain (percentages*)

	Social class (R.G.(S.E.)70)						
	1	2	3	4	5	6	All
Degree or equivalent	53	8	7	0.3	0.1	0.2	5
Higher education below degree	20	10	12	2	0.5	–	5
G.C.E.† A level or equivalent	10	9	10	4	2	1	6
G.C.E.† O level or equivalent, or C.S.E.§ grade 1	7	20	20	12	6	3	13
C.S.E.§ other grades/ commercial/apprentice-ship	1	8	8	16	7	4	10
Foreign and other	5	4	4	3	3	1	3
None	3	41	39	63	81	90	57
Social class of sample	5	14	19	41	16	6	100

*Percentages over 1 rounded
†G.C.E. = General Certificate of Education
§C.S.E. = Certificate of Secondary Education
(*Devised from table 4.7,* General Household Survey 1972 *1975*)

differences in educational qualifications and experience between the social classes, each level of qualification and of full-time education is represented in every social class. Perhaps surprisingly, some 3 per cent of social class 1 have no qualifications, and 13 per cent left full-time education at less than 15 (note however that eleven years separate the two sets of data). At the other extreme 0.2 per cent of class 6 (unskilled manual workers) had terminal educational ages of 20 or more and held degrees or their equivalents. It is also clear from table 6.2 that successful completion of some form of higher education is almost exclusively associated with membership of the non-manual or middle classes (1 to 3), and consequently the lack of it with membership of the manual or working classes (4 to 6).

The same source provides comparable figures for females, which are shown in table 6.3. Two factors must be borne in mind. First, the distribution of women's employment over the

Table 6.3

Highest educational qualification by social class, females, Great Britain (percentages*)

	Social class (R.G.(S.E.)70)						
	1	2	3	4	5	6	All
Degree or equivalent	(21)	4	3	0.5	0.1	–	2
Higher education below degree	(1)	11	11	0.7	0.4	–	6
G.C.E. A level or equivalent	(2)	3	3	2	0.5	–	2
G.C.E. O level or equivalent, or C.S.E. grade 1	(4)	11	19	8	5	1	12
C.S.E. other grades/ commercial/apprentice- ship	(1)	8	14	8	4	2	9
Foreign and other	(2)	5	4	2	2	0.4	3
None	(3)	60	46	79	88	96	66
Social class of sample	*0.6*	*4*	*50*	*8*	*28*	*9*	*100*

*Percentages over 1 rounded
( )Actual numbers, too small for conversion to percentages
(*Devised from table 4.7,* General Household Survey 1972 *1975*)

social classes is clearly different from that of men. This was pointed out in chapter 3 and can be seen again by comparing the bottom rows of tables 6.2 and 6.3:

	Social class (R.G.(S.E.)70)					
	1	2	3	4	5	6
Bottom row of table 6.2 (men)	5	14	19	41	16	6
Bottom row of table 6.3 (women)	0.6	4	50	8	28	9

Most notable here is the under-representation of women in social classes 1, 2 and 4, and their over-representation in the other classes. Secondly, the educational achievements of the sexes are clearly different. The top right-hand figures in tables 6.2 and 6.3 show that while 5 per cent of males were graduates or their equivalents, only 2 per cent of females were. Similarly 57 per cent of all men compared to 66 per cent of all women were without educational qualifications. The difference is particularly marked for women in social classes 2 and 3 where 60 and 46 per cent respectively do not have qualifications, compared with 41 and 39 per cent of men. However, as was suggested in chapter 3 (pp. 64–99), this was due not only to differences in educational qualifications and related job opportunities, but also to the fact that these social classes cover occupations which are predominantly if not exclusively filled by women. Given these two marked differences between the sexes, the relationships between social class and education are still rather similar in the two tables. Leaving aside social class 1 in table 6.3, for which the numbers are too small for analysis, it can again be seen that higher education is almost exclusively related to membership of the non-manual classes. Further, as with the men, the higher the social class the higher the level of education.

The relationship between adults' social class and their educational qualifications and experience can be explained fairly straightforwardly. Social class is defined in terms of occupation (see chapter 2), and certain jobs are only open to people with certain educational qualifications. However, as can be seen in tables 6.1, 6.2 and 6.3, the relationship between educational level and social class is not direct. Not all people with higher education are to be found in social classes I and II, nor are these classes made up exclusively of people with higher education. It may be assumed that this is due both to changes in the occupational structure of society over time (see chapter 3, pp. 96—100), to educational opportunities, and to the importance of factors other than education in getting a job.

Parental social class and children's education

As was suggested at the beginning of this chapter, the most extensively researched area of social class and education has been the relationship between parental social class and the educational experience and achievements of children. The present treatment is therefore necessarily selective. It traces the progress of the social classes through the educational system, using research from the last decade and a half or so. Some of the earlier data from this period could be seen as being dated. The years since its collection have been marked by educational change, notably some reorganisation of secondary education and a considerable expansion of higher education. The extent to which these and other changes have affected the relationships outlined below is, without specific empirical evidence, open to some debate.

Pre-school education

Although the statutory age for entry into the educational system in Britain is five, some provision is made for younger children. Local authorities provide a limited number of places in nursery schools and day nurseries; the latter open for longer hours and terms than do the former, which are similar to infant schools. The most dramatic growth in such provision has been in private voluntary playgroups, which are self-supporting, and often initiated by parents. It has been argued

Table 6.4

Pre-school education by social class of father or head of household (percentages of children under five)

| | Social class (R.G.(S.E.)70) | | | | | | |
	1	2	3	4	5	6	All
Day nursery/playgroup	18	26	18	12	9	7	14
Nursery school*	14	12	9	7	8	7	8
Not yet started	68	62	73	81	84	85	78

*Including primary and independent schools for under fives
(Devised from table 4.1, General Household Survey 1972 *1975)*

that pre-school education has a beneficial effect on a child's subsequent school performance, and that it may go some way towards closing the social class gap in attainment. Though research has not as yet supported these views very strongly, a government white paper, *Education: A Framework for Expansion* (1972), put forward plans for the expansion of such provision. The figures in table 6.4 suggest that in 1972 the middle classes (1 to 3) were better catered for by, or took greater advantage of, pre-school education than the working classes. These figures are based on children aged 0—5, while pre-school education is normally associated with the age of 3 and over. On the assumption that the proportion of children over 3 is the same in each social class, the percentage attending nursery school shows a steady decline across the social classes. The percentage for social class 1 (14 per cent) is twice that for classes 4 and 6 (7 per cent). For day nurseries and playgroups the differences are more marked, though not as regular. The highest percentage is for social class 2 (26 per cent), classes 1 and 3 both having 18 per cent. Here the working class and middle class percentages differ more noticeably than for nursery schools. This may indicate middle class 'self-help' — that is, voluntary playgroups. In both forms of pre-school education the middle classes are above, and the working classes below, the average for all social classes.

Infant school

The research into social class differences in attainment at school has concentrated on performance in public examinations, notably the 11-plus exam for secondary school selection, and school-leaving examinations. The National Child Development Study (see also chapter 5), however, made a unique contribution to knowledge in the field by demonstrating the very marked social class differences in attainment in the infant school. In the course of their study Davie, Butler and Goldstein (1972) collected the test scores of some 15,000 children aged seven in Great Britain, in the basic areas of the curriculum – reading and arithmetic. The grouped results of these scores, analysed by social class, are shown in table 6.5. This table displays a clear relationship between social class and measured attainment at seven years of age. In the case of reading, social class V children are six times as likely to be poor readers (i.e. to come in the lowest 29 per cent of all children – see top row of table 6.5) than those from social class I (48 per cent compared with 8). The study also points

Table 6.5

Reading and arithmetic attainment test scores of seven-year-old children by fathers' social class (percentages)

			Social class (R.G.60/A)				
	I	II	III(N.M.)	III(M.)	IV	V	All*
Grouped Southgate reading test scores							
0–20	8	15	14	30	37	48	29
21–28	37	39	43	41	38	34	39
29–30	54	47	43	29	25	17	32
Grouped problem arithmetic test scores							
0–3	12	19	19	30	34	41	29
4–6	38	39	43	42	42	37	41
7–10	50	42	38	28	24	22	31

*Of whole sample, including those without father or social class information
(*Devised from tables A165 and A168, Davie, Butler and Goldstein 1972*)

out that the lower the level at which a 'poor reader' is defined, the more marked is the imbalance in terms of social class. Hence a social class V child is some fifteen times more likely to be a *non*-reader at age seven than a child from social class I. The table also shows that the gradients across the social classes for the percentage gaining marks for reading and arithmetic in the lowest 29 per cent of the whole sample (top row of each section of the table) are not regular. The percentages for classes II and III(N.M.) are very close for reading and identical for arithmetic. What is very noticeable, however, is the clear division between the middle classes (I, II and III(N.M.)) and the working classes (III(M.), IV and V). For example, while the average of poor readers was some 13 per cent for the former and 34 for the latter, social class III(N.M.) had 14 per cent and III(M.) 30 per cent. Class I is distinguished from the other middle classes by having a lower percentage of poor readers, and a higher percentage of the best readers. Conversely, class V stands out from the other working classes by having markedly poorer scores.

Primary school

A longitudinal study of some 5,362 children who were born during one week of 1946 provides data which reveal how the initial differences in attainment between the social classes develop in the primary school (Douglas 1964). Note, however, that this study is quite separate from that of infant schools, and in fact preceded it. A battery of tests, including intelligence, reading and attainment tests, was administered to the children in this sample at the ages of eight and eleven. In order to allow comparison the actual scores on these tests were standardised to a mean score of 50 and a standard deviation of 10. Briefly this means that the scores were arranged so that 68 per cent fell in the range 40–60, with 16 per cent above 60, and 16 per cent below 40. Table 6.6 presents the averaged scores for the set of tests at each age by social class. The table reveals that at each age there is a steady decline in average test scores across the social classes from

Table 6.6
Change in the average test scores of children in each social class
between the ages of 8 and 11 years

Social class (N.S.)

	U.M	L.M.	U.W.	L.W.
Average test score at 8	56.64	52.96	49.99	48.05
Average test score at 11	56.99	53.88	50.05	47.55
Change in score	+0.35	+0.92	+0.06	−0.50

(Derived from table VI(d), Douglas 1964)

upper middle to lower manual working. Of particular interest, however, are the social class differences in the score changes. While the two middle classes both show increased scores (+0.35 for U.M. and +0.92 for L.M.), the working classes either show a very marginal increase (+0.06 for U.W.) or a sizeable loss (−0.50 for L.W.). The net result is a widening gap between the social classes over this period of primary education.

Another aspect of primary school education that has received considerable research interest is streaming − i.e. the division of children into classes on the basis of ability. The way in which this is done varies, but typically it involves one or more of the following: teacher's personal or professional assessment; performance on a school-based attainment test; performance on an external intelligence test and/or attainment test; and the child's age. The differing social class compositions of the various streams was demonstrated by Jackson (1964). His survey was based on 660 primary schools in England and Wales, being those that responded from a one-third sample of the 2,892 schools in the country large enough to be able to divide their children into separate classes. Nearly all such schools (96 per cent) did, in fact, stream. In the 620 schools which had from two to four streams, information about the fathers' occupations was collected for some 26,582 eleven-year-old children. Table 6.7 shows their distribution by stream and social class. What can be seen from these data is that the

Table 6.7

The social class* composition of streams in primary schools,
for 11-year-old children (percentages)

	I and II	III(N.M.)	III(M.)	IV	V	All
		Social class (R.G.60/AB)				
(a) *In 140 2-stream schools*						
'A' stream	73	61	56	42	39	53
'B' stream	27	39	44	58	61	47
(b) *In 252 3-stream schools*						
'A' stream	58	47	41	29	21	37
'B' stream	28	32	35	41	34	36
'C' stream	14	21	24	30	46	27
(c) *In 228 4-stream schools*						
'A' stream	55	40	34	20	14	30
'B' stream	27	32	30	28	24	28
'C' stream	13	17	24	31	30	25
'D' stream	5	11	12	21	32	17

*Based on teacher's report of child's father's occupation
(Derived from tables 6, 7 and 8, Jackson 1964)

higher the social class of a child's father the more likely he or she was to be in a higher stream at primary school. In the case of schools with three streams, for example, over half (58 per cent) of social classes I and II were in the 'A' stream and about a seventh (14 per cent) in the 'C' stream, whereas only about a fifth (21 per cent) of social class V were in the 'A' stream and nearly half (46 per cent) were in the 'C' stream. There are two further points of interest. One is a certain blurring of the differences between the middle and working classes. Social class III(M.) had a majority of its children in the 'A' stream in two-stream schools (section (a) in table 6.7), albeit a smaller majority (56 per cent) than those of classes I and II (73 per cent) and III(N.M.) (61 per cent). It was however in marked contrast to the minorities in the 'A' streams of social classes IV (42 per cent) and V (39 per cent). Similarly, in the other schools social class III(M.) had its largest proportion in the 'A' stream, but classes IV and V had theirs in the lower streams. Secondly, one should notice that the streams are of unequal size, the top streams being larger, and the lower smaller, than if the children were equally divided (in which case, for example, the streams in section (*c*) of the table would each contain 25 per cent of all children).

A view of the way in which social class and streaming operate together over time in the primary school is given by Douglas (1964). Part of his study was concerned with children in two-stream primary schools. He found that on the basis of measured ability (the tests referred to above), there were 11 per cent more middle class children than expected in the 'A' streams, and 26 per cent fewer than expected in the 'B' streams. He further revealed that the experience of being in an 'A' or 'B' stream had different effects on the performance of children from the two broad social classes. Hence in the 'A' stream, while both social classes improved their scores between the ages of 8 and 11, it was the middle class children who improved them most. In the 'B' streams the scores of the middle class children also improved, but not as much as in the 'A' stream, while the working class children's scores actually deteriorated. Over all the effect of 'A'-stream experience was an improvement in average test scores (+0.71 marks), and of 'B'-stream experience, a decline (−0.49 marks).

Many primary schools do not now have streaming by ability as such. Barker Lunn (1970) surveyed a matched sample of 72 primary schools, of which 36 streamed and 36 did not. The reading test scores in the first and fourth years of primary schooling produced very similar findings to those of Douglas (1964) reported above. In both streamed and unstreamed schools the performance of the middle classes (R.G. I, II and III) improved, and that of the working classes (IV and V) deteriorated. The changes were very marked, and were again true for all ability groups. This study suggests that different school organisation does not necessarily affect social class differences in achievement. Perhaps, though, its major contribution was to review teachers' ratings of children's abilities in comparison with the children's actual test scores, by social class (based on teachers' categorisation of fathers' occupation).

Table 6.8

Teachers' ability ratings of pupils compared to objective ratings
of pupils' ability based on English test scores, by social class*
(percentages)

Social class (R.G.60/F)

Teachers' rating	I,II,III	IV,V	I,II,III	IV,V	I,II,III	IV,V
			Test score			
	Above average		Average		Below average	
Above average	74	60	19	14	1	1
Average	25	39	69	68	34	28
Below average	1	1	12	18	65	71

*Based on teacher's categorisation of fathers' occupations
(Derived from table 5.4A, Barker Lunn 1970, appendix 6)

Table 6.8 reveals a tendency for teachers to overestimate the
ability of children from social classes I, II and III and to
underestimate that of children from classes IV and V. For
example, only 26 per cent of middle class children who were,
on test scores, 'above average' were not so rated by their
teachers, compared with 40 per cent of the 'above average'
working class children. Barker Lunn argues that this under-
estimation by teachers of working class ability may be a factor
affecting the social class composition of streams. In unstreamed schools also, she suggests, teachers' different expectations about a child's ability, depending on whether the child is
middle class or working class, may affect his attainment.

Type of secondary school.

The empirical research interest in the secondary schooling of
the social classes in Britain really stems from the 1944
Education Act. After this Act secondary schools were either
selective, offering chances of public examination, or non-
selective, normally leading to termination of schooling at the
minimum school-leaving age. A Central Advisory Council for
Education document published at the height of this period of
concern, *15–18* (1960) – often referred to as the Crowther
Report – contained two surveys which revealed sharp social

class differences in secondary schooling. The first was an analysis by social class of a sample (N = 1,455) of children in selective schools and of some 1,811 children educated at non-selective schools. Both groups left school in the period 1954–5. The second survey involved the analysis of schooling by social class of some 7,221 recruits to National Service in 1956–8.

Table 6.9A suggests that the social class compositions of selective and non-selective schools were quite different, the former type of school having a much higher percentage of social class 1 (18 compared to 4) and a lower percentage of social class 4 (10 compared to 23) than the latter. Similar

Table 6.9A
The social class of fathers of children who attended (*a*) grammar and technical schools, (*b*) secondary modern schools (percentages)

	Social class (R.G.(S.E.)50/B)					
	1	2	3	4	Unclassified	All
(*a*) Grammar and technical	18	19	41	10	12	100
(*b*) Secondary modern and all age	4	11	49	23	13	100

(Derived from table 1, 15–18 1960, vol. 2)

Table 6.9B
Type of secondary school attended, by father's social class, National Service recruits, 1956–8 (percentages)

	Social class (R.G.50)					
	I	II	III	IV	V	All
Independent efficient*	22	4	—	—	—	3
Grammar	40	30	17	12	7	20
Technical	9	10	7	6	5	7
Secondary modern and all age	24	52	74	81	86	68
Other types	5	4	2	1	2	2
All	All columns = 100					

*Recognised as such by the Ministry of Education (now the Department of Education and Science)
(Derived from table 9, 15–18 1960, vol. 2, part 2)

though smaller differences can be observed between the schools in the percentage of classes 2 and 3. Table 6.9B shows that male children from different social classes had very different school experiences. Whereas in social class I only about a quarter (24 per cent) attended non-selective schools, while nearly half (49 per cent) went to selective schools and 22 per cent to independent schools, in social classes IV and V over 80 per cent went to non-selective, less than 20 per cent to selective, and virtually none to independent schools.

Since these researches two main changes have taken place in secondary schools. First, before the raising of the statutory minimum school-leaving age to 16 years in 1973, many of the non-selective schools introduced opportunities for education beyond the minimum leaving age, and for sitting public examinations. Secondly, many areas have introduced comprehensive secondary education, in some cases ending the coexistence of selective and non-selective schooling. There is, however, wide variety in the comprehensive schemes existing in different areas of Britain (see, for example, Benn and Simon 1972). Some areas have yet to introduce such schemes, and those which have been introduced are still at varying stages of development. These changes need to be borne in mind when looking at table 6.10, which shows the percentage of each social class (based on fathers) of some 1,688 11- to 14-year-old children surveyed in the *General Household Survey 1972* (1975). Caution is necessary, since the type of school attended was identified by the parent involved. Given the state of flux in school organisation, some schools have probably been misidentified (for example, some might still have been known by their old names, while others might have been in the process of changing). Further, because of differences in the definitions of social class, and particularly in the types of school mentioned, direct comparisons between tables 6.9B and 6.10 are somewhat suspect.

Given the limitations of the survey and the rapidly changing situation that was being reviewed, the data in table 6.10 can be construed in a number of ways. Perhaps the fairest way is to

Table 6.10

Type of secondary school attended by children aged
11—14 years by social class of father or head of household
(percentages)

	Social class (R.G.(S.E.)70)						
	1	2	3	4	5	6	All
Secondary modern	29	34	32	49	53	49	44
Comprehensive	20	29	34	32	29	30	30
Grammar	19	19	24	12	9	6	15
Direct grant/independent	30	15	4	1	—	—	5
Other/special	1	3	6	6	8	15	6
All	6	16	17	41	15	5	100

(Devised from table 4.1, General Household Survey 1972 *1975)*

compare the percentage of each social class in each type of
school with the overall figure (far right-hand column of the
table). In this way one can see that the middle classes have a
higher percentage in the remaining selective schools, that is
grammar, direct grant and independent, and a somewhat lower
percentage in secondary modern schools. The opposite is true
of the working classes. The social classes other than class 1 all
have remarkably similar percentages in comprehensive
schools — around the average for all social classes of 30 per
cent.

Given the strictures pointed out above, some general
observations can be made about the effects of secondary
school reorganisation, by comparing tables 6.9B and 6.10. If
the secondary modern and comprehensive schools are
accepted, by definition, as non-selective, then while the
proportion of working class children in such schools has
remained at around 80 per cent, the percentage of social class
1 children has risen from 24 to 49 per cent. (This does not
necessarily mean that any particular school is now attended by
children from more social classes than before. Many comprehensive schools are neighbourhood schools — they cater for
children from a limited area surrounding the school —
and as was shown in chapter 2 many such areas are

occupied predominantly by one social class or another. Hence some comprehensives could be described as working class, and others as middle class.) At the same time it can also be seen that a considerable proportion of middle class children, particularly in social class 1, are educated in schools other than those provided by a local education authority.

Given the local variations in the development and organisation of comprehensive schools, together with the lack of research, it would be very difficult either to substantiate or to refute the suggestion that secondary school reorganisation is bringing together the educational experience of the social classes. A survey carried out some ten years ago on behalf of the National Foundation for Educational Research (Monks 1968) suggested that the early reorganisations produced a comprehensive school intake which was not representative, in terms of social class, of the population at large. The study, which was based on 331 comprehensive schools, had two main limitations. One was that only a third of the schools were fully developed as comprehensives. The other was the reliance on headteachers' estimates of the social class backgrounds of the children in their schools. As can be seen from table 6.11, social classes 1 and 2 appeared to be under-represented and classes 4 and 5 over-represented in comprehensive schools in relation to

Table 6.11

Estimated social class* of fathers of children attending
comprehensive schools in 1965, England and Wales
(percentages)

	Social class (R.G.(S.E.)60/D)					
	1	**2**	**3**	**4**	**5**	Not classified
Comprehensive pupils	9	12	37	30	17†	—
Approximate national proportions	13	17	40	19	8	1.7

*Estimated by headteachers, who reported proportion of fathers of children in their schools in each social class
†Broadness of N.F.E.R. categories accounts for total percentage of over 100
(Devised from table 8, Monks 1968)

their approximate proportions in society as a whole. The figures were drawn from a large number of schools, widely distributed, and the social class distributions depicted are likely to have ranged from real reflections of a catchment area's social structure to extremely distorted ones.

The exclusively middle class nature of public and independent schools which can be seen from tables 6.9B and 6.10 above was highlighted by the Public Schools Commission (*Public Schools Commission: First Report* 1968). Here an analysis of the social class of the fathers of 17,787 children attending public and 950 children attending independent schools which were 'recognised as efficient' produced the results shown in table 6.12. The table shows that over 80 per cent of pupils in such schools came from social classes I and II, which comprised about 18 per cent of the adult male population of the country. In stark contrast classes IV and V, which made up some 28 per cent of the population, provided only around 1 per cent of the pupils in these schools.

The importance of public schools in relation to social class

Table 6.12

Social class of the fathers of pupils attending public and recognised-as-efficient independent schools (percentages)

	Social class (R.G.60/AB)				
	I and II	III(N.M.)	III(M.)	IV and V	Armed forces
Public schools					
Boarding pupils	84	4	1	–	11
Day pupils	85	8	3	1	3
Recognised independent					
Boarding pupils	82	5	1	–	12
Day pupils	82	7	4	2	5
Approximate male population	18	50		28	4*

*All the unclassified males, including armed forces
(*Derived from table 5*, Public Schools Commission: First Report *1968*, vol. 2, appendix 6, section 3; source — Kalton 1966 and commission questionnaire)

does not only lie in the almost exclusively upper middle class nature of their intakes. A number of recent publications have put forward evidence that public school products are particularly successful at gaining high-status and high-income occupations, often called élite jobs (Boyd 1973; Stanworth and Giddens 1974; Urry and Wakeford 1973). Table 6.13 below presents a selection of such élite jobs together with the percentage of public-school-educated people in them. While

Table 6.13
Percentage* of public-school-educated holders of various élite jobs in Britain (percentages)

(a) The establishment

The Civil Service, under-secretary and above (1970)	62
High court and appeal judges (1971)	80
Church of England bishops (1971)	67

(b) Education

Vice-chancellors, principals and professors in English and Welsh universities (1967)	33
Heads of colleges and professors at Oxford and Cambridge (1967)	49

(c) Commerce and industry

Directors of 40 major industrial firms (1971)	68
Directors of clearing banks (1971)	80
Directors of major insurance companies (1971)	83

(d) Politics

Conservative Members of Parliament (1970)	64
Conservative Members of Parliament (1974)	73
Conservative Cabinet (1970)	78
Labour Members of Parliament (1970)	8
Labour Members of Parliament (1974)	9
Labour Cabinet (1970)	29

(e) Base line

14-year-olds at school in England and Wales (1967)	2.6

*Percentages rounded. The percentages are the total in each group whose education is known. All public schools are included, but not other independent or direct grant grammar schools
(Devised from: (a) *tables 4—11, Boyd 1973;* (b) *and* (e) *vol. II, appendix 8, section 4,* Public Schools Commission: First Report *1968;* (c) *Whitley 1973;* (d) *p. 257,* The Times House of Commons *1970 and 1974, and table XX, Punnett 1971)*

looking at these figures, remember that only some 2.6 per cent of children in England and Wales were educated at such schools (see 'base line' in table).

Secondary school achievement

The bulk of the existing research in this area has been concerned with the O level General Certificate of Education performance of children at maintained (local authority) selective (mainly grammar) schools. Although somewhat dated, this research has a number of advantages for our purposes. It holds constant the type of school attended and the measured ability of the children, two variables of obvious importance in educational achievement. This allows the central variable under consideration, that of social class, to be isolated to some degree. Even so, two other factors need to be considered. As has been shown, the social classes vary in their achievement on tests in primary school; hence, opportunity to sit for public examinations was, at the time of these studies, affected by the difference in social class chances of gaining entry to selective secondary schools. It is also true that, until the raising of the school-leaving age in 1973, social class differences in secondary school achievement were affected by early leaving. Douglas, Ross and Simpson (1968) point out that, whereas there were no social class differences among the brightest 16 per cent of primary school children entering grammar school, such differences were observed in the proportion of these children who completed the course. Of the top 16 per cent of lower manual working class children in their sample, 50 per cent left before the age of sixteen, compared with 10 per cent of the upper middle and 22 per cent of the lower middle class children. Thus part of the explanation of the following data consists simply in the fact that different proportions of social classes actually sat examinations. Table 6.14 shows this in relation to the differences in O and A level G.C.E. success. The larger gap between the two sets of figures for 'manual' and for 'non-manual' children is due in part to the lower level of entry into the sixth form by the former, and the

Table 6.14

Academic achievement of children born 1940–1, at maintained grammar schools, by grouped I.Q. scores at age 11 and fathers' social class, England and Wales (percentages)

		Social class (R.G.60/C)	
I.Q. scores	Achievement	Non-manual	Manual
130+	Degree-level course*	37	18
	At least 2 A levels†	43	30
	At least 5 O levels†	73	75
115–29	Degree-level course*	17	8
	At least 2 A levels	23	14
	At least 5 O levels	56	45
100–14	Degree-level course*	6	2
	At least 2 A levels	9	6
	At least 5 O levels	37	22

*Figures in this row relate to Great Britain
†In the General Certificate of Education (G.C.E.)
(Derived from table 5, Higher Education 1963, appendix 1, part 2)

same can be observed in the case of entry to degree-level courses after A level success. The percentage of the most able group (I.Q. of 130 or more) who gained two or more A levels and who went on to degree-level courses was 86 per cent for the 'non-manual' and only 60 per cent for the 'manual' children. In the less able groups the differences are even more marked. Except for children in the highest I.Q. range (130 or more) at the O level stage, the table shows that differences existed in the achievements of children of the same measured ability, attending the same type of school, but from differing social class backgrounds. In the 115–29 range of I.Q. scores this meant that a quarter as many more children from the non-manual classes gained 5 O levels than from the manual classes, two-thirds as many more gained 2 A levels, and over twice as many entered degree-level courses.

A very similar situation was recorded by a Ministry of Education survey of 5 per cent of leavers from maintained grammar schools some six years later (*Statistics of Education 1961: Supplement* 1962). In this survey ability was defined in

Table 6.15

Percentage of maintained grammar school children gaining 5 or more G.C.E. O level passes in each social class by 11-plus grading, England and Wales 1960—1

	Social class (R.G.(S.E.)50/B)				
11-plus grading	1	2	3	4	All
Upper third	91	79	77	49	78
Middle third	68	60	55	46	56
Lower third	53	47	32	22	36
All	72	60	55	37	55

(Derived from table 14, Higher Education *1963, appendix 1, part 2, and* Statistics in Education 1961: Supplement *1962)*

terms of scores in the 11-plus secondary school selection examination, which normally involved school attainment tests as well as I.Q. tests. It also used a more sophisticated, and unique, classification of social class (see p. 42 above). Table 6.15 displays a steady decline across the social classes (1 to 4) in the percentage of children in each ability band who gained 5 or more O levels. At each ability level the middle classes (1 and 2) had higher percentages than the working classes (3 and 4). However, the differences between classes 1 and 2, and between 3 and 4, are greater than those between 2 and 3. Clearly, the most marked differences occurred at the extremes. In the upper third of the ability range (the top row in the table) 91 per cent of social class 1 gained 5 or more O levels compared with just under half (49 per cent) in class 4. The comparable figures in the lower third of the ability range were 53 and 22 per cent.

A final view of this situation can be gained from the work of Douglas, Ross and Simpson (1968). This study involved the same sample as that mentioned above in the section on primary education (Douglas 1964). The main contribution of this study is that it used, as the measure of ability, an intelligence test administered at the age of 15, that is, only one year before the majority of the sample sat G.C.E. O level. Hence, unlike the two studies above, it takes some account of any changes in measured ability which may have taken place between selection at 11 and the G.C.E. O level examination. The study further distinguishes between the 'quality' of O level certificates, and takes account of all passes rather than merely '5 or more' (for definition of 'good' and 'general' certificates see footnotes to table 6.16). In the case of 'good' certificates there are very marked differences between the social classes (see table 6.16). In the top 16 per cent of the ability range (ability score of 60 and over) the percentage of upper middle class children gaining such certificates is more than twice that of the lower manual working class (77 per cent compared to 37 per cent). At the ability level just above the average for the whole group (marks of 50—4) the upper middle

Table 6.16

Percentage of children in each ability* band gaining (*a*) good certificates,† (*b*) general certificates,§ by social class of parents

	Social class (N.S.)			
(*a*) *Good certificates*	U.M.	L.M.	U.W.	L.W.
Ability scores				
60+	77	60	53	37
55—9	33	18	15	9
50—4	11	6	2	3
45—9	4	—	1	—
44 and less	—	—	—	—
(*b*) *General certificates*				
Ability scores				
60+	94	87	86	69
55—9	79	59	45	31
50—4	54	38	17	12
45—9	27	13	5	2
44 and less	20	1	—	—

*Based on intelligence test, standardised on the sample involved so that the scores have a mean of 50 and a standard deviation of 10 (i.e. 68 per cent of scores fell between 40 and 60; see also p. 174 above)
†A G.C.E. O level certificate of at least four passes including three of the following: English language, mathematics, science, a foreign language
§At least one G.C.E. O level pass, and any number and combination of passes other than those which constitute a good certificate (see previous footnote)
(*Derived from table 4, Douglas, Ross and Simpson 1968*)

class percentage is nearly four times the lower working class one (11 per cent and 3 per cent respectively). In the case of 'general' certificates the social class differences in the top ability range were smaller: for the upper middle class the percentage was 94 and for the lower manual working 69. At the just-above-average ability level (50−4), however, the differences between the social classes are of the same order as those for 'good' certificates (54 per cent compared to 12 per cent). The starkest differences to be observed occur in the lower ability ranges: while 27 per cent of the upper middle class in the just-below-average ability group (45−9) gained some O level passes, and 20 per cent in the lowest ability range, the comparable percentages for the lower manual working class were 2 per cent and nil.

Higher and further education

The most comprehensive research in this area was that conducted for the Committee on Higher Education (*Higher Education* 1963, often referred to as the Robbins Report), a survey of 21-year-olds born in 1940−1. Part of this was concerned with the highest level of education reached by the sample. The survey covered about 1 in 200 of the age group (N = 3,008). Table 6.17 shows their educational achievements in terms of social class (based on fathers' occupation at the time the sample left school). This table shows how very sharply separate the social classes were in terms of entry to higher and further education. At each level of education the percentage entering declines across the social classes from I to IV-and-V. Some 33 per cent of social class I undertook degree courses compared to only 1 per cent of classes IV and V. Put another way, the chances of a child from social class I entering degree-level education were 33 times greater than that of a child from classes IV and V. At the other extreme, while almost two thirds (65 per cent) of classes IV and V neither gained qualifications nor entered post-school education, this was true of only 7 per cent of class I and 20 per cent of class II.

Table 6.17

Highest level of education, by social class of father, attained
by children born in 1940—1 in Great Britain (percentages)

| | *Social class (R.G.60/AB)* | | | | | |
	I	II	III(N.M.)	III(M.)	IV and V	All
Higher education						
Degree-level full-time	33	11	6	2	1	4
Other full-time	12	8	4	2	1	3
Part-time	7	6	3	3	2	4
A level or S.L.C.*	16	7	7	2	1	3
Other post-school course, or O level	25	48	51	42	30	40
No post-school course or O level/S.L.C.*	7	20	29	49	65	47

*Scottish School Leaving Certificate
(*Derived from table 2*, Higher Education *1963, appendix 1, part 2,
section 2*)

One rather interesting innovation in this research was that
mothers' as well as fathers' occupation was related to children's
educational achievements (mothers' occupation before marriage
was used). Table 6.18 allows for comparison, in terms of a
simple non-manual/manual dichotomy, of both parents' social
class with their children's level of education. Note that the
mothers and fathers are not matched with each other. Given
the crudity involved in combining the social classes contained
in table 6.17 to produce those in table 6.18, the two tables
clearly present a very similar picture with respect to fathers'
social class. What is important to recognise here is that the
sample's educational attainment is related nearly as closely to
mothers' social class, defined by occupation before marriage,
as it is to that of fathers at their children's school-leaving age.
In *Higher Education* the authors suggest that a mother's
occupation is an indirect measure of her education, and
comment in a footnote (p. 38): 'But his [the father's]
occupation . . . presumably affects his family income and
children's education directly, whereas in the case of the

mother the effect of her education, rather than that of her occupation before marriage, is presumably the more direct.'

Given the relative social class chances for entry into higher and further education outlined above, the subsequent further findings of the Committee on Higher Education hold few surprises. The social class composition of various groups of students were traced from a number of sample surveys. This research involved some 9,452 students, comprising 568 post-graduates, 3,725 undergraduates, 1,223 teacher trainees, 2,178 in full-time further education, 837 part-time day students, and 921 part-time evening students. Table 6.19 gives the fathers' social class for these groups of students, together with the social class distribution of economically active males at the same period, for purposes of comparison.

There are several ways of looking at this table. One way is to compare the base line — the percentages of economically active males — with the rest of the table — the percentages of each type of student — in each social class. This reveals that in each type of higher and further education, social classes I and II were over-represented, while the proportions of social class III(N.M.) in each were rather similar. In contrast, the working

Table 6.18

Highest level of education, by social class of father and mother, of children born in 1940—1 in Great Britain (percentages)

| | Social class (R.G.60/C) | | | |
| | Non-manual | | Manual | |
	Fathers	Mothers	Fathers	Mothers
Degree-level full-time	12.0	14.8	1.5	1.9
Other full-time	7.5	8.3	1.7	2.4
Part-time	5.5	4.8	3.0	3.6
A level or S.L.C.*	7.9	9.3	1.7	2.0
Other post-school or O level	46.0	44.3	37.5	39.0
No post-school course O level/ S.L.C.*	21.0	18.2	54.5	51.0

*Scottish School Leaving Certificate
(Derived from tables 1 and 3, Higher Education *1963, appendix 1, part 2, section 2)*

Table 6.19

Higher and further education students† by social class of father, Great Britain 1960—1
(percentages)

| | Social class (R.G.60/A) | | | | | | | Percentage of 19-year-olds |
	I	II	III(N.M.)	III(M.)	IV	V	Not known	
Postgraduate	10	37	14	25	7	2	6	—
Undergraduate	18	41	12	18	6	1	4	3.3
3-year teacher training	7	33	14	29	9	2	6	1.7
Full-time further education	12	32	14	28	8	2	4	0.9
Part-time day	6	20	16	39	12	4	3	0.7
Part-time evening	5	22	14	39	12	3	4	0.1
*Economically active males**	4	11	17	39	18	8	3	

*Social class R.G.(S.E.)60
†Overseas students not included
(*Devised from tables 5, 65, 81, 102 and 135, Higher Education 1963, appendix 2 (B), part 1; table 3, Higher Education 1963, appendix 2 (A); and table 1, Census 1961, Socio-Economic Group Tables 1966*)

classes, particularly classes IV and V, were under-represented in each type. The skilled manual class – III(M.) – was also under-represented, except in part-time further education, where the percentage was identical with that of economically active males. The social class composition of undergraduates, 71 per cent middle class and 25 per cent working class, was somewhat different from that of teacher trainees, where the percentages were 54 and 40 per cent respectively, and from further education, particularly part-time, where the working classes were in the majority. The table also reveals an interesting fact about postgraduates. Although their social composition is somewhat similar to that of undergraduates, comparison between the two reveals a difference. The percentage of postgraduates in social classes I and II is lower than that of undergraduates, whereas in all the other social classes it is higher. At this educational level, then, there may be some advantage for the working class. It is also interesting to note here that, in spite of the vastly differing social class chances of university entry, performance once at university is apparently not affected by social class. Certainly research in this field has failed to show any consistent relationship between social class and class of degree (Brockington and Stein 1963; Kelsall 1963; chapters by Newfield and Dale in Halmos 1963).

A study of a large percentage of all those who graduated (N = 8,284) from universities in 1960 (Kelsall, Poole and Kuhn 1972, perhaps aptly sub-titled *The Sociology of an Elite*) demonstrated their social class composition by sex. Table 6.20 once again displays the disparity in the social origins of graduates. In the case of both sexes the majority of graduates came from the middle classes, which are a minority of society at large. What is particularly noticeable here is that, as a group, the female graduates appear to come more frequently from the higher social classes than do the males. While 26 per cent of male graduates came from the working classes this is true of only 19 per cent of the females. A higher proportion of the latter came from social classes I and II – 54 per cent compared to 46 per cent of male graduates.

Table 6.20

University graduates by social class of fathers,* and sex
(percentages)

Social class (R.G.60/A)

	I	II	III(N.M.)	III(M.)	IV	V	Unknown
Male graduates	12	34	14	19	6	1	14
Female graduates	15	39	13	14	5	–	12
Economically active males	4	11	17	39	18	8	3

*At time of graduates' entry to university
*(Derived from table 1, Kelsall, Poole and Kubn 1972, and table 1,
Census 1961*, Socio–Economic Group Tables *1966)*

A number of studies of individual universities have displayed considerable differences in the social origins of their
students. This could indicate social class differences in choice
of, or opportunity to enter, particular universities. In 1960–1
the average proportion of undergraduates from the manual
classes for all universities was 25 per cent (*Higher Education*
1963). At one extreme 13 per cent of male and 6 per cent of
female undergraduates were from the manual classes in Oxford
and Cambridge (Kelsall, Poole and Kuhn 1972, table 22). This
matches the figures of 10 and 12 per cent for both sexes in
two Cambridge colleges (anonymous) reported elsewhere
(Hatch and Reich 1970). At the other extreme Musgrove
(Musgrove, Cooper, Derrick, Foy and Willig 1967) showed that
41 per cent of the entrants to Bradford University, then a
newly emerging technological university, came from manual
backgrounds. Of particular interest here is the Open
University, which had as one of its aims the provision of higher
educational opportunities for those who had 'missed out' on
the conventional ones. The top row of table 6.21 shows that
its first intake was, in terms of the students' own social class,
even more heavily biased towards the middle classes than that
of a conventional university. Indeed some 93 per cent came
from social classes I, II and III(N.), the vast majority, 62 per

Table 6.21
The 1971 intake of the Open University by social class of
students and students' fathers (percentages)

	Social class (R.G.60/A)					
	I	II	III(N.M.)	III(M.)	IV	V
Students	20	62	11	5	1	0
Students' fathers	8	26	13	34	13	4

(Derived from table 4, McIntosh and Woodley 1974)

cent, coming from class II. In fact the bulk of the entrants had
been previously successful in the educational system. Many
were, for example, non-graduate teachers (hence the very large
proportion of social class II). However, as the second row of
the table shows, just over half the students' fathers (51 per
cent) were from the working classes. Since this latter measure
is the one used in the earlier tables, it is perhaps the most
appropriate here. Clearly, at this stage of the Open University's
development, the majority of students were those who had
been intra-generationally socially mobile (see p. 90 above).

A major area of expansion in higher education over the last
decade or so has been the polytechnics. Only small scale
single-institution investigations of students' social class have as
yet been undertaken. One such study (Donaldson 1971) was
concerned with entrants to read for degrees at a college of
technology, which was subsequently elevated to polytechnic
status. Given that in table 6.22 the middle/working class divide

Table 6.22
Entrants into Enfield College of Technology* in 1968 to read
for C.N.A.A. degrees, by fathers' social class (percentages)

	Social class (H.J.)						
	1	2	3	4	5	6	7
Entrants 1968	24	16	13	21	22†	3	2

*Now a polytechnic
†Non-manual, 12; manual, 10
(Derived from table 2, Donaldson 1971)

is in social class 5, the relevant percentages, 85 and 15 per cent, once again reveal a strong middle class bias. This may be due to the nature of the courses for which the students were enrolled (many were courses leading to business studies degrees, and it may be that these are more attractive to students from middle class backgrounds). This study shows the difficulties of attempting to generalise from a study of a single institution. Donaldson's findings, for example, contrast with those of Hatch and Reich (1971), who produced figures for an anonymous polytechnic, showing that 33 per cent of the students had manual social class backgrounds.

7

Politics, religion, leisure and opinion

Whichever way you turn this curse of class difference confronts you like a wall of stone. Or rather it is not so much like a stone wall as the plate glass pane of an aquarium: it is so easy to pretend that it isn't there, and so impossible to get through it.

George Orwell (1937)

This chapter deals with a number of topics which at first glance seem rather diverse and perhaps unrelated. They have to do with areas of life which are typically seen as more personal and intimate than many of the others reviewed in this book. This is because they involve belief and feeling, and are surrounded by social values. For example, in politics and religion there exists a profound social acceptance of the individual's right to his own views, and also his right to secrecy, in voting and in his relationship with his God. Again, while most of us appreciate that money, time, age and ability must limit our leisure activities, we jealously regard how we spend our spare time as a matter of individual choice. It is not surprising, therefore, that these areas are often emotionally charged: they arouse passion and enthusiasm, particularly when like-minded people gather, or attempt to bring new recruits into the fold.

Probably most of us who are involved in a social organisation centering on politics, religion or leisure are aware to some degree of a social class exclusiveness or emphasis. Certainly many of the organisations themselves exhibit such an awareness. Sometimes this is explicit and assertive as in the case of some golf clubs, working men's clubs, trade unions, chambers of commerce, professional associations and so on. More typically the awareness is expressed defensively, and exclusive social class labels or associations are deliberately avoided. Political parties and churches are in general careful to avoid, or to reject, such labels (for example, the working class label of the Labour party, or the middle class/aristocratic/ establishment image of the Conservative party and the Church of England). An alternative tack is to emphasise the existence of minority groups within the organisation — a very good example, though from a somewhat different sphere, is the claim by many public schools, in the face of evidence to the contrary (see chapter 6 above), that they contain children from all walks of life and social classes.

Such factors as individuals' desire for privacy of beliefs and feelings, and the concern of institutions with their public image, may partly explain why empirical research in these fields tends to be limited, both in scope and depth (in contrast to the wealth of research in the last chapter). A further explanation for the comparative paucity of empirical research in this area is that there are recognised methodological problems associated with the investigation of opinion and attitudes (for a review of these see Oppenheim 1966). This is particularly true of large-scale research, the concern of this book, since private and deep-seated factors can perhaps only really be explored by using long in-depth interviews, which are not a feature of social surveys. Finally, the institutions involved are often not particularly research-minded. A good case in point are the churches, whose information about the numbers of their members and attenders is often based only on rather dubious estimates. Gaine (1975), in reviewing the literature on religious practice and belief, concludes: 'It must be strongly emphasised that the above conclusions are highly tentative and cannot be made more definite due to the absence of agreed statistics and scientific study of the factors involved. In particular, the effects of social class, education, and locality need to be studied . . .'

Politics

Popular belief has it that politics is all about social class. This belief has been shared by some academics. Pulzer (1968) is quoted by Butler and Stokes (1969) in their study, subtitled *Forces Shaping Electoral Choice*, as having claimed that 'class is the basis of British party politics, all else is embellishment and detail'. This is not to suggest that the situation is simple. If the working classes voted Labour, and the middle classes voted Conservative, then Britain would have had Labour government ever since the creation of the Labour party, because the working classes are in a clear majority (see above, p. 64). In fact the situation is confounded not only by non-conforming voters, but also by the existence of other political parties, by shifts in allegiance, and by failure to vote.

Voting behaviour is the most rigorously researched area of political activity. A growing number of commercial firms now conduct polls (or surveys) of the voting intentions of samples of the public, both continuously and during election campaigns. During campaigns the polls hope to predict, and some say they affect, the outcome. They bring out some of the problems involved in this type of social research: their predictive powers vary in accuracy, in relation both to other polls and to subsequent events. Over all, however, their track record is quite good. Table 7.1 shows the combined results of

Table 7.1

Percentage* of each social class by voting intentions,† general election, October 1974

Social class (M.R./A)

	A	B	C1	C2	D	E	All
Conservative	68	60	46	30	25	34	37
Labour	14	20	28	50	59	52	43
Liberal	19	19	23	18	14	12	18
Nationalist	–	2	2	2	2	2	2
Other	–	0.5	1	1	1	1	1

*Percentages over 1 rounded
†Figures are the combined results of Gallup Election Surveys
(Derived from Gallup Polls 1974)

a series of pre-election polls conducted by Gallup Polls Ltd up to the October 1974 general election. The table is particularly useful because it uses the full range of social classes and five political party categories. Looking first at the support for the major parties (the first two rows of the table) it can be seen that no social class is completely aligned to one party in its voting intentions. Hence 14 per cent of the highest class (A) intended to vote Labour, while a quarter of class D and a third (34 per cent) of class E intended to vote Conservative. There is, however, a clear divide between the middle class and the working class in terms of support for the major parties. In each of the middle classes the percentage intending to vote Conservative is much larger than that intending to vote Labour. In classes A and B the Conservatives have a clear majority over all the other parties put together. On the other hand in the working classes (C2, D and E) the opposite is true, since at least 50 per cent of each class intended to vote Labour. The percentages involved for classes C1 and C2, on either side of the middle/working class divide, are almost a direct mirror image of each other. Social class variations in Liberal party support are less marked, the highest percentage (23 per cent) being in social class C1, and the lowest (12 per cent) in class E. Nationalist and 'other' parties are supported equally by very small overall percentages of each of the social classes. It is noticeable, however, that social class A voters had no intention of voting for any party other than the three main ones.

Voting is for most people their only political activity. Other political activities are very much minority affairs. Butler and Stokes (1969) show, in their table 2.1, that while some 77 per cent of the eligible population voted in the general election of 1964, only about 25 per cent were nominal members of a political party, 14 per cent actually subscribed to a local party, 8 per cent attended an election meeting, and 3 per cent actually campaigned. Unfortunately for our purposes these data are not analysed by social class. However, National Opinion Polls have enquired into the general level of interest in

Table 7.2

Level of interest in politics by social class (percentages)

	Social class (M.R.)				
	AB	C1	C2	DE	All
Very interested	15	12	6	6	8
Quite interested	46	38	34	27	34
Not very interested	32	40	43	41	41
Not at all interested/no opinion	7	10	17	26	17

(Derived from p. 5, National Opinion Polls 1969b)

politics. Table 7.2 gives the results of their enquiry, in which respondents were asked merely to indicate their level of interest. Over all, most (58 per cent) of those interviewed were 'not very' or 'not at all' interested in politics. A majority of classes C2 and DE, 60 and 67 per cent respectively, fell into these categories, compared with half of C1, and a minority, 39 per cent, of AB. There were similar social class differences among those who classified themselves as interested in politics. 61 per cent of class AB, but only a third of class DE were 'quite' or 'very' interested. The starkest difference is that between the 15 per cent of social class AB and the 6 per cent of classes C2 and DE who were 'very interested'. Clearly the middle classes saw themselves as more interested in politics than did the working classes.

Party support and interest in politics have been investigated together. Another National Opinion Poll (National Opinion Polls 1972) asked a sample (N = 1,000) 'Would you describe yourself as a supporter of one political party? Which is that?' Table 7.3 shows that two in every five (39 per cent) did not see themselves as supporters of any party, and a further 4 per cent were 'don't knows'. There were no real social class differences among those counting themselves as supporters. Over all, as can be seen from the top two rows of the right-hand column in the table, support was equally split between Labour and Conservative parties. If we look at the social class differences in the support for the two main parties in table 7.3, and compare them with voting intentions in

Table 7.3

Percentage in each social class who see themselves as supporters
of political parties

	Social class (M.R.)				
	AB	C1	C2	DE	All
Conservative	45	36	23	16	26
Labour	8	16	32	36	27
Liberal	3	2	5	4	4
Other	0	1	*	0	*
Don't know	6	5	3	4	4
Not a supporter	38	40	37	40	39

*Less than 1 per cent
(Derived from p.30, National Opinion Polls 1972a)

table 7.1, a somewhat similar picture emerges. Some people
from each social class supported each major party, but there is
a clear divide between the middle classes, who supported the
Conservatives, and the working classes, who supported Labour.
It is, however, noticeable that the middle classes supported the
Conservatives somewhat more strongly than the working
classes supported Labour. In the first case 45 per cent of class
AB and 36 per cent of class C1 supported the Conservatives,
compared to the 32 per cent of class C2 and 36 per cent of
class DE who supported Labour. Finally, a slightly higher
percentage of classes C2 and DE (5 and 4 per cent) saw
themselves as Liberal supporters, compared to 3 and 2 per cent
of classes AB and C1. The only class with any supporters of
'other' parties to speak of was C1.

Following the recent local government reorganisations,
local authorities have taken steps to involve the public more in
their affairs. In most areas this has included mounting
exhibitions, holding public meetings, and issuing questionnaires. A National Opinion Poll (National Opinion Polls
1975a) investigated the level of public participation in these.
Only 12 per cent of those surveyed had been involved, as can
be seen in table 7.4. The social class composition of the
participants (the top row of the table) shows that the bulk

Table 7.4

Social class profiles of active participants* and non-participants
in local government (percentages)

Social class (M.R.)

	AB	C1	C2	DE	Percentage of sample
Participants	27	28	27	17	12
Non-participants	12	19	39	30	88
All	14	21	37	28	100

*Attended a public meeting or exhibition, or completed a questionnaire
(Derived from table 3, p. 22, National Opinion Polls 1975a)

were from the middle classes. For example, social class AB
provided 27 per cent of the participants, but only 14 per cent
of those interviewed (see bottom line of the table). In
contrast, social class DE provided 28 per cent of the sample,
but only 17 per cent of the participants.

As has been shown above, interest and involvement in
politics vary along social class lines. Social class differences are
even more dramatically marked among those who become
politicians. A listing of the occupations of Members of the
House of Commons in 1974 (*The Times House of Commons*
1974) revealed the following: 8 per cent had had what could
be termed manual jobs – they were trade union officials, or
mine, rail or other manual workers – another 8 per cent had
had clerical, technical and engineering jobs, and the remaining
84 per cent had been professionals, managers, administrators
or landowners.

A further major area of politics is obviously opinion, and
some aspects of political opinion are dealt with below in the
general section on opinion (pp. 225–33).

Religion

As Matthijssen (1959) has pointed out, 'It is one of the
idiosyncrasies of the English people to regard enquiries into a

person's religion as something unheard of.' This idiosyncrasy may go some way towards explaining the relative dearth of empirical research in this field in Britain. For example it was only in the 1851 census that attendance at religious worship was investigated, and then only on a voluntary basis. This is in marked contrast to the Northern Ireland census, which has always produced a volume of *Religion Tables* (1976), analysed by social class except on this latest occasion. Such extensive and systematic data do not exist for the rest of Britain, even for a particular denomination. Consequently reliance has to be placed on smaller-scale researches. A number of social surveys have shown that the general public are quite willing to be associated with religious, mainly Christian, denominations. For example, a National Opinion Polls study (1970) found less than 1 per cent who refused to answer or 'did not know', and around 3 per cent who claimed to be 'non-religious' — that is atheist or agnostic (see table 7.5). Over all the table shows that almost two-thirds of the sample saw themselves as being Church of England, and there was little variation between the social classes. This is very similar to the results of other studies — for example that by Butler and Stokes (1969), who found that 64 per cent of their sample claimed to belong to the Church of England (footnote to their p. 160). Indeed the only noticeable social class differences in table 7.5 are to be

Table 7.5
Religion by social class (percentages)

	Social class (M.R.)				
	AB	C1	C2	DE	All
Church of England	67	64	67	63	65
Roman Catholic	9	7	10	12	10
Presbyterian Church of Scotland	9	9	6	10	8
Nonconformist	9	11	8	8	8
Atheist/agnostic 16	5	4	3	1	3
Other	4	4	5	6	5
Don't know/refused	—	1	1	—	1

(Derived from p. 23, National Opinion Polls 1970)

found among Roman Catholics, where the percentages show an increase from social classes AB (9 per cent) to DE (12 per cent), and among atheists and agnostics, where the reverse is true (AB, 5 per cent; DE, 1 per cent).

Obviously there is quite a difference between claiming an allegiance to a denomination and actual involvement in its activities. Butler and Stokes (1969), for example, found that of those claiming to belong to the Church of England only 16 per cent attended church at least once a month, while 45 per cent of nonconformists and 73 per cent of Roman Catholics did so. Sex differences were apparent, with 47 per cent of males compared to 32 per cent of females stating that they never attended church. A National Opinion Polls survey in 1972 (1972b) asked the direct question 'Could you tell me how often, if at all, you attend religious services these days?' Most surprisingly, a third of the sample replied that they 'did not know'. This figure makes it difficult to draw any real conclusions, though it seems reasonable to assume that few, if any, who so replied were frequent attenders. Over all table 7.6 shows that almost two out of five of those questioned said that they never attended religious services, the highest percentage (46) being in class C2. At the other extreme – those who attended more than once a week – the percentage for class AB

Table 7.6
Attendance at religious services by social class (percentages)

| | *Social class (M.R.)* | | | | |
	AB	C1	C2	DE	All
More than once a week	6	4	4	3	4
Once a week	13	10	8	12	11
Less than once a fortnight, more than once a month	4	3	1	2	3
Less than once a month, more than once in 3 months	6	7	5	4	5
Less than once in 3 months	14	7	3	5	6
Never	31	36	46	33	38
Don't know	26	33	33	41	33

(Derived from p.19, National Opinion Polls 1972b)

was twice that for class DE, 6 compared to 3 per cent. Similarly social class AB had the highest percentage (23) of those who attended more than once a month, followed by classes C1 and DE, both with 17 per cent, while class C2 had the lowest at 13 per cent

Less direct questioning in the context of enquiries into other areas, notably leisure, has produced what might well be more valuable evidence of religious involvement. Sillitoe's study (1969) of leisure asked questions about club membership, including membership of religious organisations. Note that in table 7.7 social class 4 is junior non-manual and is positioned between skilled manual (3), and semi- and unskilled manual (5). In general there was a decline in membership across the social classes, the only exceptions being males in social class 2, whose percentage was higher than that in class 1, and females of class 2, whose percentage was identical to that in class 1. In the case of both sexes the middle classes (1, 2 and 4) have much higher percentages than do the working classes (3 and 5). Sex differences are quite marked, females being more likely, over all, to be members, though the reverse is true in classes 2 and 5.

In somewhat similar fashion Young and Willmott's study (1973) of the family asked the married working males to report which of a list of leisure activities, one of which was attending church, they had engaged in twelve or more times during the previous year. Table 7.8 shows their replies,

•

Table 7.7
Membership of religious organisations by sex and social class
(percentages)

	Social class (R.G.(S.E.)60/A)					
	1	2	3	4	5	All*
Female members	14	14	9	15	5	11
Male members	9	17	4	8	6	7

*Including those not classified
(Derived from table 19, Sillitoe 1969)

Table 7.8

Church attendance of married men, working full time, by
social class

Social class (R.G.66/AB)

	I and II	III(N.M.)	III(M.)	IV and V	All
Percentage who reported attendance 12 or more times in previous year	22	20	12	7	15

(Derived from table 38, Young and Willmott 1973)

analysed by social class. Very clear social class differences can
be observed here, particularly between the middle classes and
the working classes. At the extremes, males in classes I and II
are three times as likely to attend church as those in classes IV
and V.

A most useful study of social class and religious behaviour
for our purposes is the analysis of the Roman Catholic Pastoral
Research Census data by Moulin (1968). A door-to-door
census was conducted in six parishes, four in Southwark and
one in Westminster (both in London), and one in
Northampton. This identified 15,851 Roman Catholics, of
whom 42 per cent were observed at mass at their parish
churches on the subsequent Sunday. Detailed analysis of the
3,661 working men in the survey by social class is presented in
table 7.9. It is interesting to note that among the Catholics
social classes I and V are over-represented in relation to the
population of the regions within which the parishes are
situated, while classes II and III(N.M.) are under-represented
(compare the bottom two rows of the table). It should also be
noted that the social class distribution of Catholics here is at
some variance with that in table 7.5 above.

There are very apparent social class differences in attendance at mass, which ranges from 61 per cent in social class I
down to 36 per cent in classes IV and V, together with a
noticeable difference between the middle classes, with attendance percentages of around 50 and upwards, and the working
classes, with percentages around 36. Similar though less

Table 7.9

Church attendance and involvement of Roman Catholics* by
social class (percentages)

	I	II	III(N.M.)	III(M.)	IV	V	All†
			Social class (R.G.60/A)				
Attended Mass	61	51	49	37	36	36	42
Married to Catholic women	79	74	72	67	70	77	73
Not confirmed	4	4	5	6	6	6	5
Members of Catholic organisations	16	18	24	17	11	5	16
All education at Catholic schools	49	50	45	58	66	71	62
Social class distribution							
Catholics in the six parishes	7	13	14	28	17	11	100†
Population of the 3 regions	5	16	20	28	18	8	100†

*Working males only
†Including those whose occupation was not stated/classified
(Devised from tables 1, 2, 5 and 7, and pp. 27 and 28, Moulin 1968
[Clergy Review])

marked differences can be observed in relation to confirma-
tion, where a slightly higher percentage of the working classes
(III(M.), IV and V) had not been confirmed, and in membership of Catholic organisations. In the latter case it is social
class III(N.M.) which had the highest percentage of members
(24), and only classes IV and V which had noticeably lower
rates than the other classes. Marriage within the faith shows
some variation, though here (second row of the table) social
classes I and V are very similar, and social class III(M.) has the
lowest percentage. A reversed situation is found in the case of
Catholic school education, the percentages increasing across
the social classes from 49 per cent for social class I to 71 for
class V. While this may well reflect the provision of, and
opportunity to attend, such schools, the survey also indicates
that the majority of Catholics who were converts came from

the higher social classes, and obviously would not have attended Catholic schools. The study shows that all the factors outlined above (rows 2 to 5 in the table) are related to attendance at mass. This supports Moulin's view that, since religious behaviour is a social act, only people integrated — through such factors as education, marriage and organisations — into the religious community will display such behaviour (in this case, attending mass).

There are, of course, some sizeable non-Christian religious minorities in Britain. One of these, Anglo-Jewry, has had its social class structure investigated in a particularly novel way (Prais and Schmool 1975). The study involved collecting information about Jewish burials and then securing social class information, via the Registrar General, from the death certificates of those involved (N = 1,216). By comparing the top and bottom rows of table 7.10 one can see differences between the social class structure of Jews and of the general population. What is very noticeable is that none of the Jewish sample were in social class V, whereas 13 per cent of the general population were. Jews were also under-represented in class IV (14 compared to 22 per cent), equally represented in class III, and over-represented in classes I and II (34 compared to 14, and 4 compared to 2 per cent) in comparison with the

Table 7.10
Jews, synagogue members and others by social class*
(percentages)

Social class (R.G.60)

	I	II	III	IV	V	Unclassified
Jews†	4	34	46	14	0	3
Synagogue members §	4	34	46	14	0	2
Non-members §	3	30	40	22	1	5
General population	2	14	46	22	13	3

*Married women classified by husband's occupation
†Sample aged 15–64
§ Sample aged 15–74
(Derived from tables 1 and 2, Prais and Schmool 1975)

general population. The table also reveals differences between the two-thirds of the sample (second row of table) who were synagogue members and those who were not (third row). Non-members were rather more similar to the general population in social class than were members. In particular, the non-members were more likely to have been in social classes IV (22 compared to 14 per cent) and V (1 compared to 0 per cent) than the members. The authors suggest that this may be due to the greater difficulty encountered by the lower classes in meeting the expenses of membership.

Leisure

Strictly, this section should be concerned with all activities other than work. In fact such a simple distinction is neither easy to apply, nor particularly desirable. Many activities do not fall simply into the category of work or non-work, but span both. Nor does space, our present purpose, or the available research allow for such a comprehensive treatment. Therefore, as will be seen below, a somewhat loose and selective approach has been adopted.

It is important to appreciate at the outset that all leisure activities demand time, and many money, for their pursuit. Since the manual classes spend longer at work and earn less money than the non-manual (see chapter 3), the social classes differ in the amount of time and money they have available for leisure. These factors, while not necessarily determinants of leisure behaviour, should be borne in mind when looking at the social class differences in involvement in the activities dealt with below.

Television

Household ownership of a television set is now almost universal in Britain. Table 22 in Nissel and Lewis 1974 shows that in 1973 some 93 per cent of all households in Britain had one. Research suggests that television-watching is a, if not the, major leisure-time pursuit of the population as a whole (see for example Sillitoe 1969 and Young and Willmott 1973). The

Table 7.11

Average weekly hours of television viewing by social class

	Social class (B.B.C.)		
	A	B	C
February 1973	15.1	16.8	19.3
August 1973	11.2	12.8	14.4

(Derived from table 109, Facts in Focus *1974; source –
unpublished B.B.C. data)*

B.B.C.'s evidence, from their panel research, shows that the amount of time spent viewing varies along social class lines (table 7.11). The higher the social class the less time spent watching television. Note, however, that in the social class classification used by the B.B.C. 'C' represents 70 per cent of the population (see p. 48 above). It is interesting to note from the table that the seasonal differences in viewing (the difference between the two rows) are similar in all the social classes.

Apart from the time spent watching T.V. there are some social class differences in what is watched (see table 7.12). The National Readership Survey 1975 asked three questions (see the footnotes to the table) which concerned the amount of

Table 7.12

Amount of Independent Television viewing* by social class

	Social class (M.R./A)						
	A	B	C1	C2	D	E	All
Heavy*	3	5	12	23	31	33	21
Heavy–medium	9	13	19	25	26	24	22
Medium	19	22	25	24	20	19	22
Light–medium	26	24	20	15	11	8	16
Light	31	26	18	10	7	5	13
Never†	11	9	6	4	5	12	6

*Sample divided into five approximately equal groups based on three factors: (*a*) number of days in week, (*b*) number of hours in day they watched any T.V., (*c*) hours out of each 10 of viewing they watched I.T.V.
†Included: (*a*) those without I.T.V. reception, (*b*) those who never watched any T.V., (*c*) those who never watched I.T.V.
(Derived from table 101, National Readership Survey 1975 *1976)*

viewing and the proportion of I.T.V. watched as opposed to
B.B.C. The table reveals quite marked social class differences,
especially at the extremes. While only 3 per cent of social class
A and 5 per cent of class B are 'heavy' I.T.V. viewers, and 31
and 26 per cent of them are 'light', the comparable figures for
classes D and E are 31 and 33 per cent 'heavy', and 7 and 5 per
cent 'light'. A somewhat similar percentage of each social class,
around 20 per cent, are to be found in the 'medium' I.T.V.
viewing group.

Reading

The most comprehensively surveyed area is that of newspapers
and periodicals. The Joint Industry Committee produces
regular National Readership Surveys which are widely used by
advertising and commercial concerns. This research is extensive
and continuous, involving some 30,000 interviews in a full
year. Table 7.13, based on research during 1975 (N = 30,570),
gives data on readership by social class in two separate but
related ways. The unbracketed figures in the table are the
percentages of respondents in each social class who claimed to
have read or looked at a copy of the publications listed, in a
period up to the interview corresponding to the length of time
between publications: for example, in the case of weeklies, in
the previous seven days. The figures in brackets give the social
class composition (profile) of all the readers of each publication. Hence the figures in the left hand column of the top row
of the table reveal that 6 per cent of social class A claimed to
have read the Daily Mirror and that of all the readers of that
paper less than 0.5 per cent came from social class A. The rest
of the table can be read in the same way. As can be seen from
the bottom row of each section of the table (in italics), the
readership of each kind of publication other than women's
weeklies declines across the social classes. While 84 per cent of
class A read daily newspapers, only 60 per cent of class E did.
It should be noted that class E includes the very poorest paid
sections of society, and state pensioners, so that here the
inability to pay for publications may be a major factor limiting

Table 7.13

The percentage of each social class claiming readership of
newspapers and selected periodicals, and the latter's social
class readership profiles* 1975

Social class (M.R./A)

	A	B	C1	C2	D	E	All†
Daily newspapers							
Daily Mirror	6(§)	11(4)	24(19)	39(42)	39(28)	22(7)	30
The Sun	5(§)	10(4)	22(18)	37(42)	38(29)	18(6)	29
Daily Express	23(3)	22(12)	24(29)	18(31)	16(18)	17(8)	19
Daily Mail	15(3)	16(14)	16(32)	10(28)	9(16)	9(7)	12
Daily Telegraph	42(11)	28(34)	12(34)	4(14)	2(5)	3(3)	9
Daily Record¶	1(§)	2(4)	3(16)	6(43)	6(28)	4(9)	5
The Times	20(18)	8(33)	3(30)	1(11)	1(6)	§(2)	3
The Guardian	7(7)	18(32)	4(39)	1(14)	1(6)	§(2)	2
Financial Times	11(15)	6(34)	2(31)	1(12)	1(7)	§(1)	2
Any daily paper	*84(3)*	*77(11)*	*75(23)*	*79(34)*	*77(22)*	*60(7)*	*75*
Sunday newspapers							
News of the World	6(§)	12(4)	24(17)	42(40)	47(30)	31(9)	34
Sunday Mirror	9(1)	14(5)	27(21)	38(42)	35(26)	18(6)	30
Sunday People	5(§)	12(4)	23(19)	35(40)	37(28)	24(8)	29
Sunday Express	41(4)	39(18)	33(34)	18(25)	13(13)	14(6)	23
Sunday Post	4(1)	8(7)	9(20)	12(34)	13(26)	14(12)	11
Sunday Times	42(10)	28(31)	14(35)	5(17)	2(5)	2(2)	9
Observer	22(9)	16(29)	9(36)	3(16)	2(8)	1(2)	6
Sunday Mail	1(1)	2(5)	4(18)	7(42)	6(26)	5(8)	5
Sunday Telegraph	24(11)	15(31)	8(34)	3(16)	1(5)	2(3)	5
Any Sunday paper	*87(2)*	*84(10)*	*83(23)*	*87(34)*	*84(22)*	*72(8)*	*84*
General weeklies							
T.V. Times	22(2)	24(11)	25(26)	23(32)	23(21)	20(8)	23
Radio Times	39(4)	36(16)	28(29)	19(27)	17(17)	17(7)	23
Reveille	1(§)	3(4)	5(17)	8(40)	8(29)	5(8)	6
New Musical Express	3(2)	3(4)	3(26)	3(36)	3(22)	1(3)	3
Punch	9(9)	6(25)	3(33)	2(21)	1(10)	§(2)	2
The Economist	5(10)	4(38)	2(33)	§(14)	§(5)	§(1)	1
Investor's Chronicle	3(18)	1(32)	1(32)	§(11)	§(5)	§(2)	§
Any general weekly	*61(3)*	*57(12)*	*52(25)*	*49(32)*	*47(21)*	*40(8)*	*50*

(continued overleaf)

Table 7.13 (*continued*)

Social class (M.R./A)

	A	B	C1	C2	D	E	All†
Women's weeklies							
Woman	15(2)	17(10)	20(28)	16(32)	15(19)	14(8)	17
Woman's Realm	5(1)	9(10)	11(27)	10(33)	8(19)	9(9)	10
Jackie	3(2)	3(8)	3(20)	4(40)	4(26)	2(4)	4
Mirabelle	§(1)	§(6)	1(16)	2(36)	2(38)	§(4)	1
Any women's weekly	27(2)	33(9)	41(26)	37(32)	35(32)	40(10)	37
General monthlies							
Reader's Digest	28(3)	28(15)	24(29)	19(32)	14(16)	10(5)	19
Do It Yourself	4(2)	6(13)	5(28)	5(36)	4(18)	2(3)	4
Penthouse	3(2)	4(11)	4(24)	5(41)	4(20)	1(2)	4
Mayfair	§(§)	5(12)	4(24)	5(43)	3(18)	1(2)	4
Football Monthly	§(§)	1(4)	1(16)	2(43)	2(32)	1(4)	2
The Director	5(23)	2(40)	1(27)	§(7)	§(3)	0(0)	1
Film Review	1(1)	2(8)	2(26)	2(37)	2(23)	1(5)	2
Any general monthly	54(3)	51(15)	43(28)	37(33)	28(17)	16(4)	36

*Readership profiles are the figures in brackets, which should be read across the table, each row adding up to 100 (approximately)
†Columns add up to more than 100 because many respondents read more than one
§ Less than 0.5 per cent
¶ Scottish newspaper, asked about only in Scotland

Estimated population over 15 years of age (percentages)

A	B	C1	C2	D	E	All
2.3	10.4	23.5	32.5	21.8	9.5	100

(Derived from: (dailies and Sundays) tables 5 and 69, (general and women's weeklies) tables 9 and 71, (general monthlies) tables 13 and 73, National Readership Survey 1975 1976)

readership. Certainly the figures for classes A to D display less marked differences. Sunday paper readership has very similar appeal for all classes, the 87 per cent of class A being matched by that of class C2 — with B, C1 and D only marginally lower. It is interesting that women's weeklies are read by 40 per cent of social class E, a figure only matched by class C1. This may reflect the pensioners within the former class, of whom a majority are female.

Perhaps surprisingly, the table reveals not only the social class differences in readership which might have been expected, but a considerable breadth of readership in each social class. For example, a small minority (less than 1 per cent) of the working classes (C2, D and E) read *The Financial Times*, *Investor's Chronicle* and *The Director*. Overall, and with respect to newspapers in particular, the social classes display quite different choices. Around 40 per cent of classes C2 and D read the *Daily Mirror*, and they form 70 per cent of its readers, while 42 per cent of class A, 28 per cent of class B and 12 per cent of C1 read *The Daily Telegraph* and form together 79 per cent of its readers. Similar percentages of each of the social classes read some publications, for example the *Daily Express*, *T.V. Times*, *Woman* and *Reader's Digest*. Note that the bottom row of the table provides as a base line for comparison the social class distribution of the national population.

Some general observations can also be made. Social class differences between the readerships of the *T.V. Times* and *Radio Times* probably reflect differences in viewing (see the section above on television, pp. 210–12). Social class differences in women's weeklies are less marked than in other types of publication. While the middle classes provide some three-quarters of the readers of so-called 'quality' newspapers (the *Guardian*, *The Daily Telegraph* and *The Times*), readership of such papers is only really widespread in social class A. Adding together the percentage of readers of each 'quality' paper in the middle classes (which assumes that no individual read more than one of the three) reveals that 69 per cent of social class A, 54 per cent of class B, and 19 per cent of class C1 read 'quality' newspapers.

Book readership has not been similarly researched, but such evidence as exists suggests that book reading also declines across the social classes. For example Young and Willmott (1973) (and see pp. 207 and 224) found that it was only in book reading and gardening that marked social class differences were to be found in the leisure activities of their sample.

Of the married working men in their sample (N = 588) 67 per cent of social classes (R.G.) I and II, 63 per cent of III(N.), 33 per cent of III(M.) and 28 per cent of classes IV and V reported reading a book twelve or more times in the year previous to the interview. A similar and clear middle class bias is reported by Mann (1971) in his analysis of non-student users of a central lending library and of bookshop customers.

Drinking

A government survey (Bradley and Fenwick 1974) looked at the consumption of, and attitudes to, alcoholic drink. Particularly interesting here are the figures showing where such consumption took place. Table 7.14 shows that drinking at home declines across the social classes, from some three-quarters of social class I to a quarter of social class V. While similar percentages of all social classes visit public houses to drink, consumption in clubs is more frequent among the working classes, and in restaurants and hotels among the middle classes — particularly class I. The same source reveals differences between the classes in the type of drinks consumed, but not in the percentage (around 92) who had drunk alcohol at some time or other. Unfortunately for our purposes, differences in the amounts consumed, and in frequency of drinking, were not investigated.

Table 7.14
Percentage in each social class who are frequent visitors to licensed premises* and/or frequent drinkers at home

			Social class (R.G.70/B)			
	I	II	III(N.)	III(M.) and IV	V	All
Public house	40	44	46	47	47	46
Club	22	25	23	28	33	27
Restaurant	39	28	15	11	8	16
Hotel	19	13	8	6	5	8
Home	77	58	44	45	25	49

*Once a month or more often
(Derived from table 10, Bradley and Fenwick 1974)

Table 7.15

Persons over the age of 15 years who smoked (age-standardised percentages)*

	Social class (R.G.(S.E.)70)						
	1	**2**	**3**	**4**	**5**	**6**	**All**
Male							
Cigarette smokers	32	43	46	57	57	66	52
All tobacco smokers	48	58	57	66	65	73	62
Female							
Cigarette smokers	29	36	39	45	45	47	42

*See note on p. 112
(Derived from table 5.53(b), General Household Survey 1972 *1975)*

Smoking

Although smoking is not simply a leisure activity, smoking and drinking are often related in the public eye. *The General Household Survey 1972* (1975) reviewed smoking by social class, and the results are given in table 7.15. The table shows that cigarette smoking for both sexes increases steadily across the social classes from 1 to 6. In the case of males, 32 per cent of class 1 smoked cigarettes, compared to 66 per cent of class 6. Male cigar and pipe smokers can be identified by subtracting the top from the second row. This shows a decline in the incidence from social class 1, with 16 per cent, to class 6, where the percentage is 7. If we look at all male tobacco smokers together, it can be seen that half (48 per cent) of social class 1 smoked compared to nearly three quarters (73 per cent) of class 6. The male and female figures clearly follow the same pattern, but are of a different magnitude. In general, female middle class (1 to 3) cigarette smokers are more similar to their male equivalents than are working class women smokers.

Cinema and theatre

The National Readership Survey asked its sample about cinema-going. As will be seen in table 7.16, regular, that is

Table 7.16

Frequency of cinema attendance by social class (percentages)

	Social class (M.R./A)						
	A	B	C1	C2	D	E	All
Once a week or more	2	2	2	2	3	1	2
More than once a month	13	12	12	10	8	3	9
Less than once a month	50	47	39	37	27	10	34
Never	35	40	47	51	62	86	54

(Derived from table 101, National Readership Survey 1975 *1976)*

weekly or more frequent, attendance was very rare — only 2 per cent over all. Only social class D had a higher rate, and class E a lower rate, than the overall one. Social class differences are more apparent in the rest of the table, the percentage who never attended increasing across the social classes from just over a third (35 per cent) of class A to more than four-fifths (86 per cent) of class E.

A survey of the audiences at a provincial theatre over a six-week period in 1965 revealed that theatre attendance was a predominantly middle class activity (Mann 1967). Table 7.17 shows the social class of some 9,601 persons who completed the questionnaire. No indication is given of what percentage this was of the actual audiences. A comparison of the social class compositions of the audiences (the top two rows of the table) with that of the general population (bottom row)

Table 7.17

Social class of members of audience at Sheffield Playhouse over a six-week period (percentages)

	Social class (M.R./A)						
	A	B	C1	C2	D	E	All
Young people's play	21	29	33	14	3	—	100
General play	18	32	39	9	2	—	100
National distribution of classes	3	9	17	38	28	5	100

(Derived from table 6, Mann 1967)

Table 7.18

Social class composition of performing arts* audiences†
(percentages)

Social class (U.S.A.)

	Professional	Managerial	Clerical sales	Blue collar
Male audience†	61	19	16	5
Male population	8	11	13	69
Female audience†	55	5	37	3
Female population	10	4	37	48

*London performances: 2 National Theatre, 1 ballet, 3 orchestra, 1 opera
†Classified persons only, excluding students and housewives
(Derived from table IV-2, Baumol and Bowen 1966)

reveals a contrast. In the middle classes — A, B and C1 — the audience percentage is far larger than that of the population. For example, social class A provided 21 per cent of the audience for the young people's play, but formed only 3 per cent of the population as a whole. The opposite was true of the working classes: social class D provided only 3 per cent of the audience, but formed 28 per cent of the population, while class E was unrepresented in the audiences.

A survey of the London audiences at drama, ballet and orchestra performances produced a similar picture. Table 7.18 is based on 2,295 responses — 50.3 per cent of the audiences involved. This table can be read in the same way as table 7.17. Going to watch the performing arts is an almost exclusively middle class, particularly professional class, activity. As can be seen in the table, only 5 per cent of the males and 3 per cent of the females in such audiences were from the working class, who represented some 69 and 48 per cent respectively of the adult population as a whole.

Clubs and organisations

Most of the literature in this area suggests that joining clubs and organisations is more of a middle class trait than a working class one. A large national survey (N = 5,275) found that club

Table 7.19

Membership of any kind of club by sex and social class
(percentages)

	Social class (R.G.(S.E.)60/A)					
	1	2	3	4	5	All*
Club members						
Male	69	72	52	56	46	55
Female	50	45	29	36	23	33
Average clubs per person						
Male	1.0	1.2	0.7	0.9	0.7	0.8
Female	0.9	0.7	0.3	0.5	0.4	0.4

*Including unclassified
(Derived from table 19, Sillitoe 1969)

membership declined across the social classes (Sillitoe 1969).
Table 7.19 shows that this was true of both males and females,
and that it applied both to the percentage of each social class
who were club members (top two rows) and to the average
number of clubs per person (bottom two rows). It should be
noted that in the social class classification used in table 7.19
class 4 is junior non-manual, and class 3 is skilled manual. The
predominance of male club members was found to occur in all
types of clubs except 'religious', where females predominated
(see section above on religion, pp. 203—10).

A rather similar picture emerges from a study of youth club
attenders (Bone and Ross 1972). The top row of table 7.20
shows that 85 per cent of social class I were attached to a club
as opposed to 56 per cent of class V. The table also displays a
big difference between length of schooling and club attach-
ment: in each social class the percentage attached is around 20
points higher (e.g. 75 compared with 55 per cent in class II)
for those who stayed on beyond the minimum school-leaving
age. Similar differences can be seen between the sexes (bottom
two rows), the boys' percentages being in the 60s and the girls
in the 40s.

Social class differences in joining organisations can be seen
at even earlier ages. A survey of children in eight primary

Table 7.20

Percentage of 14- to 20-year-olds attached to youth clubs by social class

	Social class (R.G.60/A)					
	I	III	III(N.M.)	III(M.)	IV	V
Boys and girls						
All attached	85	73	71	64	55	56
Attached and left/leaving school at 15	—	55	50	52	44	50
Attached and left/leaving school at over 15	86	75	78	74	67	67
Boys attached						
Left/leaving at 15	—	61	61	62	53	62
Girls attached						
Left/leaving at 15	—	46	43	43	36	40

(Derived from table 2.8, Bone and Ross 1972)

schools (N = 1,791) found differences in membership of the Cubs and Brownies (Dearnaley and Fletcher 1968). The schools were selected as representative of the variety of environments found in Stockport, which is south of Manchester. The study revealed that almost half (49 per cent) of children from social class I homes were members compared to about one in seven (15 per cent) from class V (table 7.21).

Table 7.21

Percentage of children aged 7—11 years in each social class who were members of the Cubs or Brownies

	Social class (R.G.60)					
	I	II	III	IV	V	All
Cubs and Brownies	49	41	37	22	15	36
Non-members	51	59	63	78	85	64

(Derived from table 1, Dearnaley and Fletcher 1968)

Holidays

A survey commissioned by the British Travel Association surveyed the holidays of some 4,000 representative people. As

Table 7.22
Social class profiles of various groups of holiday makers, 1974
(percentages)

	Social class (M.R.)				
	AB	**C1**	**C2**	**DE**	**All**
No holidays	8	17	35	40	
*Great Britain**					
Main holidays	16	22	41	22	Each
Additional	26	26	33	15	row
Abroad†					= 100
Main holidays	26	28	29	17	
Additional	35	30	25	10	
All adults	14	21	37	28	

*4 or more nights
†1 or more nights
(Derived from table 5, The British on Holiday 1974˗1975)

can be seen in table 7.22, 8 per cent of non-holiday-makers were from social class AB, and the percentage increases across the social classes to 40 per cent from class DE. Note that since these figures are social class profiles of the groups involved they do not indicate that 40 per cent of social class DE did not go on holiday in 1974, but that 40 per cent of those who did not go on holiday were from class DE.

Briefly, the rest of the rows in the table show social class differences in type and place of holidays. The bottom row gives the population profile for comparison purposes — if there were no social class differences, then each of the other rows would be similar. The only one which approximates to it is entitled 'Great Britain, Main holidays'.

Sport
Involvement in or with sport — as in the case of politics — can be identified at several levels. The most general of these is that of interest. This was surveyed by a National Opinion Poll in 1971. This asked the sample 'Could you tell me which, if any,

Table 7.23

Percentages of males in each social class claiming interest in
various sports

Social class (M.R.)

	AB	C1	C2	DE	All
Football	43	49	57	56	53
Athletics	41	40	36	31	36
Cricket	30	32	24	23	27
Boxing	20	23	29	30	26
Horse racing	14	18	22	30	22
Swimming	18	18	16	25	19
Golf	27	19	13	13	16
Rugby Union	24	19	12	11	15
Rugby League	12	14	15	13	13
Greyhound racing	4	4	5	10	6
None/don't know	19	19	17	27	20

(Derived from p. 16, National Opinion Polls 1971)

of these sports you are interested in at all. I mean sports which
you make a point of following whether you go to watch them
or not.' Table 7.23 reveals that sports attract the interest of
the social classes differentially — for example, compare golf
and greyhound racing. It is worth noting too that lack of
interest in any of the sports is only markedly different in social
class DE where 27 per cent of the sample said they were
uninterested, compared with 17 per cent for C1 and 19 per
cent for the other two classes.

A second level of involvement with sport is being a
spectator. Sillitoe (1969) investigated this, and table 7.24
shows the percentage of each social class and sex who attended
selected sports as a spectator at least once a month for at least
part of the year previous to the interview. Being a spectator is
clearly a minority activity, particularly on the part of women.
Thus, while over a quarter of the men went to the most
popular male spectator sport, soccer, only 4 per cent of
women went to the most popular female sports. In the male
part of the table there are no substantial social class
differences, other than at the extremes in the case of rugby.

Table 7.24

Percentage of each social class who were spectators* at various sports

Social class (R.G.(S.E.)60/A)

Men	1	2	3	4	5	All
Soccer	25	31	26	28	26	27
Cricket	12	13	14	21	10	14
Rugby	10	8	5	7	4	6
Tennis	2	9	4	5	1	5
Boxing and wrestling	2	5	2	2	4	4
Women						
Soccer	6	3	4	5	3	4
Cricket	8	7	4	4	4	4
Swimming	6	6	5	4	2	4
Tennis	2	5	3	1	3	3
Boxing and wrestling	3	1	2	3	3	2

*At least once a month for part of previous year
(*Derived from tables A42 and A43, Sillitoe 1969*)

Here 10 per cent of class 1 compared to 4 per cent of class 5 were spectators. Among females, however, the percentage of spectators of football, cricket, and swimming clearly declines across the social classes, whereas for tennis, boxing and wrestling this is not the case.

The last level of involvement in sport is actual participation. Young and Willmott asked their sample of married working men which of a list of twelve sports they had actually played or taken part in in the twelve months previous to the interview. Table 7.25 shows the nine most popular sports and the percentage in each social class who had been active in them. Over all, participation in sport is clearly related to social class. The higher the social class the higher the percentage active in each sport and the higher the average number of sports per person. The only noticeable exception is soccer, where social class III(M.) has the highest percentage (8), and classes IV and V have figures very similar to those of the middle classes.

Tables 7.25

Activity* in sport by social class, married males working full
time in London (percentages)

Social class (R.G.66/AB)

	I and II	III(N.M.)	III(M.)	IV and V	All
Swimming	34	25	20	8	22
Fishing	9	3	9	5	8
Soccer	6	6	8	5	7
Golf	9	11	4	2	6
Table tennis	10	10	4	2	6
Cricket	8	0	6	4	5
Tennis	8	7	2	0	4
Badminton or squash	7	6	2	0	4
Sailing	6	0	1	0	2
Average number of sports	1.1	0.8	0.6	0.3	0.7

*At least 12 times in previous year
(Derived from table 37, Young and Willmott 1973)

Opinion

The investigation of the public's opinion on various matters
has been a developing enterprise in Britain since the Second
World War. Even the Government involved itself over the
Common Market issue. Quite apart from academic research in
this field, a number of commercial social research organisations attempt to maintain a continuous picture of various areas
of public opinion, particularly political, while some also under-
take specific research. The possible range of research that
could be reported in this section, then, is very large. The small
selection here has been made with a view to topicality and
relevance. It should be noted that the term 'opinion' has been
used in preference to 'attitude' because of the type of research
reported here. The data have been produced from responses to
quite direct questions and are unlikely therefore to illuminate
or explain, in any depth, the areas of attitudes, beliefs and
understanding.

As has already been pointed out, political opinion is very
widely, and continuously, surveyed in Britain. For example,

National Opinion Polls ask a series of standard political questions in their regular surveys, of which there were nine
between May and December in 1975. Table 7.26 shows the
answers given to these in the last survey in 1975, which
involved some 3,827 electors in 240 parliamentary constit-
uencies in Great Britain, analysed by social class. (The actual
questions for the first three sections of the table are given in
a footnote.) The 'voting intention' section of the table has
been included mainly to allow for comparison with table 7.1
above, which records voting intentions just before the October
1974 general election. Together the tables show quite marked
changes of intention. Over all there is a swing to the Conservatives, from 37 to 45 per cent, and to the Nationalists, from 2
to 4 per cent, and a swing away from Labour, from 43 to 38
per cent, and from the Liberals, from 18 to 12 per cent. The
social classes displaying the largest changes in intention are C1
and C2. If we look at the two main parties only, we see that
46 per cent of social class C1 were for the Conservatives and
28 per cent for Labour in 1974, compared with 61 and 22 per
cent respectively in 1975.

The table also reveals that the majority of those interviewed
(63 per cent) were dissatisfied with the way in which the
Government was running the country. In social class AB this
amounted to almost four in every five (79 per cent), and the
percentages decrease across the social classes to just over half
of class DE. This probably reflects the differences in social
class support for the Labour Party, who were in Government
(see table 7.1). Similarly, such differences in party support
may partly explain the social class differences in satisfaction
with the Prime Minister and Leader of the Opposition. Over all
there was 'dissatisfaction' with Mr Wilson (51 per cent), but
this declined from 72 per cent of class AB through the classes
to 39 per cent of class DE. And while 43 per cent over all
expressed satisfaction with Mrs Thatcher, this reflects a range
which fell from 50 per cent of social class AB to only 35 per
cent of class DE. However, opinion about Mrs Thatcher was
less definite than about Mr Wilson. In her case almost a quarter
(24 per cent) had no answer, or no opinion, compared with

Table 7.26

Level of satisfaction with the Government, Mr Wilson and
Mrs Thatcher,* and voting intention by social class 1975
(percentages)

| | *Social class (M.R.)* | | | | |
	AB	C1	C2	DE	All
The Government					
Satisfied	14	21	28	31	25
Dissatisfied	79	70	60	51	63
Don't know/ no answer	7	9	12	18	12
Mr Wilson					
Satisfied	22	32	46	49	40
Dissatisfied	72	60	45	39	51
Don't know/ no answer	7	8	9	12	9
Mrs Thatcher					
Satisfied	50	49	41	35	43
Dissatisfied	30	31	35	35	33
Don't know/ no answer	20	20	24	30	24
Voting intention†					
Conservative	69	61	38	30	45
Labour	15	22	45	55	38
Liberal	14	14	11	9	12
Nationalist	2	3	5	4	4
Other	—	1	1	1	1

*Answers to questions 'Are you satisfied or dissatisfied with (*a*) the way
the Government is running the country? (*b*) Mr Wilson as Prime
Minister? (*c*) the way Mrs Thatcher is doing her job as Leader of the
Opposition?'
†These are percentages of those giving a voting intention (6 per cent
said they would not vote, and 5 per cent refused to answer or were
undecided)
(Derived from tables 1 and 3, National Opinion Polls 1976)

only 9 per cent in the case of Mr Wilson. It should be noted
that the social classes differed in their use of this reply category, the percentage of 'don't knows' and 'no answer' increasing in each case quite markedly across the social classes from
AB to DE. This pattern can also be observed in the tables that

follow. It suggests that in comparison with the middle classes the working classes are less ready to give definite answers to questions of opinion, at least in the research situations and on the topics involved here.

Two areas which have been the centre of considerable debate in political and general arenas over the last decade are trade unions and company profits. Opinion on these has been separately surveyed by National Opinion Polls (1969a and 1970). A social class analysis of opinion about the type of influence and the amount of power of the trade unions can be seen in table 7.27. While social class differences can be observed in the table, they are not as great as might have been expected, given the differential involvement and interest of the social classes in trade unions. For example, the majority overall opinion was that the unions were a bad influence, though the middle class majority was more substantial — at about two-thirds — than the working class one of just over half. In a parallel way the overall majority of respondents thought the unions had too much power, but here the social classes were somewhat wider apart, at around three-quarters

Table 7.27

Percentage of each social class holding certain opinions* about trade unions

	Social class (M.R.)				
	AB	C1	C2	DE	All
Good influence	21	21	30	30	27
Bad influence	67	66	54	51	57
Don't know	12	13	16	19	16
Too much power	76	75	61	53	63
Too little power	6	4	7	9	7
About right	12	14	21	25	19
Don't know	6	7	11	13	11

*Answers to questions (a) 'On the whole would you say the unions have a good or bad influence on Britain?' (b) 'Do you think the unions have too much power, too little power or about the right amount of power?' (Derived from pp. 5 and 6, National Opinion Polls 1969a)

Table 7.28

Opinion regarding companies' profits by social class
(percentages*)

| | Social class (M.R.) | | | | |
	AB	C1	C2	DE	All†
Too much profit	9	27	38	39	29
Reasonable profit	52	46	44	40	41
Not enough profit	25	12	4	8	8
Don't know	14	15	14	13	22

*Social class percentages are of people interviewed who were in full-time employment only
†'All' refers to all who were interviewed
(Derived from p. 2, National Opinion Polls 1970)

for the middle, and between 50 and 60 per cent for the working classes.

Social class differences of opinion differed more in relation to company profits, as can be seen in table 7.28. In this case while the largest proportion of the respondents in each social class thought that profits were reasonable (this is only just true of DE) there was a marked divergence among the remainder as to whether too much or not enough profit was being made. The middle classes, AB and C1, were much more likely to say 'not enough' rather than 'too much' (e.g. 25 compared to 9 per cent of class AB), while the opposite was true of the working classes (e.g. 8 compared to 39 per cent of class DE).

Gallup Polls regularly ask samples of the public this question: 'There used to be a lot of talk in politics about the class struggle. Do you think there is a class struggle in this country?' As can be seen in table 7.29, the majority (60 per cent) said that they thought there was a class struggle, and this proportion varied little between the social classes. At the same time it can be seen that a slightly higher percentage of the middle class (ABC1) than of class DE did not think that there was a class struggle (32 per cent compared to 25 per cent), while in DE a larger percentage claimed not to know.

A further area in which opinions tend to run high is education — particularly where type of secondary schools is

Table 7.29

Percentage of each social class who thought a class struggle
existed in Britain

	Social class (M.R./B)			
	ABC1	C2	DE	All
Is a class struggle	60	63	59	60
Is not	32	29	25	29
Don't know	8	9	16	11

(Derived from table 4, Gallup Polls 1975a)

concerned. The existence of public schools and the introduction of comprehensive schools have been, and are, widely
debated. As might be anticipated, the social classes hold varying views on this topic (see table 7.30). The overriding middle
class approval of public schools is not shared by the working
classes, though their abolition was only agreed to by one in
three of social class C1 and 27 per cent of DE. Over all,
approval is less marked for comprehensive schools (40 per
cent) than for public schools (55 per cent). In the case of
comprehensives, however, approval was higher in the working
classes, while disapproval was the majority view (56 per cent)

Table 7.30

Opinion concerning public and comprehensive schools, by
social class (percentages)

	Social class (M.R./B.)			
	ABC1	C2	DE	All
Public schools				
Approve	70	48	46	55
Should be abolished	19	33	27	26
Don't know	11	19	28	19
Comprehensive schools				
Approve	32	48	41	40
Disapprove	56	33	25	39
Don't know	12	19	34	21

*(Derived from table 6, Gallup Polls 1973, and table 3, Gallup Polls
1975b)*

Table 7.31

Percentage of each social class agreeing* (or disagreeing†) with statements concerning controversial topics

	Social class (M.R.)				
	AB	C1	C2	DE	All
1 The death penalty should be reintroduced for all murders	49(41)	59(31)	67(23)	71(18)	64(26)
2 Abortion should be made legally available for all who want it	50(38)	51(38)	55(30)	48(35)	52(34)
3 Maintaining law and order is one of Britain's biggest problems	71(23)	76(20)	79(12)	82(10)	77(14)
4 Divorce should be made easier	25(56)	35(52)	36(48)	40(41)	35(48)
5 Homosexual couples should be able to live together openly	45(28)	49(25)	41(31)	31(37)	40(31)
6 All further immigration to Britain should be stopped	50(36)	62(23)	78(12)	77(14)	70(18)
7 Birth control should be provided free for all who ask for it	63(28)	70(21)	75(16)	69(18)	70(20)
8 Censorship laws should be made stricter	37(45)	44(40)	53(33)	55(28)	48(34)
9 Students who take part in political demonstrations should have their grants stopped	42(46)	48(40)	50(33)	58(27)	51(35)
10 Homosexuals should be allowed to marry each other	20(50)	12(50)	15(53)	15(54)	16(52)
11 There are certain occupations that homosexuals should never be allowed to have like being teachers or doctors	43(39)	48(31)	50(38)	48(28)	48(30)

Respondents replied to each statement in one of the following categories: 1 Agree very strongly, 2 Agree strongly, 3 Agree, 4 Neither agree nor disagree, 5 Disagree, 6 Disagree strongly, 7 Disagree very strongly, 8 Don't know
*Unbracketed figures are those in categories 1, 2 and 3
†Bracketed figures are those in categories 5, 6 and 7
(Devised from N.O.P. data from study reported in National Opinion Polls 1975b)

of the middle class. About a third of class DE did not know whether they approved or disapproved of comprehensive schools.

Finally, a view of social class differences in a more general area of public opinion. A recent inquiry by National Opinion Polls (1975b), ostensibly into homosexuality, was in fact concerned with a range of controversial topics, chosen to gain an overall indication of the 'liberalism' of the sample. Respondents were asked to respond to the statements in one of seven categories (details of which can be seen in table 7.31). The unbracketed figures in the table give the percentages who agreed — in varying degrees — with the statement, and the ones in brackets those who disagreed. The percentages who neither agreed nor disagreed, or who did not reply, can be worked out by adding the unbracketed and bracketed figures together and subtracting from 100. For example, in the case of the first statement, 49 per cent of class AB agreed, and 41 per cent disagreed, so 10 per cent did neither.

There are a number of ways in which the data in table 7.31 could be viewed. If one limits oneself to the approval rates, one can say that on abortion and homosexuality (items 2, 5, 10 and 11) there is little social class variation in opinion. The same is true of free birth control. While it is the majority opinion of all the social classes (77 per cent) that maintaining law and order is one of the country's biggest problems, the percentage rises from 71 per cent in class AB to 82 per cent in class DE. More marked differences can be seen in relation to the remaining topics. The working classes (C2 and DE) have higher percentages who agreed that divorce should be made easier, immigration laws made stricter and students punished for taking part in political demonstrations. The explanation of these differences is complex. In some cases, for example that of immigration, it could be argued that this merely represents reaction to the different experiences of the social classes, rather than differing ways of thinking. It is the working classes who are most likely to live in areas with immigrants and to compete with them for jobs and homes and so on, and perhaps this affects opinion. However, in the face of lack of proper evidence, this must remain speculative. In any case, as is apparent from the table and discussion above, there is no evidence here of consistent social class differences in overall 'liberalism'.

8

Afterword

This book has presented what amounts to a catalogue of social class differences in Britain. Having finished it, the reader is in a position to echo the words of Berger (1963), quoted in chapter 2, 'Different classes in our society . . . live in different styles qualitatively', and to give evidence to support that view. While the actual differences between the separate classes have varied in magnitude, an abiding impression must be of the very substantial extent of the differences between the middle (non-manual) and the working (manual) classes, and of the stark differences between the extremes — the professional and the unskilled manual classes. It is now relatively simple to compile a list of contrasting differences. We can state that middle class people, in comparison with the working classes, enjoy better health; live longer; live in superior homes, with more amenities; have more money to spend; work shorter hours; receive different and longer education, and are educationally more successful; marry later in life; rear fewer children; attend church more frequently; belong to clubs more often; have different tastes in the mass media and the arts; are politically more involved — to mention only a few examples. Not only could a reader add to this list, but he could rewrite it from the working-class perspective. Further, he has some knowledge both of the size of such differences and of the basis on which the evidence rests.

In the face of the data contained in this book it would be difficult to deny that social class, in spite of the considerations discussed in chapter 2, is a meaningful and useful concept. If it were only a spurious and artificial concept of social scientists it is difficult to imagine that its research application would so consistently turn up differences. Indeed it is hard to think of any other variable which would perform in the same way. Perhaps, as was suggested in chapter 2, only other forms of social stratification or categorisation — namely sex and age — would do so. Actually, as was seen, these categories too are intimately related to social class. In chapter 3 there was a discussion of how the sexual composition of the social classes contributed to and maintained class differences in income. In chapter 4 it was necessary to standardise the classes for age before relating them to measures of health.

Many if not all social class differences can be seen to stem from basic economic inequalities, and their effects, both long- and short-term, on the people involved. In spite of changes in our society, the realities of life for people in different social classes have remained pretty constant. As Field (1973) has written, 'Despite the growth in national wealth the age-old inequalities remain. The position of the poor has improved. But so, too, has that of the rich.' As somebody who read an early draft of this book remarked, 'What does it tell us other than that there are some very big economic differences in our society?' However tempting such a conclusion may be, it is almost certainly only partially true. Not only are some social class differences difficult to explain directly, if at all, in such terms — for example, differences in opinion, child-rearing customs and religious observance — but such research as has been done suggests that increased wealth does not, at least initially, make working class people into middle class people (see Goldthorpe, Lockwood, Bechhofer and Platt 1969). Again, the relative increase in the wealth (in real terms) of many working class people, together with increased opportunities for higher education, have not significantly affected the proportion of working class university students. This proportion has remained stubbornly constant at around 25 per cent since the 1930s. However, as we have seen, there is a degree of social mobility in our society, and in the long term people who have been mobile, or whose economic situation has changed, do merge successfully into their new milieu (or perhaps, at least, their children do).

It seems reasonable to conclude, then, by accepting that a root cause of social class differences is economic differentiation. At the same time, it is necessary to recognise that the economic structure of our society has not changed, and is unlikely to change, dramatically. Even if it were to change, the concept of social class would still have considerable utility. In societies with more economic equality than ours — for example, the Soviet Union and China — social differences similar to ours have far from disappeared.

All the obvious things have been done which were fought and argued about. And yet, mysteriously enough . . . the ideal, the pattern of values, has not been achieved. We have done them, we have created the means to the good life which they all laid down and said 'If you do all these things, after that there'll be a classless society.' Well, there isn't.   (Crossman 1950)

Appendix

This is a complete list of all the studies from which the tables in this text have been derived. These are alphabetically listed by author or source, together with brief, systematic information about the research involved. The following general comments explain how the appendix works.

The first two columns, headed *Study* and *Date of publication*, are designed to be used in conjunction with the list of references in the bibliography, pp. 246–58. This provides full details of each publication involved. In the rest of the columns a dash (–) indicates that information is either unavailable, insufficient or inappropriate. *Sample size* is, wherever possible, the effective sample size, that is the number actually surveyed (excluding non-contacts, refusals etc.). In some studies the sample size in one part of the research is different from that in the others. In these cases the sample size is followed by '(varies)'. Where the exact sample size is unknown this is indicated by 'approx.'. *Sample type, Research technique*, and *Social class definition* are identified in the appropriate columns by a code. Keys to these codes are to be found in chapter 2 and on pp. 55, 59 and 49 respectively. Further explanations of these areas are to be found in the relevant sections of chapter 2. These are headed by the terms above and are on pp. 49, 56 and 34. Under *Table references* are listed all the tables in this text that have been derived from the source in question. The *Notes* column contains certain other specific information relevant to the study in question, for example unusual or modified procedures.

Obviously the information provided here is very limited. Generally, further information will be found either in the text relating to the particular tables, or by reference to the original source.

Study	Date of publication	Date of data	Sample type	Sample size	Research technique	Social class definition	Table reference	Notes
Annual Report for Scotland 1973	1974	1973	P	75,265	DE	R.G.70/E	4.3, 4.4	Population was all births in 1973
Barker Lunn	1970	1964/7	See notes (varies)	5,045	QPO, QP, QG etc.	R.G.60/F	6.8	Matched pairs of schools were used; number of schools and number of children in sample varied
Baumol and Bowen	1969	1965	P	2,295	QG	U.S.A.	7.18	Sample was those who replied to QG
Bone	1973	1970	MSS	3,494	IS	R.G.66/D	5.11	
Bone and Ross	1972	1969	MSS	3,916	QPO, IS, QP	R.G.66/A	7.20	
Bradley and Fenwick	1974	1970	MSR	2,747	IS	R.G.70/B	7.14	Four separate samples used
British Broadcasting Corporation (unpublished)	1974	1974	Pan	3,100	QP	B.B.C.	7.11	
British Labour Statistics Year Book 1973	1975			See *New Earnings Survey 1973*			3.8	
Butler and Stokes	1969	1963/4/6	MSS	2,009 (varies)	IS	M.R./C	2.1, 2.3, 2.4, 3.23	3 separate interviews; some respondents involved in all

Butler and Bonham	1963	1958	P	17,205	QP, IS	R.G.(S.E.)50/A	4.1, 4.2	QP filled up by midwives with mothers
Carstairs	1966	1963	P	–	DE	R.G.60	4.15	Population was all hospital admissions in Scotland other than maternal and mental
Census (listed in bibliography under specific titles, asterisked in this column)	From date of each census	1971 1966 1961	P P P	– – –	QP QP QP	R.G.70 R.G.(S.E.)70 R.G.66 R.G.(S.E.)66 R.G.60 R.G.(S.E.)60		Questionnaire was to head of household; census published separately for England and Wales, Scotland, Northern Ireland, some volumes for Great Britain and few for United Kingdom
Davie, Butler and Goldstein	1972	1965/6	P	15,496	IS,QP,DER	R.G.60/A	5.6, 5.15, 5.17, 5.18, 5.19, 5.22, 5.27, 5.32, 6.5	Population was all children born in a week in 1958
Dearnaley and Fletcher	1968	1964	P	1,791	QG	R.G.60	7.21	Sample was children aged 7–11 years from eight primary schools

Study	Date of publication	Date of data	Sample type	Sample size	Research technique	Social class definition	Table reference	Notes
Decennial Supplement, England and Wales, 1961	1971	1959/63	P	—	DE	R.G.60	3.24, 4.7, 4.8, 4.17, 4.18, 4.19, 4.20, 4.21	Used census data (1961) and death certificates (1959–63)
Department of Employment Gazette	1975	1975	P	798,855	DE	D.E.	3.17	Sample was returns from un-employment offices
Donaldson	1971	1968	P	252	QP	H.J.	6.22	
Douglas	1964	1954/7	P	5,362 (varies)	QP, IS, DER N.S.	6.6	Population was all children born in a week in 1946
Douglas, Ross and Simpson	1968	1962	P	4,720 (varies)	QP, IS, DER N.S.	6.16	
Dunnell and Cartwright	1972	1969	MSR	1,412 (varies)	IS(PC), DC	R.G.66/A	4.13	
*Economic Activity 1973/5 (10% Sample)		1971	SR	—	QP	R.G.70	3.1, 3.2, 3.3, 3.4, 3.5, 3.6, 3.7, 3.25, 3.26	Sample was 10% of census returns
*Education Tables (10% Sample)	1966	1961	SR	—	QP	R.G.(S.E.)60	6.1	Information from 10% of population survey in the census of 1961
Family Expenditure Survey: Report for 1974	1975	1974	MSR	6,695 (varies)	IS, DC	F.E.S.	3.12, 3.13	Sample is households, and rotates, each area being used four times, and then changed

15–18	1960		MP R Q	—	QPO I(PC), QG I(PC)	R.G.(S.E.)50/B	6.9	
Gallup Polls	Various – see table concerned: results published within a month of research	1954/5 1956/8		8,475 Monthly 1,000+ approx. (varies) See text to tables	I(PC)	M.R./A, M.R./B	7.1, 7.29, 7.30	
General Household Survey Introductory Report	1973		MSR	10,929	IS	R.G.(S.E.)70	3.19, 5.25, 5.26, 5.28, 5.29	Sample was households who co-operated
General Household Survey 1972	1975		MSR	10,584	IS	R.G.(S.E.)70	4.5, 4.6, 4.12, 4.14, 6.2, 6.3, 6.4, 6.10, 7.15	
Gibson	1974	1961	DR	598	DE	R.G.60/A	5.3	
Glass	1954	1949	MSR	9,296 (varies)	IS	H.J., H.J./A	3.22, 5.4	
Goldberg and Morrison	1963	1956	D	369	DE	R.G.50	4.10	Sample not random: surnames A–M of male patients, 15–34 years
Gorer	1965		MP	1,628 (359)	IS	M.R.	4.22	Higher sample was first phase
Gray, Todd, Slack and Bulman	1970	1969	MSR	2,932	IS	R.G.66/A	4.11	Also examined sample's teeth
Grey	1971	1969	MSR	3,400	DE	R.G.66/AB	5.13	Sample was application files for adoption
Harris and Clausen	1967	1953/63	MSS	19,975	IS	R.G.60/A	3.20, 3.21	

Study	Date of publication	Date of data	Sample type	Sample size	Research technique	Social class definition	Table reference	Notes
Higher Education 21-year-olds	1963	1962	MS, Q	3,169	IS	R.G.60/AB (varies)	6.14, 6.15, 6.17, 6.18, 6.19	Only final stage of sampling was quota
Undergraduates and post-graduates		1962	DR	4,293	IS, QP	R.G.(S.E.)50/B R.G.60/A		
Teacher training		1962	MS	1,223	IS, QP	R.G.60/A		
Further education		1962	MS	3,936	IS	R.G.60/A		
Holman	1973	1968	P	217	IS	R.G.66	5.14	Matched sample of private and local authority foster children in two local authority areas
Household Composition Tables (10% sample)	1975	1971	SR	—	QP	R.G.70	3.9, 3.10, 3.11, 3.14, 5.1	Sample was 10% of census returns
Jackson	1964	1962	P	26,528	QPO	R.G.60/AB	6.7	Sample was children from schools which replied
Kahan, Butler and Stokes	1966			See Butler and Stokes Males 4,702 Females 3,582				
Kelsall, Poole and Kuhn	1972	1966	P		QPO	R.G.60/A	6.20	Male sample was doubled to put figures on same footing

McIntosh and Woodley	1974		P	19,581	DE	R.G.60/A	6.21	
Mann	1967	1965	P	9,601	QG	M.R./A	7.17	
Monks	1968	1966	P	331 schools	QPO	R.G.(S.E.)60/D	6.11	
Moulin	1968	1962/4	P	3,661	IS	R.G.60/A	7.9	Inquiry was based on house-to-house census and census at places of worship
National Opinion Polls	Various — see tables: results published within a month of research		SR	Monthly 1,500+ (varies)	I(PC)	M.R.	2.2, 2.3, 2.5, 7.2, 7.3, 7.4, 7.5, 7.6, 7.23, 7.26, 7.27, 7.28, 7.31	
National Readership Survey 1975	1976	1975	MSR	30,570	I(PC)	M.R./A	7.12, 7.13, 7.16	Sample was continuous, i.e. initially of polling districts, then allocated to a month, then to a day; sample takes one year to complete Sample of National Insurance cards
New Earnings Survey 1973	1974	1973	DR	172,000	QPO	D.E.	3.18	

Study	Date of publication	Date of data	Sample type	Sample size	Research technique	Social class definition	Table reference	Notes
Newson and Newson	1963, 1968		DR	700	IS	R.G.60/AB	5.9, 5.16 5.20, 5.21, 5.23, 5.24	
Nissel and Lewis *Occupational Pensions Schemes 1971*	1972	1971	P	See Census 1971 (1) 33 (2) ½ million (approx.)	QPO	D.E.	5.5 3.16	Sample sizes: (1) firms in private sector, (2) their employees
Prais and Schmool	1975	1961	P	1,216 (varies)	DER	R.G.60	7.10	Sample was derived from certain Jewish burial societies
Public Schools Commission: First Report	1968 (1966)	1962/3 1965/6	P	(varies)	QPO	R.G.60/AB	6.12, part of 6.13	H.M.C. schools were surveyed by Kalton (1966)
Report on an Enquiry into the Incidence of Incapacity for Work	1964, 1965	1961/2	SR	708,132 (varies)	QPO	R.G.60/B	3.15, 4.9	Sample was 5% of male and 2½% of female registered unemployed
Sillitoe	1969	1965/6	MSR	6,275 (varies)	IS	R.G.(S.E.)60/A	7.7, 7.19, 7.24	

Statistical Review of England and Wales 1967	1971	1966	SR	4,152	DE	R.G.60	5.2	Sample was of first marriage divorces in 1966
Statistical Review of England and Wales 1972, 'Supplement on Abortion'	1974	1972	P	108,505 (varies)	DE	R.G.66	5.12	
The British on Holiday 1974	1975	1974	SR	4,000 (see note)	IS	M.R.	7.22	Further 18,000 contacts made for holidays abroad realised 2,290 such holidaymakers
The New Housewife 1967	1967	1967	SR	1,172	IS	M.R./B	5.31	
Wakefield and Sansom	1966	1965	P	4,048	DE	R.G.60/A	4.16	
Woman and the National Market	1967	1967	—	—	IS	M.R./D	5.30	
Woolf	1971	1967	MSS	6,248	IS	R.G.(S.E.)66/B	5.7, 5.8, 5.10	
Young and Willmott	1973	1970	MS, MP	1,928 (varies)	IS	R.G.66/AB	7.8, 7.25	Number of smaller samples also used

*See under census above

Bibliography *and* Author index

All these sources are followed by page references, to show where they are mentioned or discussed in this book, except that references to tables, which are to be found in the appendix, are not duplicated here. Works are referenced, wherever possible, by author(s), and otherwise (with the exception of the publications of the Consumer Council and The Open University, qq.v., National Opinion Polls Market Research Ltd (see National Opinion Polls) and Social Surveys (Gallup Polls) Ltd (see Gallup Polls)) by their full title. 'Her Majesty's Stationery Office' has been abbreviated to 'H.M.S.O.', 'National Foundation for Educational Research' to 'N.F.E.R.', and 'Office of Population Censuses and Surveys' to 'O.P.C.S.'.

ABRAMS, M. (1951) *Social Surveys and Social Actions* (London: Heinemann) 102

Age Marital Conditon and General Tables (1974) Census 1971, England and Wales, O.P.C.S. (London: H.M.S.O.) 129, 130

Annual Report for Scotland 1973 (1974) Part 1, *Mortality Statistics*; part 2, *Population and Vital Statistics*; Registrar General for Scotland (Edinburgh: H.M.S.O.) 106, 129

ATKINSON, J. (1971) *A Handbook for Interviewers* (London: H.M.S.O.) 155

BANKS, O. (1968) *The Sociology of Education* (London: Batsford) 166

BARKER LUNN, J.C. (1970) *Streaming in the Primary School* (Slough: N.F.E.R.) 37, 57, 177

BAUMOL, W.J., and BOWEN, W.G. (1969) *Performing Arts Economic Dilemma* (Cambridge, Massachusetts: Massachusetts Institute of Technology) 48

BENDIX, R. and LIPSET, S.M. (1967) *Class Status and Power* (London: Routledge and Kegan Paul) 62

BENJAMIN, B. (1970) *The Population Census* (London: Heinemann) 101

BENN, C., and SIMON, B. (1972) *Half Way There*, 2nd ed. (Harmondsworth: Penguin) 180

BERENT, J. (1954) 'Social Mobility and Marriage: A Study of Trends in England and Wales', in Glass 1954 44, 134, 135

BERGER, P.L. (1963) *Invitation to Sociology* (New York: Doubleday; Harmondsworth, 1966: Penguin) 18, 234

BLISHEN, E. (1969) *The School that I'd Like* (Harmondsworth: Penguin) 164

BONE, M. (1973) *Family Planning Services in England and Wales* (London: H.M.S.O.) 141

BONE, M., and ROSS, E. (1972) *The Youth Service and Similar Provision for Young People* (London: H.M.S.O.) 220

BOTTOMORE, T.B. (1965) *Classes in Modern Society* (London: Allen and Unwin) 62

BOYD, D. (1973) *Elites and their Education* (Slough: N.F.E.R.) 184

BRADLEY, M., and FENWICK, D. (1974) *Public Attitudes to Liquor Licensing Laws in Great Britain* (London: H.M.S.O.) 216

BRIGGS, A. (1960) 'The Language of Class of Early Nineteenth Century England', in Briggs, A., and Saville, J. (eds), *Essays in Labour History in Memory of G.D.H. Cole* (London: Macmillan) 19

British Labour Statistics Year Book 1973 (1975) Department of Employment (London: H.M.S.O.) 42

BROCKINGTON, F., and STEIN, Z. (1963) 'Admission, Achievement and Social Class', *Universities Quarterly* 18, 52–73 193

BROWN, G., CHERRINGTON, D. H., and COHEN, L. (1975) *Experiments in the Social Sciences* (London: Harper and Row) 10

BURT, C. (1937) *The Backward Child* (London: University of London Press) 165

BURT, C. (1943) 'Ability and Income', *British Journal of Educational Psychology* 13, 83–98 165

BUTLER, D., and STOKES, D. (1969) *Political Change in Britain* (London: Macmillan; Harmondsworth, 1971: Penguin) 41, 47, 94, 200, 204, 205

BUTLER, N. R., and ALBERMAN, E. D. (1969) *Perinatal Problems* (London: Livingstone)

BUTLER, N. R. and BONHAM, D. G. (1963) *Perinatal Mortality* (London: Livingstone) 103

CARSTAIRS, V. (1966) 'Distribution of Hospital Patients by Social Class', *Health Bulletin* 24, 59–64 121

CARTWRIGHT, A. (1964) *Human Relations and Hospital Care* (London: Routledge and Kegan Paul) 123

CARTWRIGHT, A. (1967) *Patients and their Doctors* (London: Routledge and Kegan Paul) 119, 123

CARTWRIGHT, A., HOCKEY, L., and ANDERSON, J. L. (1973) *Life Before Death* (London: Routledge and Kegan Paul) 127

Children and Their Primary Schools (1967) (The Plowden Report) Department of Education and Science (London: H.M.S.O.) 143

Classification of Occupations (1950, 1960, 1966, 1970) O.P.C.S. (London: H.M.S.O.) 33, 34, 35, 37, 38, 96

COATES, B. E., and RAWSTRON, E. M. (1971) *Regional Variations in Britain – Studies in Economic Social Geography* (London: Batsford) 4

CONSUMER COUNCIL (1967) *Living in a Caravan* (London: H.M.S.O.) 158

CONWAY, F. (1967) *Sampling* (London: Allen and Unwin) 51, 56

COX, P. R. (1970) *Demography*, 4th ed. (Cambridge: Cambridge University Press) 101

COXON, A. P. M., and JONES, C. L. (1973) 'Occupational

Similarities: Some Subjective Aspects of Social Stratific-ation', British Sociological Association conference paper (unpublished) 32

COXON, A. P. M., and JONES, C. L. (1974) 'Occupational Similarities', *Quality and Quantity* 8, 139–58 (published version of Coxon and Jones 1973) 32

CROSSMAN, R. H. S. (1950) 'Socialist Values in a Changing Civilization', in *Fabian Tract 286* (London: Gollancz) 236

DAVIE, R. (1969) 'The First Follow-up of the Children Born in the Control Week', in Butler and Alberman (1969) 105

DAVIE, R., BUTLER, M., and GOLDSTEIN, H. (1972) *From Birth to Seven* (London: Longman) 105, 137, 144, 151, 152, 158, 162, 173

DEARNALEY, E. J., and FLETCHER, M. H. (1968) 'Cubs and Brownies – Social Class, Intelligence, and Interests', *Educational Research* 10, 149–51 221

Decennial Supplement, England and Wales, 1961 (1971) 'Occupational Mortality Tables', Registrar General (London: H.M.S.O.) 95, 112, 113

Department of Employment Gazette (August 1975) (published monthly) (London: H.M.S.O.) 42

DONALDSON, L. (1971) 'Social Class and the Polytechnics', *Higher Education Review* 4, 44–68 195

DOUGLAS, J. W. B. (1948) *Maternity in Great Britain* (London: Oxford University Press) 103, 144

DOUGLAS, J. W. B. (1964) *The Home and the School* (London: MacGibbon and Kee) 174, 177, 187

DOUGLAS, J. W. B., ROSS, J. M., and SIMPSON, H. R. (1968) *All Our Future* (London: Peter Davies) 185, 187

DUNNELL, K., and CARTWRIGHT, A. (1972) *Medicine Takers, Prescribers and Hoarders* (London: Routledge and Kegan Paul) 119

DURKHEIM, E. (1952) *Suicide* (London: Routledge and Kegan Paul) 125, 127, 164

DURKHEIM, E. (1956) *Education and Sociology* (Glencoe, Illinois: Free Press) 164

Economic Activity (10% Sample) (1975) Census 1971, Great Britain, O.P.C.S. (London: H.M.S.O.)

Education: A Framework for Expansion (1972) (London: H.M.S.O.)   172

Education Tables (10% Sample) (1966) Census 1961, England and Wales, O.P.C.S. (London: H.M.S.O.)   166

ELIOT, T. S. (1932) *Sweeny Agonistes: Fragments of an Aristophanic Melodrama* (London: Faber and Faber)   102

Facts in Focus (1974) (2nd ed.) Central Statistical Office (Harmondsworth: Penguin and H.M.S.O.)   221

Family Expenditure Survey: Report for 1973 (1974) Department of Employment (London: H.M.S.O.)   43

Family Expenditure Survey: Report for 1974 (1975) Department of Employment (London: H.M.S.O.)   43, 60, 80

FIELD, F. (1973) *Unequal Britain* (London: Hutchinson; London, 1974: Arrow Books)   235

15–18 (1960) (The Crowther Report) Central Advisory Council for Education, Ministry of Education (London: H.M.S.O.)   178

GAINE, J. J. (1975) *Young Adults Today and the Future of the Faith* (Upholland: Secretariat for Non-Believers)   198

GALLUP POLLS (1973) Report No 157; (1974) Report No 171; (1975a) Report No 178; (1975b) Report No 185 (London: Social Surveys (Gallup Polls) Ltd)   200, 229

GAVRON, H. (1966) *The Captive Wife* (London: Routledge and Kegan Paul)   131

General Household Survey Introductory Report (1973) O.P.C.S., Social Surveys Division (London: H.M.S.O.)   89, 90, 111, 155, 156, 158, 159

General Household Survey 1972 (1975) O.P.C.S., Social Surveys Division (London: H.M.S.O.)   86, 108, 110, 119, 121, 161, 168, 180, 217

GIBSON, C. (1974) 'The Association between Divorce and Social Class in England and Wales', *British Journal of Sociology* 25, 79–93   133

GIDDENS, A. (1971) *The Sociology of Suicide* (London: Cass)   126

GIDDENS, A. (1973) *The Class Structure of the Advanced Societies* (London: Hutchinson)   62

GLASS, D. V. (1954) *Social Mobility in Britain* (London: Routledge and Kegan Paul) 44, 93, 134

GOLDBERG, E. M., and MORRISON, S. L. (1963) 'Schizophrenia and Social Class', *British Journal of Psychiatry* 109, 785–802 117

GOLDTHORPE, J. H., LOCKWOOD, D., BECHHOFER, F., and PLATT, J. (1969) *The Affluent Worker* (Cambridge: Cambridge University Press) 29, 44, 235

GOLDTHORPE, J. H., and HOPE, K. (1972) 'Occupational Grading and Occupational Prestige', in Hope 1972 31

GOLDTHORPE, J. H., and HOPE, K. (1974) *The Social Grading of Occupations* (London: Oxford University Press) 31, 60

GORDON, M. M. (1963) *Social Class in American Sociology* (Cambridge, Massachusetts/London: McGraw-Hill) 16

GORER, G. (1965) *Death, Grief, and Mourning* (London: Cresset Press) 128

GORER .G. (1971) *Sex and Marriage in England Today* (London: Nelson; London, 1973: Panther) 131

GRAY, P. G., and RUSSELL, R. (1962) *The Housing Situation in 1960* (London: H.M.S.O.) 159

GRAY, P. G., TODD, J. E., SLACK, G. L., and BULMAN, J. S. (1970) *Adult Dental Health in England and Wales in 1968* (London: H.M.S.O.) 118

GREY, E. (1971) *A Survey of Adoption in Great Britain* (London: H.M.S.O.)

HALL, J., and JONES, D. C. (1950) 'The Social Grading of Occupations', *British Journal of Sociology* 1, 31–55 30, 44

HALMOS, P. (1963) *Sociological Studies in British University Education* (Keele: Keele University Press) 193

HALSEY, A. H. (1972) *Trends in British Society since 1900* (London: Macmillan) 4

HARRIS, A. I., and CLAUSEN, R. (1967) *Labour Mobility in Great Britain, 1953–63* (London: H.M.S.O.) 90, 92

HART, J. T. (1971) 'The Inverse Care Law', *The Lancet* 1971 vol. 1, 405–12 123

HATCH, S., and REICH, D. (1970) 'Unsuccessful

Sandwiches?', *New Society* 15 No 389 (14 May 1970), 824–5   194, 196

Higher Education (1963) (The Robbins Report) Command Paper 2154 (London: H.M.S.O.)   189, 190, 194

HOLMAN, R. (1973) *Trading in Children* (London: Routledge and Kegan Paul)

HOPE, K. (1972) *The Analysis of Social Mobility* (Oxford: Clarendon Press)

HOPE, K. (1973) 'What are People Doing When they Grade Occupations?', British Sociological Association conference paper (unpublished)   31

Household Composition Tables (10% Sample) (1975) Census 1971, England and Wales, O.P.C.S. (London: H.M.S.O.)   131

Household Composition Tables (1975) Census 1971, Scotland, O.P.C.S. (Edinburgh: H.M.S.O.)   131

Hymns Ancient and Modern (1950) (revised ed.; original ed. 1861) (London: Clowes)   129

JACKSON, B. (1964) *Streaming: An Education System in Miniature* (London: Routledge and Kegan Paul)   175

JONES, D. C. (1934) *Social Survey of Merseyside*, vol. 2 (Liverpool: Liverpool University Press)   43

KAHAN, M., BUTLER, D., and STOKES, D. (1966) 'On the Analytical Division of Social Class', *British Journal of Sociology* 17, 122–32   23, 26, 28

KALTON, G. (1966) *The Public Schools* (London: Longman)   183

KELSALL, R. K. (1963) 'Survey of all Graduates', *Sociological Review Monographs* No 7   193

KELSALL, R. K., POOLE, A., and KUHN, A. (1972) *Graduates* (London: Methuen)   193, 194

KIPLING, R. (1902) *The Wage Slaves*, repr. in *Rudyard Kipling's Verse* (London, 1940: Hodder and Stoughton)   63

LINDLEY, D. V., and MILLER, J. C. P. (1971) *Cambridge Elementary Statistical Tables* (Cambridge: Cambridge University Press)   51

LIPSET, S. M., and BENDIX, R. (1959) *Social Mobility in*

Industrial Society (Berkeley, California: University of California Press) 31

LOGAN, W. P. D., and CUSHIONS, A. A. (1962) *Morbidity Statistics from General Practice* (London: H.M.S.O.) 119

McGREGOR, O. R. (1957) *Divorce in Britain* (London: Heinemann) 132

McINTOSH, M. E., and WOODLEY, A. (1974) 'The Open University and Second Chance Education', *Paedagogica Europaea* 9, 85–100

MADGE, J. (1953) *The Tools of Social Science* (London: Longman) 50, 54, 56, 60

MANN, P. H. (1967) 'Surveying a Theatre Audience: Findings', *British Journal of Sociology* 18, 75–90   218

MANN, P. H. (1968) *Methods of Sociological Enquiry* (Oxford: Blackwell)   56, 60

MANN, P. H. (1971) *Books, Buyers and Borrowers* (London: Deutsch)   216

MARSH, D. C. (1965) *The Changing Structure of England and Wales 1871–1961*, 2nd ed. (London: Routledge and Kegan Paul)   4

MARTIN, F. M. (1954) 'Some Subjective Aspects of Social Stratification', in Glass 1954   22, 26

MARX, K., and ENGELS, F. (1848) *Manifesto of the Communist Party* (Contemporary editions – Moscow: Foreign Languages Publishing House)   62

MATTHIJSSEN, M. A. J. M. (1959) 'Catholic Intellectual Emancipation in the Western Countries of Mixed Religion', *Social Compass* 6, 91–113   203

MAUSNER, J. S., and BAHN, A. K. (1974) *Epidemiology* (London: Saunders)   108

MONK, D. (1970) *Social Grading on the National Readership Survey* (London: Joint Industry Committee for National Readership Surveys)   13, 15, 47

MONKS, T. G. (1968) *Comprehensive Education in England and Wales* (Slough: N.F.E.R.)   182

MORRIS, J. N. (1964) *Uses of Epidemiology* (London: Livingstone)   108

MOSER, C. A. (1958) *Survey Methods in Social Investigation* (London: Heinemann)   56, 60

MOSER, C. A., and KALTON, G. (1971) *Survey Methods in Social Investigation* (London: Hutchinson)   56, 60

MOULIN, L. DE S. (1968) 'Social Class and Religious Behaviour', *The Clergy Review* 53, 20—35   207, 209

MUSGROVE, F., COOPER, B., DERRICK, T., FOY, J. M., and WILLIG, C. J. (1967) 'Preliminary Studies of a Technological University', Bradford University mimeograph   194

NATIONAL OPINION POLLS (1969a) August *Bulletin*; (1969b) November *Bulletin*; (1970) February *Bulletin*; (1971) *Bulletin No 101*; (1972a) *Bulletin No 109*; (1972b) *Bulletin No 110*; (1975a) *Political Social Economic Review No 1*; (1975b) *Political Social Economic Review No 3*; (1976) *Political Social Economic Review No 5* (London: National Opinion Polls Market Research Ltd)   23, 27, 28, 201, 202, 204, 205, 222, 226, 228, 232

National Readership Survey 1975 (1976) (London: Joint Industry Committee for National Readership Surveys)   211, 212, 217

New Earnings Survey 1973 (1974) Department of Employment (London: H.M.S.O.)   76, 92

NEWSON, J., and NEWSON, E. (1963) *Infant Care in an Urban Community* (London: Allen and Unwin)   139, 144, 145, 149, 153

NEWSON, J., and NEWSON, E. (1968) *Four Years Old in an Urban Community* (London: Allen and Unwin; Harmondsworth, 1970: Penguin)   57, 144, 149—54

NISSEL, M. (1971) *Social Trends No 2* (London: H.M.S.O.)   112

NISSEL, M., and LEWIS, C. (1974) *Social Trends No 5* (London: H.M.S.O.)   123, 210

NORTH, G. (1948) *Matters of Life and Death* (London: H.M.S.O.)   1

Occupational Mortality 1959—63 (1970) Registrar General for Scotland (Edinburgh: H.M.S.O.)

Occupational Pension Schemes 1971 (1972) Government Actuary (London: H.M.S.O.)

OPPENHEIM, A. N. (1966) *Questionnaire Design and Attitude Measurement* (London: Heinemann)   60, 198

ORWELL, G. (1937) *The Road to Wigan Pier* (London: Gollancz)   63, 197

PIERCE, R. M. (1963) 'Marriage in the Fifties', *Sociological Review* 11, 215–40   131

PLATT, J. (1971) 'Variations in Answers to Different Questions on Perceptions of Class', *Sociological Review* 19, 409–19   29

PRAIS, S. J., and SCHMOOL, M. (1975) 'The Social-Class Structure of Anglo-Jewry, 1961', *Jewish Journal of Sociology* 17, 5–15   209

Public Schools Commission: First Report (1968) Department of Education and Science (London: H.M.S.O.)   183

PULZER, P. G. J. (1968) *Political Representation and Elections in Britain* (London: Allen and Unwin)   199

PUNNETT, R. M. (1971) *British Government and Politics* (London: Heinemann)   184

REIN, M. (1972) 'Social Class and the Health Service', in Butterworth, E., and Weir, D., *Social Problems of Modern Britain* (London: Fontana) (repr. from *New Society* 14 No 373 (20 November 1969), 807–10)   123

Religion Tables (1976) Census 1971, Northern Ireland, O.P.C.S. (Belfast: H.M.S.O.)   204

Report on an Enquiry into the Incidence of Incapacity for Work (1964, 1965) Part 1 (1964), *Scope and Characteristics of Employers' Sick Pay Schemes*; part 2 (1965), *Incidence of Incapacity for Work in Different Areas and Occupations*; Ministry of Pensions and National Insurance (London: H.M.S.O.)   114

RILEY, M. W. (1963) *Sociological Research – A Case Approach* (New York: Harcourt Brace and World)   56

ROSSER, C., and HARRIS, C. C. (1965) *The Family and Social Change* (London: Routledge and Kegan Paul)   23

Royal Commission on Population (1949) Command Paper 7965 (London: H.M.S.O.)   137

RUNCIMAN, W. G. (1964) 'Embourgeoisement, Self-Rated Class, and Party Preference', *Sociological Review* 12, 137–54   *23*

SILLITOE, K. K. (1969) *Planning for Leisure* (London: H.M.S.O)   39, 206, 210, 220, 223

SILVER, H. (1973) *Equal Opportunity in Education* (London: Methuen)   164

Small Area Statistics (Ward Library) (1975) Census 1971, England and Wales, O.P.C.S. (London: H.M.S.O.)   72

Socio-Economic Group Tables (1966) Census 1961, England and Wales, O.P.C.S. (London: H.M.S.O.)

STANWORTH, P., and GIDDENS, A. (1974) *Elites and Power in British Society* (Cambridge: Cambridge University Press)   184

Statistical Review of England and Wales 1967 (1971) Part 3, 'Commentary', Registrar General (London: H.M.S.O.)   132, 135

Statistical Review of England and Wales 1972 (1974) 'Supplement on Abortion', Registrar General (London: H.M.S.O.)

Statistical Review of England and Wales 1973 (1975) Registrar General (London: H.M.S.O.)   106

Statistics of Education 1961: Supplement (1962) Ministry of Education (London: H.M.S.O.)   186

STEVENSON, T. H. C. (1928) 'The Vital Statistics of Wealth and Poverty', *Journal of the Royal Statistical Society* 91, 207–30   20, 30, 34, 102

STOTT, D. H. (1963) *The Social Adjustment of Children: Manual to the Bristol Social-Adjustment Guides* (London: University of London Press)   148

STRAUS, M. A., and NELSON, J. I. (1968) *Sociological Analysis* (New York: Harper and Row)   10

TAYLOR, G., and AYRES, N. (1970) *Born and Bred Unequai* (London: Longman)   4

The British on Holiday 1974 (1975) (London: British Tourist Authority)   221

The New Housewife (1967) Vol. 3 (London: British Market Research Bureau)

THE OPEN UNIVERSITY (1972) D283 *Sociological Perspectives*, Block 3 *Stratification and Social Class*, Unit 9 *Major Theories of Stratification* [by G. Salamon] (Milton Keynes: The Open University Press)   62

The Times House of Commons (1970) (London: Times Newspapers)   184

The Times House of Commons (1974) (London: Times Newspapers)   184, 203

THOMPSON, K., and TUNSTALL, J. (1971) *Sociological Perspectives* (Harmondsworth: Penguin)   62

TITMUSS, R. M. (1968) *Commitment to Welfare* (London: Allen and Unwin)   123

TOWNSEND, P. (1974) 'Inequality and the Health Service', *The Lancet* 1974 vol. 1, 1179–90   114

URRY, J., and WAKEFORD, J. (1973) *Power in Britain* (London: Heinemann)   184

WAKEFIELD, J., and SANSOM, C. D. (1966) 'Profile of a Population of Women who have Undergone a Cervical Smear Examination', *The Medical Officer* 116, 145–6; repr. in Wakefield 1972   122

WAKEFIELD, J. (1972) *Seek Wisely to Prevent* (London: H.M.S.O.)

WAKEFORD, J. (1968) *The Strategy of Social Enquiry* (London: Macmillan)   10

WEBB, D. (1973) 'Some Reservations on the Use of Self-Rated Class', *Sociological Review* 21, 321–30   28

WHITLEY, R. (1973) 'Commonalities and Connections among Directors of Large Financial Institutions', *Sociological Review* 21, 613–32; repr. in Stanworth and Giddens 1974   184

Woman and the National Market (1967) (London: Odhams)

WOOLF, M. (1971) *Family Intentions* (London: H.M.S.O.) 40, 137, 139

YARROW, M. R., CAMPBELL, J. D., and BURTON, R. V. (1964) 'Reliability of Maternal Retrospection; A Preliminary Report', *Family Process* 3, 207–18   144

YOUNG, M., and WILLMOTT, P. (1956) 'Social Grading by Manual Workers', *British Journal of Sociology* 7, 337–45 31

YOUNG, M., and WILLMOTT, P. (1973) *The Symmetrical Family* (London: Routledge and Kegan Paul; Harmondsworth, 1975: Penguin)   206, 210, 215, 224

Subject index

abortion, 141–2; 5.12
absence from work, 110–11,
    114–17; 4.6, 4.9
  absenteeism, 111
accommodation
  bedrooms, 159–60; 5.28
  overcrowding, 158–9; 5.27
adoption, 142–3; 5.13
age
  and health, 99, 109; 4.5
  and social class, 96–101;
    3.25–6
alcohol, *see* drinking
awareness of class, *see* recognition
    of social class, self-rating,
    subjective existence of
    social class

B.B.C., *see* British Broadcasting
    Corporation
bedrooms, *see* accommodation
bias in sampling, 54–5
birth, 102, 103–8 *and see* birth
    weight, child-rearing,
    children, gestation, infant
    mortality
birth rate, 102
birth weight, 105–6; 4.2 *and see*
    birth
  later development, 106
  length of gestation, 106
  mortality ratio, 105–6; 4.2
bottle-feeding, 145; 5.16
breast-feeding, 144–5; 5.15–16
British Broadcasting Corporation,
    48–9

cancer, *see* disease

caste, 14
census
  characteristics of data, 2, 3,
    49–50, 54, 63–4,
    95–6, 100–101
  education, treatment of,
    166–7
  marriage, treatment of,
    129–30
  re-classification, effects of,
    95–6
Certificate of Secondary
    Education, *see* secondary
    schools
cervical smears, *see* medical
    facilities
child-rearing (*see also* birth,
    children, health)
  dental care, 147; 5.17
  discipline, 151–2; 5.22
  employment and, 99
  facts of life, 151; 5.21
  father's involvement, 153; 5.34
  feeding infants
    bottle-feeding, 144; 5.16
    breast-feeding, 144–5;
      5.15–16
  genital play, attitudes to,
    149–50; 5.20
  immunisation, 123, 146, 147;
    5.17
  medical facilities, use of,
    146–7; 5.17
  nakedness, attitudes to,
    150–1; 5.21
  punishment, 152–3; 5.23
  reliability of existing research,
    144

social adjustment, 148—9; 5.19
  and gestation, 105
social mobility, 92
speech development, 147—8;
  5.18
children, 136—55 *and see* birth,
  child-rearing
  adoption, 142—3; 5.13
  average family size, 137
  expected number, 138—9; 5.8
  family planning
    abortion, 141—2; 5.12
    contraception, 140—1; 5.11
  fostering, 143; 5.14
  length of marriage, 139; 5.10
  mother's age, 139; 5.9
  number per household, 136—7;
    5.5—6
Church of England, 20, 198,
  204—5; 7.5
cinema attendance, 217—8; 7.16
clinics, *see* medical facilities
club membership, 219—21; 7.19
  Cubs and Brownies, 220—1; 7.21
  youth clubs, 220; 7.20
comprehensive schools, *see*
  secondary schools
consumer durables, possession of,
  161—2; 5.30—1
contraception, *see* family planning

data
  graphical presentation, 10—12;
    figs 1.1—3
  interpretation of, 8—9
death (*see also* infant mortality)
  causes of death, 111—14,
    124—7; 4.7—8, 4.19—21
  maternity, 125; 4.19
  suicide, 125—7; 4.20—1
  death rate (mortality), 123—4
    mortality ratio, defined,
      104
    standardised mortality
      ratios, 112—14,
      124—7; 4.7—8,
      4.18—20
  mourning, 127—8; 4.22
  and wealth, 102, 103

dental health, 118, 123; 4.11 *and
  see* health
  and children, 147; 5.17
Department of Employment,
  occupational classification
  by, 42—3
direct sampling, 50—1
disease (*see also* health)
  cancer, 113; 4.7
  death from, 111—14; 4.7—8
  epidemiology, 108
  and wealth, 102
  and work, 114—17; 4.9
discipline, *see* child rearing
divorce (*see also* family, marriage)
  endogamy and, 135—6
  incidence, 132—4; 5.2
  rate, 133; 5.3
doctors, use of, *see* general
  practitioners
documents (*see also* research
  methods)
  created, 59—60
  existing, 58—9
  research, 59
domestic amenities, *see* consumer
  durables
drinking, 216—17; 7.14
dwellings, *see* households

earners and earnings, *see* income
economically active persons (*see
  also* employment,
  geographical distribution of
  social class, retired persons)
  and age structure of classes,
    96—100
  class distribution, 63—72; 3.1—3,
    3.5—6, figs 3.1—2
  and education, 167—8; 6.1
  geographical distribution,
    63—72; 3.1—3, 3.5—6,
    figs 3.1—2
  and marriage, 82—5; 3.14
  and social mobility, 90—6;
    3.20—4
  and unemployment, 87—8
education, 164—96 *and see*
  children, educational

achievement, higher education, infant schools, pre-school education, primary schools, secondary schools
census data, 166–7; 6.1
1944 Education Act, effects of, 165
historical interest in, 164–6
and occupation, 97, 99, 170–1, 184–5; 6.13
opinion on, 229–32; 7.30
qualifications, 168–71; 6.2–3
and occupation, 99, 170–1
sex differences, 170
school-leaving age, 180, 185–6
structural functionalism and, 165–6
terminal education age, 167–8; 6.1
educational achievement (performance)
higher, 189–91; 6.17
infant, 173–4; 6.5
primary, 174–5; 6.6
secondary, 185–9; 6.17
élite jobs and public schools, 184–5; 6.13
employment (*see also* economically active persons, unemployment, social mobility)
employers, change of, 92
employment offices, 87–8; 3.17
endogamy, class, 134–6; 5.4 *and see* divorce, marriage
epidemiology, *see* disease
error, in sampling, 50, 54–5
estate, 14
expenditure (financial), 80–2 *and see* households, income
average weekly (households), 80–2; 3.12
per person, 81–2; 3.13

facts of life, *see* child rearing
false conciousness, 22

family, 129–30, 155–6 *and see* child-rearing, children, divorce, endogamy, households, income, marriage
family planning (*see also* children, medical facilities)
abortion, 141; 5.12
contraception, 140–1; 5.11
fathers
child-rearing, involvement in, 153; 5.24
child's educational achievement, 85
occupation, classification by, 45–6, 63, 65
son's social class, 92–5; 3.22–3
feeding of children, *see* child-rearing
fostering, 143; 5.14 *and see* adoption
functionalism and education, 165–6
further education, 189–93; 6.17–19 *and see* education, higher education

Gallup Polls, 47
general practitioners, use of, 118–21; 4.12–14
General Certificate of Education, *see* secondary schools
genital play, *see* child-rearing
geographical distribution of social class (*see also* economically active persons)
local, 71–3; 3.6, fig. 3.2
national 63–5; 3.1
regional 65–70; 3.2–5, fig. 3.1
gestation, 103–8
duration, 103–5; 4.1
infant mortality, 104; 4.1

and reading ability, 105
and social adjustment, 105
gradients (of distribution), 103
graduates, *see* higher education
grammar schools, *see* secondary
    schools

Hall-Jones scale, 30, 43–5
health (*see also* death, dental
    health, disease, medical
    facilities, sickness)
    and age, 99
    self-rating, 119; 4.13
    symptom reporting, 119; 4.13
    National Health Service, 114
    and wealth, 102–3
    welfare state, 111, 114
higher education (*see also*
    education, further
    education)
    achievement in, 189–91; 6.17
    expansion of, 171
    polytechnics, 195–6; 6.22
    students, 193; 6.2–3, 6.19–20
    universities, 193–5; 6.20–1
        Bradford, 194
        Cambridge, 194
        Open, 194–5; 6.21
        Oxford, 194
holidays, 221; 7.22
hospitals, use of, *see* medical
    facilities
hours of work, 88–9; 3.18 *and see*
    pay
households
    amenities, 160–1; 5.29
    children per household, 136–7;
        5.5–6
    consumer durables, 161–2;
        5.30–1
    defined, 155
    dwellings (*see also*
        accommodation)

accommodation, 158–60;
    5.27–8
    tenure, 156–8; 5.26
    type, 156–8; 5.25
earners per household, 77–8;
    3.9
expenditure, average weekly,
    80–1; 3.12
    per person, 81; 3.13
moving, 162–3; 5.32
housing, *see* households, dwellings
husband's occupation
    classification by, 63, 65
    and wives' social mobility, 92

image of class, 29–30
immunisation, 123, 146, 147;
    5.17 *and see* health
income, 75–9 *and see* expenditure,
    households, pay
    earners, 77–9
        number per family, 78–9;
            3.10–11
        number per household,
            77–8; 3.9
    earnings, 75–7, 80
        average gross weekly,
            76–7; 3.8
        inflation, effects of, 76
        pay legislation, 77
        sex differences, 76–7
    overtime, 77; 3.8
independent schools, *see* secondary
    schools
indirect sampling, 52–5
industry
    social class composition,
        74–5; 3.7
    status of, 95
infant mortality, 106–8 *and see*
    gestation
    duration of gestation, 104; 4.1
    maternity deaths, 125; 4.19
    neonatal, 106; 4.4

post-neonatal, 106—7; 4.4
stillbirths, 106—7; 4.4
infant schools, 173—4 *and see*
        education
    adjustment to, 148; 5.19
    arithmetic ability, 174; 6.5
    reading ability, 173—4; 6.5
injury at work, 111
interviews (*see also* research
        methods)
    structured, 57
    unstructured, 56—7
I.Q., *see* secondary schools

jobs (*see also* employment,
        unemployment, occupation)
    élite jobs and public schools,
        184—5; 6.13
    job mobility, 92
    opportunities, 93—4, 98,
        99—100
    satisfaction, 89—90; 3.19
    vacancies at employment
        offices, 87—8; 3.19

large scale studies, 4, 56
leisure, *see* cinema attendance,
        club membership, drinking,
        holidays, reading, smoking,
        sport, television, theatre
        attendance
local distribution of social class,
        71; 3.6, fig. 3.2
longitudinal studies, 99, 174

maladjustment, *see* child-rearing
market research, 1, 20, 46—7, 53
marital breakdown, *see* divorce
marriage (*see also* children,
        divorce, family)
    age at, 131—2; 5.1
    incidence, 130—1
    married couples, 82—5, 134—6

economically active, 82—5;
        3.14
    social origins, 134—6; 5.4
Marx, Karl, 19—20, 21—2
medical facilities (*see also* child
        rearing, health)
    availability, 114
    cervical smears, 122; 4.16
    clinics
        family planning, 123
        infant welfare, 123, 146;
            5.17
        local authority, 123
        toddlers, 146; 5.17
    general practitioners, use of,
        118—21; 4.12—14
    hospitals
        in-patients, 121—2; 4.15
        out-patients, 119; 4.12
        private services, 122
    quality of treatment, 123
    use of, 108, 114, 118—23
money model of social class, 29
mortality, *see* death, infant
        mortality
mother's occupation and
        educational performance of
        child, 65, 190—1; 6.18
multi-dimensional meausres of
        social class, 15—16
multi-phase sampling, 52—3
multi-stage sampling, 52

nakedness, attitudes to, *see* child-
        rearing
natality, *see* birth rate
National Child Development
        Study, 147, 173
National Children's Bureau, 144
national distribution of social class,
        63—5; 3.1
National Health Service, 114 *and
        see* health

National Survey of Health and Development, 45—6
nursery schools, *see* pre-school education

obedience, *see* child-rearing, discipline
objective existence of social class, 20—1
occupation
    and education, 97, 99, 170—1, 184—5; 6.13
    hazards of, 111, 113—14
    and health, 111
    ranking of, 29—32, 44
and social class, 15—18, 26—8 *and passim*
Open University students, 194—5; 6.21
operationalisation of social class, 32—49
opinion
    on class struggle, 229; 7.29
    on company profits, 229; 7.28
    on controversial topics, 232—3; 7.31
    on education, 229—32; 7.30
    on politics, 225—8; 7.26
    on trade unions, 228—9; 7.27
overcrowding, *see* accommodation
overtime, 77; 3.8 *and see* income

panel sampling, 54—5
parents, *see* child-rearing
pay(*see also* income)
    hourly rates, 88—9
    legislation, 77
pensions, 85, 86—7; 3.16 *and see* retired persons
politics (*see also* opinion)
    interest in, 200—1; 7.2
    opinion, political, 225—8; 7.26
    participation in, 203; 7.4
    support of, 200, 201—2; 7.3

voting behaviour, 199—200; 7.1
polls, 47, 225
polytechnics, *see* higher education
postgraduates, *see* higher education
power model of social class, 29
pregnancy, *see* gestation
pre-school education, 171—2
    nursery school, 172; 6.4
    playgroups, 171—2; 6.4
prestige
    of occupations, 31
    model of social class, 29
primary schools (*see also* education)
    attainment in, 174—5; 6.6
    streaming, 175—8; 6.7
    teachers' ability ratings, 177—8; 6.8
public recognition of social class, 22—32, 94; 2.1—3, 3.23
public schools, *see* secondary schools
punishment, *see* child-rearing

qualifications, *see* education
questionnaires, 57—8 *and see* research methods
quota sampling, 53—4

random sampling, 50—1
ranking of occupations, 29—32, 44
reading
    ability, 173—4; 6.5
    and gestation, 105
    readership surveys
        books, 215—16
        newspapers and periodicals, 212—15; 7.13
recognition of social class, 22—32, 94; 2.1—5, 3.23
regional distribution of social class, 65—70; 3.2—5
Registrar General, 30, 33, 34—42 *and passim*
reliability of existing research, 28—32, 144

religion
  attendance at religious services,
    205–8; 7.6, 7.8–9
    Roman Catholics, 207–9;
    7.9
  denominational affiliation,
    204–5; 7.5
  lack of research, 204
  membership of religious
    organisations, 206; 7.7
  religious groups
    Church of England, 20,
    204–5; 7.5
    Jews, 209–10; 7.10
    Roman Catholics, 207–9;
    7.5, 7.9
    other, 204–5; 7.5
research methods, 56–61 *and see*
    data, documents, interviews,
    questionnaires
  methodological problems,
    28–32, 95–6, 198
  reliability of existing research,
    28–32, 144
retired persons (*see also*
    economically active persons)
  class distribution, 63–72; 3.1,
    3.3–4
  geographical distribution,
    63–72; 3.1–4, fig. 3.1
return to work of women, 100
rooms in dwellings, *see*
    accommodation, households

sampling techniques, 49–56
  direct, 50–1
    random, 50–1
  error, bias in, 50, 54–6
  indirect, 52–5
    multi-phase, 52–3
    multi-stage, 52
    panel, 54–5
    quota, 53–4
    stratified, 52
  sample frame, 51
  variable sampling fraction, 52
satisfaction at work, *see* job
    satisfaction

schizophrenia, 99
school-leaving age, 180, 185–6
schools, *see* education, infant
    schools, pre-school
    education, primary schools,
    secondary schools
secondary schools, 178–89
  achievement in, 185–9;
    6.14–16
  Certificate of Secondary
    Education; 6.2–3
  early leaving, 185–6
    raising of school-leaving age,
    180, 185
  General Certificate of
    Education, 185–9;
    6.2–3, 6.14, 6.17–18
  quality of passes, 188–9;
    6.16
  and I.Q., 186–7; 6.14
  re-organisation of, 181–3
  type attended, 178–85
    comprehensives, 165, 180,
    181–3; 6.11
    grammar, 178–81; 6.9,
    6.10
    independent, 183; 6.9,
    6.10, 6.12
    neighbourhood, 181–2
    public, 183–5; 6.9,
    6.12–13
    secondary modern,
    178–81; 6.9, 6.10
    technical, 178–80; 6.9
self-rating (*see also* recognition of
    social class)
  on class, 23, 94; 2.3, 3.23
  on health, 119; 4.13
sickness, 85–6, 97 *and see* death,
    health
  absence from work, 86, 100;
    4.6
  age, 109; 4.5
  attitude to, 108
  chronic, 108–10; 4.5
  disease, 111–13; 4.7–8
  National Insurance Scheme, 85
  schizophrenia, 117–18; 4.10
  sick pay schemes, 85–6; 3.15

and work
absence, 110—11, 114—17,
120; 4.6, 4.9
incapacity for, 114—17;
4.9
medical certificates, 114,
120
significance, statistical, 9
similarities between social classes,
7—8
small-scale studies, 4
smoking, 217; 7.15
social adjustment, *see* child-
rearing, gestation
social mobility, 26—7, 44, 90—6;
3.20—4 *and see* job mobility
and child-rearing, 92
inter-generational mobility,
92—5; 3.22—3
intra-generational mobility,
90—2, 98—9; 3.20—1
and schizophrenia, 117—18
socialisation of child, *see* child-
rearing
socio-economic groups and class,
38—42
sons' and fathers' social class,
92—5; 3.22—3
speech development, *see* child-
rearing
sport
interest in, 222—3; 7.23
participation in, 224—5; 7.25
spectators, 223—4; 7.24
statistical significance, 9
status levels (Hall-Jones), 44—5
Stevenson, T. H. C., 102
stratification, 13—16
defined, 14
stratified sampling, 52
streaming, 175—8; 6.7

structural functionalism, *see*
functionalism
students, *see* higher education,
further education
subjective existence of social class,
22—32; 2.1—5 *and see*
recognition of class, self-
rating
suicide, 114, 125—7; 4.20—1

teacher trainees, *see* higher
education
technical schools, *see* secondary
schools
television
ownership, 161, 210; 5.30
viewing habits, 210—12;
7.11—12
theatre attendance, 218—19;
7.18—19
trade unions, opinion on, 228—9;
7.27

unemployment, 63, 87—8; 3.17
vacancies at unemployment
offices, 87—8; 3.17
unions, *see* trade unions
universities, *see* higher education

variable sampling fraction, 52
Victorian class consciousness, 19—20
voting behaviour, *see* politics

wealth, and health, 102—3 *and see*
income
weaning, *see* child-rearing
welfare state, 111, 114
working hours, 88—9; 3.18 *and see*
pay
working population, *see*
economically active persons